PRAIRIE MURDERS

PRAIRIE MURDERS

The True Story of Three Murders and the Loss of Innocence in a Small North Dakota Town

---

Robert Dodge

North Star Press of St. Cloud, Inc.
St. Cloud, Minnesota

Dedication

To Catherine Cater for the privilege of having been your student

Copyright © 2009 Robert Dodge

ISBN: 0-87839-326-9
ISBN-13: 978-0-87839-326-8

First Edition: June 2009

Printed in the United States of America

Published by
North Star Press of St. Cloud, Inc.
P.O. Box 451
St. Cloud, Minnesota 56302
northstarpress.com

Acknowledgements

I would like to thank Craig Olson for his assistance in transport and continued interest in the topic. Carol Bursack's aid in gathering all past articles from the Fargo Forum was very valuable. Many people contributed the information necessary to complete this story. Peter Graber, Budd Warren, Mike Lyman, and Earl Larson warrant being singled out for all their assistance in guiding me in this effort and the West Fargo Police Department and the Cass County Sheriff's Offices deserve thanks for the records they provided. Additionally, the following all were talked to or contacted and I thank them for their responses on the cases and subjects related to the time: Gary Annear, Margie Bailey, Kevin Carvelle, Gary Clark, Larry Costello, Steve Gabrielson, Bryan Green, Bob Fatland, Gene Johnson, Ed Klinger, Paul Laney, Charlie Lee, Jan Maxwell, Merv Nordeng, Carin Noreiga, Cal Olson, Bruce Quick, Arland Rasmussen, Cynthia Rothe-Seeger, Kelly Rogers, John Rowell, James Samuelson, Keith Ternes, Dan Treat, and Nick Vogel. My thanks also to Corinne Dwyer at North Star Press for taking an interest in this project. The story could not have been developed without the contributions of many.

Contents

1

A REMOTE PRAIRIE STATE

A^{S THE CURTAIN CAME DOWN} on the 1960s, young people across the country were taking to the streets and protesting. Social activism sometimes got out of control over the great social and political issues of the times — civil rights and the continuing War in Vietnam. When these activities were beyond the capabilities of local law enforcement to control or they turned into riots, the National Guard was frequently called out, such as at Kent State in 1970.

It is a telling commentary on North Dakota that, in its entire history, the National Guard has only been called on once to officially disperse a riot. That happened in the middle of the era of civil consciousness and public protest on May 10, 1969. What gives this incident such a North Dakota flavor is the special nature of the student riot the National Guard was called in to control.

In that 1969 spring, a year after the assassinations of Martin Luther King, Jr., and Bobby Kennedy and the Tet Offensive in Vietnam, and as America was preparing to send a man to the moon to take command of the space race, there had been race riots and antiwar demonstrations, forcing campuses across the nation to look at new curricula and shut down at times. National Guardsmen were frequently on campuses and patrolling streets in urban areas. At North Dakota State University in Fargo, Kevin Carvell, the editor of the college newspaper *The Spectrum*, convinced some others on the staff to do something more mundane, rather than take on the great issues for the moment. It was time for a staff picnic, since spring break was coming, and they thought they'd make a bit more of the event. It could be a real joke of the North Dakota variety, which involved playing into people's stereotypes of the state and laughing at themselves while others did the same. There is a fine line between a joke about being backward hicks where others see a joke and where locals believe that, since outsiders are laughing, they really are hicks and are ashamed. Those remain individual choices prairie people like North Dakotans deal with.

Carvelle's choice for the location of college newspaper's staff spring picnic was the town of Zap, which he thought was a strange name. The staff went along with it and published their plans, and student body president Chuck Stroup took out an ad supporting it. They really did intend to have a newspaper staff gathering, but the way the idea was presented was a bit more. The paper proclaimed that while college students all over America would have the opportunity to head off to Florida and other sunny climes for spring break, what about a choice for those living in this isolated middle of the continent? Zap was the answer, and "Zip to Zap" was born with a front page story by Carvelle in *The Spectrum*. Zap, with a population of 271, had been known to state residents previously as part of a response to the puzzle, name three North Dakota towns that sound like Kellogg's Rice Krispies "snap, crackle and pop" commercial. They were "Zap, Gackle and Mott." The article promised great times for college students in Zap, concluding with, "a full program of orgies, brawls, freakouts, and arrests are being planned. Do you dare miss it?"

The story was picked up by Moorhead State University across the river from Fargo and the University of North Dakota, ninety miles north in Grand Forks. The idea moved beyond being a joke when the Associated Press got wind of it and turned it into national news. It was a time when young people congregated, expecting excitement and fun. The ultimate example would come three months after Zap at a dairy farm in New York with less facilities than Zap, but with open space and a great schedule of music, when nearly half a million would head to the Woodstock Festival.

The Zip to Zap, offering nothing, came on May 9 as an estimated 3,000 college students poured into the town, some from as far off as Florida, New Jersey, and Louisiana and outnumbering the local population by ten to one. The two local bars were soon dry and had angered the students by doubling their prices, while cafés were not nearly prepared for such numbers. As the temperature dropped in the evening, a vacant building was torn up to use as firewood for a bonfire in the center of Main Street. A number of students left and headed for other towns when the local people asked them to go, but about 1,000 refused, and some local businesses' windows were shattered as things began to get out of control. Several hundred merrymakers carried on throughout the night, vomiting and urinating in public while some passed out, as others slept anywhere they could find, in cars, on blankets, on the street. *The Fargo Forum* reported, "There were Vietnam veterans, fuzzy-cheeked teen-agers, fraternity men, long-hairs, and a minority of girls. Virtually all of the students were drinking and a majority were drunk." It was seen by this time as a riot. At dawn 500 National Guardsmen entered with fixed bayonets. Empty beer cans and broken glass crunched under the boots of the troops as they faced little resistance while they cleared out the town. Some revilers moved on to the nearby small towns of Beulah and Hazen, and at 8:30 a.m. about 1,000 students had congregated in Beaulah's main street, chanting "Open the bar. Open the bar." Again the National Guard arrived and the show was soon over.

The joke gone awry was the lead story that night on Walter Cronkite's *CBS News* and was carried by most major newspaper, including the Soviet Union's *Pravda*. News magazines told the story and their coverage made a mockery of North Dakota's provincialism and isolation. Zap submitted bills for damage caused by the young people to the student governments of North Dakota State University and the University of North Dakota and was paid.

North Dakota's only riot; the only time the National Guard has been called up to control rioting. Carvelle recalls, "Some people thought it was a left-wing commie conspiracy, but Zip to Zap was zero political. The 'commies' who showed up included the Vets Club, the football team, the Theta Chi fraternity." His comment echoes *The Fargo Forum*'s coverage from the day, even as the crowd made its attempts in the final moments to vent frustrations. They reported, "A staggering student from Pittsburgh, Pa., refused to move, yelling 'stick it to me, stick it to me.' . . . Some students tried to shout anti-establishment and anti-military rhetoric at the Guardsmen, but they were too drunk to make any coherent, well-founded statements."

What *The Spectrum* staff had done was more in the tradition of Norwegian jokes told by North Dakota's many Norwegian descendants, where they laughed at themselves and their heritage. It was still Cold War time and a typical joke was the one about the Russian, the American, and the Norwegian talking about their space programs. The American said, "We are going to go to Mars." The Russian said, "Oh, really. Well we're doing more than that. We are going to Jupiter." The Norwegian chimed in with, "We can top both of those. We are going to the sun." The American and the Russian looked at each other and chuckled, then said, "You can't do that because once you were within millions and millions of miles of it, the heat would be so great your spaceship and the people in it would disintegrate." The Norwegian replied, "We know that, so we are going at night."

This kind of joke initiated humor about themselves and their heritage that assumed they were the dull-witted, uncultured country hicks others presumed they were and they joined in the laughter. Like the Zap-in demonstrated and its coverage announced to the world,

4

this could reinforce those stereotypes and make some people in North Dakota begin to accept the beliefs as well.

A thesaurus written on America's East or West Coast that included "North Dakota" might well offer the following synonyms: "blizzard, remote, unsophisticated, farmer, hick." If the book had been produced in North Dakota, the entry would be more likely to say something like "honest, neighborly, courageous, hard working." They would both include descriptive elements that had foundations in truth, but those in the first set are interrelated, and North Dakotans have long been aware of outsiders' views of them and their home on the Canadian border and were hurt, or in some cases ashamed of their state. Some fell into holding the same disdainful views as were held by more urbanized outsiders, feeling inferior or focusing on the hardships of the weather and the lack of cultural activity, such as when Eric Severeid, a native of the small North Dakota town of Velva, who offered commentary for years on Walter Cronkite's *CBS News* did when he described the state as "a meaningless rectangle." Others wore the weather as a badge of courage that showed the strength of character and fortitude of the people who had settled the prairie and those who remained and survived what nature threw at them, helping each other through it. That difficult life had given them a common challenge and sense of community. They worked harder, worshipped more, counted on family and neighbors. Their payoff for living hard lives was longer lives. The highest number of triple-digitarians in the nation was in the state where hard work and clean air came with a pace of life that measured time in seasons.

The entry for a thesaurus that comes to mind first when one leaves Minnesota and crosses the Red River into North Dakota, is "flat." This most rural state in the nation is pancake flat in the east. It was once the bottom of the great glacial lake, Lake Agassiz, created as glaciers retreated at the end of the last ice age. The sediment deposited at the bottom of the lake created remarkably fertile soil where wheat, oats, and sunflowers grow in abundance. The flatness made for spectacularly large views of the skies to horizons in all directions and watching the weather was a major concern, as it varied dramatically and the agricultural economic base was dependent on it. "Strength from the Soil" became the appropriate words on the State Coat of Arms.

2

POLLIE JOHNSON OF NORTH DAKOTA

OLLIE JOHNSON AND KELLY ROGERS seemed like an ideal North Dakota teenage couple. Kelly was a personable, outgoing dark-haired young man with an easy smile who looked people in the eye when he talked to them and found that social acceptance came easily. Pollie was the blue-eyed blonde that other girls sometimes disliked, because she had all the qualities that assured popularity. She was pretty, confident and her enthusiasm and happiness showed in all she did. Pollie and Kelly dated when he was a junior and she was a sophomore at West Fargo High School, though the relationship had cooled down. Their friendship remained along with the embers of the romance, but Pollie always had many boys chasing her and Kelly was not without interested girls. He not only liked Pollie, but enjoyed the whole Johnson family, including her parents. Her father stood out, and the Viking of a man who was as strong as the elm trees surrounding their hidden home had become a bit of a father-figure to him.

Kelly's nonchalant personality was deceivingly remarkable,

as life at home wasn't always so easy. His father would skip work to go fishing or relax, then start drinking and vanish for periods of time, which he did during the first week of August in year of the nation's bicentennial. After he had been missing for several days, Kelly set out to find him and picked up Pollie to come along. They headed out in Kelly's maroon Chavelle in search of the absent parent, and during that excursion, talked about possibly doing something together on Friday evening. No final arrangements were made, and Kelly left it with the open-ended plan that on Friday night he would call Pollie.

That hot, dry Friday afternoon of August 8, 1976, Ruth Backstrom sat alone in front of her home on the farm north of West Fargo. She watched the light-colored car as it made yet another pass. Back and forth it seemed to go on a little-used gravel road in Cass County in the southeast of the state's Red River Valley. It was a county road, traveled most often by people she knew. The homes that lined it were other farm homes and the occasional country residence in a very sparsely settled area. It just seemed odd, so she kept watching. Odd things didn't happen here often, unless weather changes were considered odd. But there was the disconcerting fact that the blue-shirted driver seemed to be staring intensely at her each time he passed. That made it a little creepy odd. She would watch as he headed north on the road to the Maple River Bridge. Before long she would see him again, and he would see her. Youngish, she thought, maybe twenty to twenty-five, and had long brown hair. And there was this hat. It was hanging in the car, a green and white polka-dotted railroad hat. After about a half hour of repeated passes, the car was gone.

That evening Mrs. Backstrom and her husband went down to the Maple River Bridge. There was that car again, pulled off on the side of the road and parked next to the bridge. She didn't know what to make of it. Parking by the Maple River Bridge wasn't something really unusual. The bridge crossed the Maple River right where it emptied into the larger Sheyenne River. The Sheyenne was a major tributary of the north-running Red River, which it joined farther east. People liked coming out to this Maple River Bridge/Maple Dam area where the rivers met to enjoy the woods and because it was a good spot for fishing, a popular area activity. The surrounding Red River Valley was mainly treeless farmland and the woods along the rivers were pleasant. But it seemed late in the day for fishing, and just seeing that car again felt a bit too coincidental. People around there were good at noticing cars and recognizing the makes and models people drove.

The driver wasn't in the car because he had left to take a walk north along the east bank of the Maple River. Not far from where he had parked, on the opposite side of the river, was the secluded farm home of Gene and Norma Johnson. It was a home that people drove to quite often, but only those who knew the directions. Getting there wasn't simple. The Johnsons' home was hidden behind James Hoglund's farm off County Road 20, on a peninsula that extended into the water and was surrounded by heavy woods, the American elm growth bordering the river. There was a little-used country road that Johnson had built through Hoglund's farm. Along that road the location of the entrance had been marked that led to the secluded spot on the river where Norma and Gene's home was found. Two large white-painted logs standing nearly straight up as sentinels were connected by an unpainted log running between them high above the ground. From the connecting log a sign hung by chains, a single unfinished flat board that said in all capital, hand-painted letters, WELCOME TO THE JOHNSON'S HIDE-A-WAY. Beneath the sign was a quarter-mile dirt driveway through the trees edged with the same white wooden fence that would continue to surround the cleared property that was the Johnson home and farmland nestled inside. Against the fence at the entrance was the weathered wooden wheel of an old wagon, a symbol of the not so distant past in the area.

The Johnsons had their hideaway four miles north of West Fargo, and the couple had eight children, with seven still living at home. They weren't really farmers so much as country people, especially horse people. There was no wheat harvest here, but Gene spent time cutting hay for their five horses and their cow, and they also had two goats, a lamb, chickens, geese, ducks, a rabbit, and dogs. The children were members of the Cass County Cowboys and 4-H along with their church and school activities. The whole family came along to some of the high school rodeo events where Gene was actively involved as an organizer and promoter, and the Johnson children were often participants. Everyone helped out at the store on Main Avenue that the family owned, the C&C Market. It was a small convenience store, but with Fargo five miles down the road and the trailer parks nearby, plus the lack of stores in West Fargo, it did a fair business. It required everyone's help to make the store successful. Gene was a State Highway Patrolman and was commonly away cruising the area roads, but often back to close the store at night.

Norma and Gene Johnson's family was a busy one. What this all meant to the driver of the car parked by the Maple River Bridge was that he could stay hidden on the opposite bank of the river watching the Johnson home that Friday evening and count the number of people who left. Once the number reached nine, the secluded home would be empty. Then he could do what he had done in the past at other locations, break in and rob the place. The Johnson home had been robbed in the past, but not broken into. Someone walked off with some cash lying around during a party the children were having. The driver knew they had to have something he'd want, like guns. Guns were popular in North Dakota and valuable. Of course, there was a river in the way, but it had been an unusually hot summer. The river was low, and there would be a way.

It might have been an effective plan, but a friend of one of the Johnson girls had stayed over for the day. That put the count one off. It seemed as though the house was empty when the ninth person left, but one remained home. Sixteen-year-old Pollie was still in the house. Pollie hadn't felt well. It was Friday night and, in spite of earlier plans

10

with Kelly, she wasn't going out. She had a headache, and it was "her time."

Mrs. Backstrom wasn't the only person who noticed things seemed a bit odd. Kelly thought something was strange. He had called Pollie that evening at around 7:45, when he and a friend were going out. She told him she had a headache and was in bed. There were still other members of her family at home at the time. He called again when it was nearly 9:00 and after many rings the phone was picked up and, "Once it picked up there wasn't a voice there right away. I could hear a . . . I could hear ah there's a . . . to me it sounded like there was a ruckus going on or a fight." Next there was nothing but heavy breathing for a bit. The sound soon became what he described as a "panting, sluggish" noise followed by the single word, "Kelly?" Then came the dial tone, and he kept calling repeatedly, but there was no answer.

After ten calls, Kelly drove to the Johnson's C&C Market to let them know of his experience and concerns. Norma was there along with two of the boys, but they didn't seem quite as bothered as Kelly. Norma had talked to Pollie earlier in the evening and knew she wanted to get some sleep in hopes her headache would vanish. She probably didn't want to be bothered by the phone. Gene had been out haying that night and had broken an axle on his tractor, so he had returned to the store. He knew there was the chance, young girl home alone with phone calls coming; maybe she had a visitor she didn't want to have to explain to her parents. But if Kelly was really concerned, all right. They liked Kelly and if he wanted to go check things out, that was fine. He went, but didn't charge off because he had a feeling about how serious things were.

In the meantime the would-be intruder had made his way across the river by way of an old dead tree that had fallen from the east bank. Since the river was so low, it formed a bridge for crossing onto the Johnson land. From there it wasn't such a long walk to the house. The rest should be easy. Who knows, store owners would probably have money in the house and there might be other things along with guns that would be easy to carry away. With all of these kids living here, there might be a Farah Fawcett poster around. Love those blondes.

Getting in wasn't difficult in this area where there was no concern of a "passer-by" ever happening along. The Johnson place was so hidden that people had to know how to get there and the Johnsons didn't lock their doors. But what's this? The house wasn't vacant. There was someone home. That could really mess everything up. It was a good thing he had brought his rifle along. Then, as he made his way through the split-level home and discovered who it was, his thoughts changed. It was Pollie. Pollie, the cheerleader and gymnast known to the whole town, outgoing and exuberant and full of energy at the market and school and around the home, was all alone.

She was here, out in the countryside with no one nearby. The ruination of a good plan gave way to a more inviting, more exciting idea. What the intruder was considering was something more desirable than any goods he might have taken from the Johnson home. He saw opportunity, and he had a gun along to insure that things went his way.

Pollie broke a bone in her hand, received a gash in the back of her scalp and bruised her fingers and the back of the left hand putting up a fight, but he had her half naked in the kitchen when he inserted the barrel of the rifle in her mouth. Whether that was symbolic and he hadn't intended to discharge the weapon yet or at all would remain lost in that moment, but after that shot was fired he took the conclusive step. He "capped" her, as police say, to describe the finishing step in an execution as he did here when he fired a second round in her temple. This was in the kitchen where there was a phone on the wall. That slurred noise Kelly heard when she answered the phone was Pollie's final communication after her assailant fled the scene.

Kelly knew something was wrong and he was very familiar with the split-level house so he didn't barge directly in, taking a lower entrance on the side. He recalls, "I usually went through the front door. I knew something had happened and I went in that door, went up to the . . . went upstairs to the . . . to the landing at the front door and then from that landing, then went upstairs directly in front of the ah . . . upstairs where you got to the top of the steps where the door opening was to the kitchen I could see Pollie's body."

Only the kitchen light was on, illuminating the boldly geometric carpet. He entered and briefly noted a chair was out of place and the throw rugs were awry. There was Pollie, lying sprawled on the floor near the door.

He knew she was dead when he first looked at her. She was lying by a phone, and he had the presence of mind to go to a different room to call because he knew the kitchen phone was the one she had used to make her final call, and he didn't want to tamper with it. Kelly called the sheriff. Shortly before 10:00 he called the Johnsons at their store. He told them he had found Pollie and that she had been, "beaten, real bad."

The dispatch went out to several agencies, and Highway Patrolman Lyle Marcus was the first to respond. He was a friend and colleague of Gene's, and he headed from his home northwest of Fargo to the C&C Market to pick up Pollie's father before going to the home. Kelly knew it was Marcus. "Oh, I could hear that . . . I could hear that Dodge, that motor was just screaming. See and at that time when you got off of Cass 17, that one was paved but 20 wasn't. But I could hear it coming and when it turned onto 20, you could hear gravel, you could hear gravel spinning. Back then they had 440 mopars." Dodge 440 mopars were the 400-horsepower vehicles of the North Dakota Highway Patrol.

Marcus and Gene reached the house and were the first law enforcement officers at the country home. Gene says, "We might have screwed some things up ourselves being it was my daughter and my friend and me. We probably would have been more careful if it had been some other case."

13

It was his daughter and using the kitchen door or the telephone without thinking about fingerprints that could be getting compromised was a father's reaction. He wanted to get in quickly, and once he was there he needed an ambulance and to contact the Sheriff's Department. He also thought someone could still be in the house.

Kelly had been careful to avoid using the phone next to Pollie and found it strange that as more and more deputies arrived on the scene they weren't more cautious. He was detained for a long time and noticed, "They were using that same phone where the body was, and I thought, why are you doing that?"

Gene, like Kelly, called the Cass County Sheriff's Department, and they contacted an ambulance service and reached the state's attorney and the coroner. The coroner was at a lake cottage in Minnesota, which caused a bit of a delay in things, since final release of the body required his endorsement. Cass County Sheriff Dailey put all available officers on the case at the time it was reported, and work began that night. Among those who arrived was Deputy Mike Lyman, a trim, athletic Nordic who was a 1966 graduate of West Fargo High School. Lyman was celebrating his ten-year high school reunion that night and by the time the call came, playing poker at a classmate's home. He left for the Johnson home immediately without finishing the game, holding the winning hand, and began work on the case that was destined to command his attention for a considerable time.

At 10:40 p.m. Deputy Sheriff Earl Larson learned of the shooting while he was policing a dance at the Page Auditorium in Page, North Dakota, a town with 367 residents. That was the sort of duty the Sheriff's Department handled frequently. Larson, a solidly-built lieutenant, whose black hair betrayed his Scandinavian name, had done many investigations and was now chief investigator. Agencies in the Midwest often called the people who tried to solve the crimes "investigators," while that was the responsibility of detectives in urban areas. Larson was immediately ordered back. Sheriff Dailey put Larson in charge of overseeing the investigation. By 3:45 the next morning, the coroner had made it to the scene, and the body could be released and transported to a funeral home. The North Dakota Crime Bureau also assigned Special Agents Richard Rolle and Richard Olson to the case. They arrived during the night. The Crime Bureau existed because it had specialized agents and because many of North Dakota's towns were too small to support independent police forces.

That was a large turnout of inspectors for a crime, but this was North Dakota. Murders were something that happened on television and in movies. This was the safest state in the United States in terms of murders and all violent crime. That wasn't because of the lack of population. It had the lowest rates of both murder and violent crime *per capita* in the country. In the sixteen years the FBI had been keeping statistics for the crimes committed in individual states up to that time, in North Dakota the total number of murders had topped ten two years, and there had also been two years when the total number of murders committed in the state was one.

Sheriff's Deputy David Pralguske was also at the scene. He informed Kelly of his Miranda rights, then held him for questioning through much of the night. Miranda rights, which had originated ten years earlier in the case *Miranda v. Arizona* and have become familiar to almost everyone who watches television, are based on the threat of being a suspect:

1. You have the right to remain silent and refuse to answer questions.

2. Anything you do say may be used against you in a court of law.

3. You have the right to consult an attorney before speaking to the police and to have an attorney present during questioning now or in the future.

4. If you cannot afford an attorney, one will be appointed for you before any questioning if you wish. And so on.

Kelly felt as if he was the suspect in the murder, and believed part of the reason was his demeanor. It was, "probably because I knew something was wrong, that I was more ready for it . . . probably what . . . what triggered me being a suspect was that, you know, I wasn't . . . I wasn't really hugely emotional, and I just knew that what had happened and I didn't . . . I didn't really get overly emotional." It also made sense because in the trunk of his car was a shotgun and, more importantly, a .22-caliber rifle, which was confiscated to be test-fired to gather casings. There was also a cooler of beer in the backseat.

Pollie's father, though devastated by his loss, took time to find Kelly and check on him that night to see how he was holding up. He was worried about the young man in that moment of grief. That was Gene Johnson, a man who embodied a positive concern for others and their welfare in time of crisis, a tradition in prairie virtue.

Kelly was immediately the prime suspect, so his feeling like one was rational. When the officers finished interviewing him, they were thinking they had another possibility. Kelly mentioned that Pollie had a boyfriend, Lonnie, who was jealous and didn't always treat her well and that she was thinking of breaking up with him. West Fargo Police were called to go to this young man's home, but when they arrived no one was there. They maintained surveillance until his older brother drove up and told them Lonnie and his parents had gone to a lake resort in Minnesota for the weekend. He thought the place was called something that started with an "L" and was near Pelican Lake. After searching the brother's car for weapons, the sheriff's office contacted Ottertail County Sheriff's Office in the nearby Minnesota lake country and resort area that included Pelican Lake.

At 3:00 a.m. Ottertail County had located the family at the Ell's Resort grounds in a camper pickup. The family's camper was under surveillance by two county sheriff's departments and the Minnesota Highway Patrol until 4:55 a.m., when Larson arrived to wake them up. He first spoke with the parents, who expressed shock over the tragedy and said the whole family had arrived at 7:30 the previous evening.

He next spoke to Lonnie alone, beginning by advising him of his Miranda rights. When Lonnie was told of Pollie's death, he fell apart, crying to a point of near hysterics. Once he could respond, he said he owned a .22-caliber Browning rifle and mentioned a Robert Johnson, who was probably about twenty and used to go to the C&C Market. That Johnson fellow was from California, which often meant "weird" to North Dakotans, and seemed pretty interested in Pollie. He'd brought his yearbook to the store to show her.

Back at the crime scene, officers were looking around, but it had been decided to put off attempting a detailed search until daybreak and to get extra help to look for evidence in the woods and riverbank surrounding the house. There was the white outline drawn around Pollie on the carpet and her body had been covered after that with a heavy blanket until the coroner approved its removal. It appeared nothing had been taken—the guns were all still there and personal belongings intact. But things had been disheveled in the usually tidy kitchen. Deputies had begun talking to neighboring farmers about whether they had noticed anything unusual, but the Johnson's home, with all the kids and all the activities was a sort of meeting place, so cars coming and going wouldn't have been something strange.

In the morning, things moved quickly. By 8:30 a.m. Larson and three other officers had awakened Robert Johnson in West Fargo and were reading him his Miranda rights. They soon found he had been in the area for over a year, worked for Steiger Tractor and had a steady girlfriend. Of more interest, he was on probation for grand larceny, had asked Pollie out a number of times and had been at the Johnson's store the day before. But he was willing to take a lie detector test to show his involvement ended there.

Within two hours a West Fargo Police patrolman took two young people into custody for possession of a stolen pickup truck.

Now there were more possible suspects emerging and the list seemed to grow on its own. Chances were best of capturing the villain soon after a crime, so this looked good. These juveniles were from Moorhead, just across the Red River from Fargo, and the thing that provoked suspicion was they had red stains on their hands and clothes. By mid-morning Larson and Special Agent Rolle eagerly went to interrogate the young men, who were now their prime suspects. Hopes of a quick solution vanished when they found that both worked for Moorhead Street Department, painting fire hydrants. They weren't murderers covered with their victim's blood, but kids who hadn't cleaned up after the day's work.

Out at the Johnson home, careful inspection continued. Investigators took carpet samples and all the family's guns to have them test-fired. In a fold of a heavily woven, striped throw rug not far from where Pollie's left foot had been, they found a shell casing. The casing was less than a quarter of an inch in diameter, but Deputy Sheriff Lyman noticed it had an abnormal mark on the back of it. It was hard evidence, and they decided it would not be mentioned to the press. The murderer might not have disposed of his weapon, but if he heard that a casing was available to match to the weapon he used, the gun would be likely to vanish.

The sophisticated facilities for analyzing what little physical evidence they had didn't exist in North Dakota. Even the state's Crime Lab's technology wasn't as advanced as things were elsewhere. These bits would be sent to the FBI lab in Washington for the most accurate findings. Now they needed the gun. It was going to be difficult to make a case against anyone without more evidence when guns were owned by so many people and casings were so common, especially in these parts, but if they had the gun they would have the casing fired from it. Some real evidence that pointed a finger somewhere was needed.

In the afternoon Sheriff Dailey and Larson were walking along the bank of the river when they came to a place where uprooted trees had fallen across. In the mud near a fallen log on the bank where the Johnson home was located, there was a boot print. A quick check revealed no officer had visited this area during part of the search. Photographs were taken and a caste of the print was made, since it had some distinctive square and line markings that made it identifiable. This was something more for the FBI lab. There were also clay traces on branches of a tree that crossed the river to the side where Johnson's farmhouse was located. Larson found unclear boot impressions across the river. He and another officer each walked one side of the Maple River from the Maple River Bridge, but all indications were that someone had walked along the bank across the river from the Johnson home.

They had decided to try the walk from the Maple River Bridge because Gerald Buchli, a Highway Patrolman married to Pollie's oldest sister, had talked to Mrs. Backstrom and heard her story about the strange car she'd seen parked there the evening before. The Backstroms were asked to provide a composite sketch of the driver of the car. That would be something neither the Sheriff's Department nor the West Fargo Police had the capability for but Detective Lindblad of the Fargo Police Department could do. He could use their Identa Kit and get a witness to put together an image that people might identify. Backstroms each did theirs and Dr. Amidon of Fargo Clinic was called in to hypnotize them and help them sharpen the details.

The following day was Sunday, but things on the day of rest didn't slow down. Special Agent Richard Olson of the Crime Lab set up the polygraph in the sheriff's office, which was in the Court House building in Fargo. Robert Johnson had said he would take the lie detector test so he could be eliminated as a suspect, and he willingly showed up. Kelly, who kept fighting people's suspicions even though he was the first to be fearful and go to Pollie's aid, was also called in that day to see whether what he said held up. Results weren't back on his .22, so he was being looked at carefully, and considerable pressure was put on him during the exam to try to get something to slip out.

Larson's team spent the day seeking information from the Johnson family at that uncomfortable time to try to find direction for the investigation. The Johnsons came in for brief interviews. They were asked to make a list of all of their friends who had been at a party at their house earlier in the summer when some money was stolen in a small, unreported robbery. Carrie, one of Pollie's older sisters, said that she had received a number of calls where the caller would hang up immediately following her saying, "Hello." She also mentioned the names of workers who stopped in the family store and showed interest in Pollie. More information would be sought from her at another time.

Norma informed them of the pet Chihuahua that barked when there were strangers in the house. She hadn't heard it barking when she spoke with Pollie at 8:30 that evening. She had also asked Pollie to check a list of groceries she had left out on the dresser in her bedroom, and Pollie had said she couldn't find it. It had been sitting in plain view.

The topic of whether any of Gene's former arrests could have such ill feelings against him that Pollie had been made the victim of revenge was brought up. He couldn't remember any problems. He mostly arrested a few drunks and a member of some extremist group who had tried to give him some pamphlets at one time. He was known for his good nature and ability to handle arrests so that people ended out feeling treated well. At times he followed up on those he had helped put away or lose their driving rights to help them get straightened out. A suspect wasn't likely to emerge from Gene's work, but it was one rumor around town that the motive for the homicide had been revenge directed at the big, broad-shouldered man.

Investigators talked to Carrie's current boyfriend later in the afternoon, who was a construction worker nearby, and learned that on the day of the killing, Carrie and her friend Lori had been at the

Starlite Drive-in outdoor movie theater. Then Carrie went to his home in the nearby town of Grandin.

Larson and Rolle made an evening visit to talk more with Carrie, Pollie's nineteen-year-old sister. They learned that Pollie was going to break up with Lonnie because of the way he treated her and because he was so jealous. Carrie's boyfriend had come with his roommate to the Johnson farm recently to shoot their .22s. She also recalled a twenty-five- or twenty-six-year-old man who had been in their store a couple of months earlier. He had been drunk and called their home a number of times trying to get dates with the girls. She thought he lived at Dakota Estates Mobile Home Park. She told the investigators that the Chihuahua they kept indoors barked whenever anyone came in, but often it barked only if the outside dogs did.

The next morning Larson and Rolle interviewed Vicky, the oldest Johnson daughter, the one child not living at home. They asked her about her first husband and his relationship with the family. He was paying child support and tending bar at the airport in Fargo, but he had gotten along fine with the family, and there seemed to be little reason to look at him more closely.

The family knew nothing that pointed in any obvious direction, and the neighbors the deputies had visited hadn't been of any help. At this point Larson and the full-time team of fifteen he directed had no viable suspects and were short on evidence, though they still were looking at Kelly. The many immediate searches had failed to yield a murder weapon and the hopes for a quick, reassuring resolution to the murder faded.

Word was out around town. Paul Laney was a child at the time of Pollie's murder and recalled hearing the news. His reaction was, "I lived out there, I lived about five miles south of West Fargo on Route 17. . . . We went through shock waves, I mean, we lived in kind of the same situation, just opposite ends. It went from kind of a 'this could never happen here' to 'Oh, my God, it happened to a child.' Mostly what I remember . . . I mean my mom being extra careful with us."

A fragile social balance had been upset in the community. Memories reinforced this. Budd Warren's recollection of the time: "When Pollie Johnson [was killed] it was like total hysteria, paranoia in town. All the people . . . it was just unheard of." Dr. Dan Treat, who saw the countryside regularly added, "I remember driving the rural roads around West Fargo as a large animal veterinarian during the time that Pollie Johnson was murdered. I was usually alone and oftentimes it was after dark. Knowing that someone was out there who was a murderer was enough to make me a little nervous. A little piece of small town trust had been lost."

Crowds jostled uncomfortably in town Monday afternoon, the day of Pollie's funeral, as the bright afternoon sunshine made the ninety-six-degree heat more oppressive. Parking places for the funeral had filled early, and many of the people who came weren't dressed for walking far in the summer heat. The mourners were an unusual cross section of the small community plus visitors from nearby towns accompanied by law enforcement officers in formal uniforms. High school girls, all with straight hair, were joined by shaggy-headed boys, many sprouting moustaches, with ties awkwardly pulled tight and their foreheads glistening with sweat. There had been an effort by high school Principal Marvin Leidal to a contact a number of students, and a special area was roped off for them in the church.

Faith Lutheran was typical of many Lutheran churches that dotted the prairie of mid-America: a bright-white, wood-frame exterior with a steep, dark-shingled roof capped with a towering white steeple reaching high into the sky. The unadorned and uncomplicated design of these churches captured the spirit of the people who created the state — plain folks with heads held high. Faith Lutheran — the largest church in town and capable of holding nearly 500 people — would not be adequate for the turnout of mourners.

In the background, as people congregated, Deputy Sheriff Mike Lyman focused on watching the crowd. This was his home church, and he would have preferred to have been heading there as well to give support to Pollie's father, a "brother in arms," but duty called. Lyman knew Gene Johnson and was a North Dakotan who retained communal, rural values. Lyman was personally determined to do what he could to see this case resolved, to give the family some small measure of relief from the pain that would be forever with them. His duty was to make note of who came and who didn't, especially among the group of people considered suspects. He kept scanning the crowd for unusual behavior. Videotapes ran to catch what might escape immediate observation. There were, of course, too many people to keep an eye on all at once. As the church sanctuary filled and people crowded the aisles, this job became nearly impossible. Soon mourners were being directed to the basement below.

For all of these uncomfortably warm people, the disturbing truth—almost the only topic of conversation in town for the past three days—was visible in people's faces as they filed through the main entrance of the church.

On the entryway's right was an open, ivory-covered coffin with gold trim and brass ornamentation. In it lay the body of sixteen-year-old Pollie Lynn Johnson. Attractive blonde-haired, blue-eyed Pollie, with the winning smile and positive attitude that was well known in West Fargo, was at rest in her casket. Pollie, who represented so much of what was good and right about the community, and had played the clarinet in the high school band and been active in pep club. She was known to the town as a high school cheerleader and gymnast, the only one from West Fargo to qualify for the state finals. She was the friendly face at the C&C Market and had a personal welcome for everyone. And she was Gene and Norma's child. Seeing her young body so still made everything real to those who passed her. Murdered. Right here in West Fargo. One thing was certain. Pollie's murder would never end as a "cold case"—not the daughter of Gene Johnson. Whatever happened that tragic night would have to be discovered.

At 2:00 the coffin was carried to the front and Reverend C. Thomas Krangas, the pastor of the family's smaller home church in the country, Maple-Sheyenne Lutheran, conducted the brief service. A rural neighbor, Mrs. Dean Rust, asked all who had known Pollie to close their eyes and visualize her as the peaceful and happy girl she had been. Rust tried to make those memories more vivid by singing the song Pollie had often sung when she was younger. Her emotional rendition of "Jesus Loves Me" captured the simple faith and trust of the Lutheran girl from a time when her world was a safer place. It was followed by words from Reverend Krangas. He spoke of the "apparently senseless deed of violence" that had taken one of the town's favorites. His explanation to the congregation was, "The reason is evil; the reason is sin. It's frightening to us, evil in this world."

After a thirty-five-minute service, the coffin was carried into the heat of the day, where nearly thirty stoic law enforcement officers from a variety of agencies lined the sidewalk in silent tribute. The show of support for Pollie's father, a State Highway Patrolman, demonstrated the solidarity among the agencies charged with maintaining public safety. Throughout the proceedings, deputies had maintained surveillance on the family for reasons of security.

"The reason was evil." It seemed Reverend Krangas had provided a fair explanation for this senseless murder. North Dakota was the nation's most rural state, a state of mostly small towns and one where people didn't worry about their neighbors, but helped them. Pollie's murder could be seen as a wake-up call to the community to changes encroaching on it. The North Dakota prairie mentality no longer matched reality as the 1970s would demonstrate. The innocence and trust that were part of North Dakota's pioneer heritage had enduring and admirable qualities that would survive, but a more sophisticated world came with uglier, more threatening parasites and West Fargo was becoming a part of it. Reverend Krangas had offered a warning as well as an explanation, and in the near future that would become more apparent.

3

CHARACTER AND IDENTITY OF A NEW TOWN

I t had been exactly one century earlier when the most infamous deaths related to North Dakota had taken place. On May 17, 1876, the Seventh Cavalry had set out from its base in Fort Abraham Lincoln near Bismarck, Dakota Territory, under the command of George Armstrong Custer to find the Indian tribes refusing to be confined to reservations.

The tribes were viewed by some as noble savages but by the new settlers completing America's "manifest destiny" of coast to coast white settlement they were seen as impediments, obstacles to be overcome. The crushing of Custer's forces at the nearby Little Big Horn would make outsiders aware of the great chiefs Crazy Horse and Sitting Bull. In the days before media when the printing press dominated, word traveled slowly, but when the news hit the population centers, there was great reaction.

Typical and influential were the words of great American writers. Upon hearing the news of the Little Big Horn, Walt Whitman rushed out a poem entitled "A Death Sonnet for Custer," which appeared the following day in the *New York Herald* and later in *Leaves of Grass* as "From Far Dakota's Cañons." Whitman placed Custer's fall on the level of the Greeks at Thermopylae in the defense of civilization against barbarian forces. His work began:

Land of the wild ravine, the dusky Sioux, the lonesome stretch, the silence,
Haply to-day a mournful wail, haply a trumpet note for heroes.
The battle-bulletin,
The Indian ambuscade, the craft, the fatal environment,
The cavalry companies fighting to the last in sternest heroism,
In the midst of their little circle, with their slaughter'd horses for breast
      works,
The fall of Custer and all of his officers and men

Continues yet the old legend of our race,
The loftiest of life upheld in death,
The ancient banner perfectly maintain'd
O lesson O opportune, O how I welcome thee!

Soon Henry Wadsworth Longfellow published "The Revenge of Rain-in-the-Face," and embedded an unfounded but graphic image of Indian savagery in the public mind, as he wrote of the chief born on North Dakota's Sheyenne River having cut out Custer's heart after killing him, saying,

> And Rain-in-the-Face, in his flight
> Uplifted high in air
> As a ghastly trophy, bore
> The brave heart, that beat no more,
> Of the White Chief with yellow hair.

"the dusky Sioux, the lonesome stretch, the silence . . . Continues yet the old legend of our race, The loftiest in life." Whitman had defined Dakota and, with Longfellow, gave the country what it desired, a heroic figure to justify its questionable or unsavory actions and elevate them.

The crushing of Custer's forces did nothing to stop the slaughter of the buffalo, and defeat of the Indians in battle and spirit soon followed. The Homestead Act of 1862 brought sparse settlement, giving newcomers 160 acres of land with requirements that they make improvements. Once the native Sioux Indians had been successfully confined to five reservations, the railroads sought to populate the vast grants of land they had received in exchange for laying track to connect the settled East and West. A quarter of North Dakota had been given to the Northern Pacific Railroad with a substantial amount to the Great Northern Railroad. They brought in Northern European immigrants in the late nineteenth and early twentieth centuries.

Statehood was achieved in 1889, and the "sodbusters" found that many familiar crops didn't survive as well in the hostile northern prairie environment, but they did discover the glory of hard spring wheat as the greatest of crops, especially in the very fertile eastern half of the state. It could be planted in spring and harvested in fall. The territory was grassland, which made raising animals another source of income. Optimistic groups of Norwegians and Germans were sprinkled across the land, dotting it with towns and churches, and soon building schools.

By the end of the First World War, the white population was established across the state in a great number of very small communities. In 1920 the 647,000 North Dakotans lived in the countryside or in one of 279 towns, five of which had populations in excess of 5,000 while forty-six had less than 200 inhabitants. Wheat prospered in the plains environment, and the state was on its way to becoming the nation's leading producer.

The character of the state changed little over the next fifty years, as was indicated by the 1970 census when West Fargo reached a population of 5,161, making it the ninth community over 5,000, while the number of towns with populations below 200 had increased to 156. There were also the hundreds of incorporated townships and villages that people considered as their "hometowns," many with only a double-digit population. Maza was the smallest incorporated city in the United States with a population of five. The state's population had declined to 618,000 by then. "Thirty below keeps the riff-raff out" was a North Dakota expression for its failure to grow.

West Fargo's pride in being a part of the "winning of the West" and attached to the settlers who achieved it was apparent in the name of its newspaper, *The Pioneer*, and most noticeable structures on Main Avenue, which were the bars. They were the Frontier, the Lariat, the Silver Dollar. Farther west on Main Avenue was a twelve-acre visitors' attraction called Bonanzaville, built to commemorate the era of settlement. Named for the large "bonanza farms" of the late 1800s that the Northern Pacific Railroad had encouraged, the site acquired the Daughters of the Pioneers' original antique collection and moved in authentic buildings and machinery from the past and opened to the public in 1967.

While Main Avenue was the major east-west street and had Fradet's Fruit Market and a Tastee Freeze among its small businesses, the main north-south artery was Sheyenne Street. This was a mixed-use street, home to the small business district that included a convenience store called Jack-n-Jill; teen hangout, the Sheyenne Lanes bowling alley; Eckert's General Painting; Lindgren's Hardware; the State Bank and Trust; *The Pioneer*; doctor's offices; bars; and filling stations, as well as upscale housing. Industrial areas and residences, including six trailer courts and many small affordable homes, occupied the spread-out community.

The town had been a creation of laboring people—meat packers and stockyards workers, the farmhands, and people from small farms working in agricultural machinery production. Running water and a sewage systems had been added in the thirty years prior to Pollie's death. When lead inspector Earl Larson, a farm boy from nearby Hawley, Minnesota, had moved there in 1949, the community officially had changed from a village to a city two years earlier, and the only paved street was Main Street, which was actually on a state highway. The other streets were "all gravel or muck."

28

Earl's father worked at the meat-packing plant on the north side of the highway and their house was on the south, so, "If it rained it would get all muddy, and my dad would have to park at the fire hall, since there was a parking lot there, and just walk the rest of the way." Paving came in the 1950s. Earl learned cabinet making but took a job in West Fargo working part-time for Sheriff Smokey Stensrud in 1968. When Smokey died two years later, there had just been a big pay increase to $400 a month, so he became a full-time law enforcement officer.

West Fargo began the 1970s with a police force of one marked car. A few old-timers then remembered when the settlement was known as Haggart, named for the homesteader who had first claimed the land and had led other farmers in founding Equity Cooperative Packing Company, a meat packing plant sixty years earlier. That company had been bought out by Armour and Company that created the Village of West Fargo. The stockyards soon followed, and, on the land where vast herds of buffalo had once roamed, it became confinement pens for cattle and hogs awaiting slaughter and packing.

It had been hard work that created what was primarily a blue-collar town. As the 1970s progressed and grain prices dropped, the population from the countryside increasingly sought jobs in the state's cities. The inexpensive housing available was making West Fargo more of a bedroom community for workers in the larger Fargo-Moorhead area.

The sounds of country western music were likely on passing car radios or in shops, though the younger generation was more imbued with the same mass media as others their age. They cheered on Billy Jack and knew the words to "One Tin Soldier," and could name the "sweathogs" in the remedial class on *Welcome Back Kotter*.

But the frontier/pioneer mentality lingered in the area. A strong tie remained to ancestors who had taken on the weather and the difficulties of isolated prairie life with the courage to sustain their hopes and dreams. Their forefathers settled in a semiarid climate that produced conditions to shatter the will of all but the strongest and turned farmland into a shimmering velvet sea of amber wheat, despite the challenges location and weather had thrown at them. This was the stuff they were made of, and this was what brought out the best in them. Like a lot of other young people in small communities, some West Fargo students were up to milk the cows or do other chores before the school bus came in the morning and for many, there wasn't much money for social activities unless they earned it.

Weather received equal time with news and sports when people turned on television at 6:00. North Dakotans sometimes enjoyed exaggerating what life was like, but there was little need. It was the windiest of all states, with Fargo once clocking winds that were forty miles per hour *above* what qualified as hurricane speed. Temperatures in the state in one year had spanned 181 degrees, from a high of 121 to a low of sixty degrees below zero. Tornadoes, thirteen in the average year, were the most frightening weather events along with the two or three blizzards that typically struck annually and sometimes unexpectedly. Blizzards could be deadly, which had been especially true in the time of early settlement. They came with "white outs," when visibility was reduced to near zero. Being trapped in the countryside when a storm came up was a real danger. Dying of exposure or freezing was a threat pioneers in sod huts or simple wood frame houses in the countryside faced regularly, and weather-related deaths continued to occur in stalled cars or anywhere people were trapped away from shelter.

Wind chill was the term in use for the loss of heat from the body when wind was combined with low temperatures, but the temperature alone was often enough to bring deadly results. Devils Lake had a winter without equal in the United States until Alaska became a state, with five months continually below freezing and a thirty-seven-day stretch when the thermometer reached zero only one day. Thunderstorms were spectacular to watch, but hailstorms could wipe out a farmer's summer's labors in a matter of minutes. Then there were what North Dakotans called "snirt storms" when there was very little ground snow cover but strong winds. The mixture of snow and lifted dirt was swept along and made visibility difficult as well as leaving behind a considerable mess.

The state had become much more livable, with ploughed roads and electricity for furnaces and lights as well as for heated garages or headbolt or block heaters for cars so they would start in the morning after sitting out in the cold. There were still difficult days, but people descended from settlers, who had survived these conditions with little heat or shelter on the open and exposed plains, were strong and determined and willing to fight for the chance to till the land when warm weather came, and the living was good.

Deputy Mike Lyman, who was actively involved in investigating Pollie's homicide and the further "evil in our times" that struck West Fargo in the 1970s, was an example of how close people were to their frontier past and the character that past created. Mike's father was born on a homestead in Ransom County, North Dakota, and his parents, Stanley and Marion, had been married the year after Stanley returned from World War II.

His father tried his hand at running a pool hall briefly and his grandfather had sold his homestead to buy a farm near Lisbon. Mike's dad took over the farm at the beginning of the 1950s, when Mike was a child. The weather didn't cooperate. He describes this: "During the 1950s we had terrible dust storms in that area, and I have a recollection of coming home from town with my dad, and the kitchen door had been blown open, and we had to take a scoop shovel to get the dirt out that had filled up the house."

With the dry conditions they didn't have much luck with their crops and tried to get by mainly with their livestock.

It was hard work, and uncertainty on the prairie was understood from an early age. "We lived week to week with milking the cows, separating the cream from the milk and going to town every Saturday and selling the cream at the creamery and getting a check

31

for the cream. We threw all the [skim] milk away or else gave it to the pigs. But that's how we made a living, other than the annual crop, and some years my dad got virtually no crop off the land.

"When I was six, seven years old, I got up and milked cows before I went to school, and then again in the evening. I milked the cows by myself when dad was out in the field. He did a lot of custom work in the fall. He got a corn chopper and chopped a lot of corn for the neighbors for silage. So I did a lot of work, fed the livestock, I milked the cows. I drove truck during the harvest. I couldn't even see over the steering wheel. I was seven, eight years old, driving an old Ford truck, probably a 1940s-model truck with a floor shift. So I had to be able to push the clutch in order to put it in gear. I don't think I could see over the steering wheel when I was pushing the clutch in.

"Our land was really poor, and we had a lot of rocks. We used to go out and pick rocks and take a tractor and I drove the tractor, too, when I was pretty young. And I remember one time when I was doing that in the summer, it must have been on a field we just tilling for the summer and it didn't have a crop on it, other than maybe a cover crop, and a tornado came through the area fairly close, and I had to go crawl in a ditch. And the tornado passed between my dad, [who] was working in another part of the field [and me], and the tornado passed between the two of us. That was just kind of the daily hardships we endured on the farm.

"We were so much subsistence farmers. We had a huge garden. We raised our own meat, and we raised our own vegetables. We did all the canning in the fall and picked apples and picked chokecherries and made our own jelly and jam out of the chokecherries and apples and raspberries and strawberries and we had everything out there.

"My ancestry is Norwegian. My mother's dad came directly from Norway in the early 1900s, and my father's family is English and Norwegian. Yeah. We were Lutheran and dirt poor."

Milking cows before going to school, driving at age seven were farm activities that required responsibility and discipline. It was real work that mattered, and the family depended on it. This would be true of 1970s students in West Fargo who lived on farms—they would be up to do chores before going to school and they often understood what work was, whether manual labor or school assignments.

Lyman commented on the maturity that came with the responsibility of hard work. "My dad gave me a .22 rifle when I was seven years old. You'd never think of doing that today. But that was just part of the maturity you had to have on the farm. He thought I was mature enough, and I was."

His education also shows how close the frontier world was in rural North Dakota. "I went to a one room school house. It was called Springer Number Six, which was Springer Township. I went to my first four years in the country school and we had eleven or twelve students in the twelve grades. The school was a mile by road and a little over half a mile cross country. During the decent time of the year walking to school, you know the old story about walking against the wind both ways . . . in 1961 we moved up to West Fargo, and I went to seventh grade in West Fargo."

Mike got involved in sports and was one of West Fargo's premier athletes when they moved into competition with the larger schools in the east of the state. He was running around with a rougher crowd at first, but found role models in his cousin from Fargo, Ron Green, and Dave Osborn from the town of Cando. Both played football at the University of North Dakota in the early 1960s and went on to play professionally in the National Football League. Looking back, Lyman summarized, "All those sports experiences, work ethic, and values led me to the right side of the tracks and ultimately into law enforcement in 1971."

Years later in the 1980s it was painful for him to see his old one room school sold on auction for $250 to be destroyed. It was his heritage and symbolic of a time and a way of life, but he couldn't afford to buy it and move it.

At that time Lyman had moved to a home north of West Fargo and transferred from First Lutheran to Maple-Sheyenne Lutheran Church, the church the Johnson family attended, and was president of the congregation. It made Pollie's homicide an even more personal matter.

The values of those people who had worked to make the prairie their home were passed on to some like Pollie, who had been diligent, warmhearted and helpful, optimistic, energetic, and had a strong faith. People like Pollie had grown up facing uncertainty and had been taught one couldn't assume life would be easy, but they were people who could survive that life with hard work and cooperation. They were self-reliant people but trusted their neighbors and knew they could count on them. When times were tough or something tragic happened, people pulled together, as they did after Pollie's murder. Nora, Pollie's mother, said, "Everyone's been just wonderful," and Gene added later, "I don't know how we would have gotten through it without the support of everyone." Don Witham spoke for the town and the general view of support in his editorial the week of the funeral in *The Pioneer*, "Always With 'Em," as he said, "The community of West Fargo has not forgotten, nor will forget, Pollie Johnson."

Those values formed the basis of character that made the state proud and produced working people who earned their pay and achieved in school and elsewhere, in life. The example many pointed to was Theodore Roosevelt, who came to western North Dakota in his younger days in the latter 1800s to regain his health. He later said, "If it had not been for what I learned during the years I spent in North Dakota, I never would have been president of the United States."

But of course not all inherited the positive values of the tenacious settlers. By the early 1970s, the picture wasn't quite complete without including the less positive side that came as a result of North Dakota isolation and seclusion. In 1973 the Drake school board banned Kurt Vonnegut's novel *Slaughterhouse Five*. When the state

34

bragged of being "Whiter and brighter in winter," the emphasis on whiter seemed less than subtle. The heritage of West Fargo that was only a couple of generations away mirrored the heritage of the state in being German and Norwegian — West Fargo over eighty percent so and the State over seventy percent. The community had not shared in the social changes and cultural awareness that had been reshaping America, and prejudices existed, though they were being challenged by many younger community members.

At Pollie's school there were American Indian students, some of whom were rough — often sporting fresh burn marks spaced equidistant from their elbows from having played a form of chicken, putting a lit cigarette in the crux of the elbow and seeing who would be last to let it drop once it started burning skin. But there were other Indians like Ken and LuAnn Pettie who were stars, leading the sports teams and popular with students and faculty. Discrimination didn't seem to play a role as much as behavior and performance. There were some Hispanics — who encountered few difficulties — though the population generally avoided the major Hispanic invasion that occurred every summer as masses of migrant workers turned up to provide cheap labor.

With a black population, it was different. A black population was nearly non-existent in the state until large, self-contained air bases were established near the cities of Minot and Grand Forks in the 1960s. That led to another of North Dakota's popular and accurate sayings, that, if it left the Union, it would be the third greatest nuclear power on earth. There had been grumblings in West Fargo in the late 1960s when North Dakota State University in Fargo began recruiting black athletes. What was happening in the state where milk was the official state beverage?

Integration came to the West Fargo schools in 1970 when a military recruiter was assigned to Fargo and settled in West Fargo. A middle school teacher recalled the day well, as the school year had started and he was reading a short story with his class to show the hardships black Americans sometimes faced and how impressive their achievements could be in the face of adversity. The story was about Wilma Rudolph, who had been famous ten years earlier, and the new African-American girl, Bonnie, was brought in to his class just as they were about to start. She took a copy of the story and sat down to listen. Wilma Rudolph was the twentieth of the twenty-two children of a dirt-poor twice-married man, and was born prematurely in Tennessee, when segregation was standard policy. In her early years she had pneumonia, scarlet fever, and polio with less than first rate medical care. She lost the use of her left leg, and was fitted with metal leg braces when she was six. Her brothers and sisters massaged her leg every day, but she suffered from whooping cough, measles, and chicken pox, while remaining determined to be a "normal kid." At age nine, she took off her leg braces and soon discovered she could run, fast. Rather like Forest Gump she said, "I don't know why I run so fast. I just run." The track coach at Tennessee State discovered her and when she was twenty. Called the "Black Pearl" and the "Black Gazelle" in Europe, Wilma was at the 1960 Rome Olympics, where she became the first woman in history to win three gold medals. Her soft-spoken and charming manner did much for the nation's image, but when the mayor of her hometown planned a welcoming parade and banquet, she refused to attend because it was segregated. It became Clarksville, Tennessee's, first integrated public event.

After finishing the inspirational story, it was time for class discussion, and the new girl raised a long arm and spoke her first words in her new school. "That's my aunt," Bonnie said, and the teacher smiled politely and nodded. The next day Bonnie arrived with a shoebox filled with, among other things, AAU gold medals and a black-and-white photograph of Wilma Rudolph and President Kennedy at the White House that was signed, "From a grateful nation, John Kennedy." The Reeves family was accepted better than some might have been at the time in part because Bonnie's gracious mother took a job at the middle school, and the parents were such pleasant people that those who were so inclined found it difficult to fit them into their prejudicial stereotypes. Another reason was that Bonnie had a brother, Tony, a freshman who had inherited some of the Rudolph genes, so West Fargo had a scoring threat in football and points in basketball and track, which, in small-town mid-America was important.

When Tony began dating the attractive white girls . . . well that was another matter. For some, a line was being crossed that was not tolerable. *Guess Who's Coming to Dinner* might have been a good movie, but racism was still pervasive and the town of 5,000 not really cosmopolitan. For many, this was their first exposure to African-Americans and a very constructive one. The 1970s brought change and broadening of horizons to West Fargo and some of it was positive, as many young people took it in stride and the presence of the Reeves family as normal.

Open spaces with opening minds, such as the prairie offered much of its younger population, could be a strong combination when the foundations were solid. But there were the exceptions, and sometimes the necessity of being strong enough was twisted by insecurity into the need to show how tough and dominant a person could be.

It was an intimidated and intimidating man who came home all muddy that night of August 8, 1976, when the town had been struck by the "evil in this world." His wife noticed his clothes and heard his explanation about having fallen down. In her mind there was something more to the story, and in fears she only shared quietly and privately, she wondered about muddy clothes during the driest summer in thirty years.

4

Investigating Pollie's Murder

O ne down, seven to go," said an unknown caller to the Johnson home during the week of Pollie's funeral. Horrified, the family wasn't taking chances on whether the called might have been the killer or whether he was serious. "We have eight children," Nora explained. Gene added, "We lock all the doors now. Before this happened, we didn't even know where the keys to the house were."

Country living wasn't the same. At least one male member of the family had be in the home at all times. As for father's work, "I've turned down a lot of assignments that would have taken me away from home at night. And when I'm on patrol at night, I make sure to swing by here a few times."

With no leads or real suspects and with little physical evidence to go on, Pollie's murder was going to be a case that would require Larson to start at square one and seek to find a direction to follow. The tension the Johnsons felt was felt by many others, and community pressure on the investigators for results was intense. The investigation needed to be organized, both to narrow down possible suspects and find leads to pursue, unless it happened to get a lucky break. Finding the weapon would be one focus, and searches of woods would continue, plus frogmen were ready to search the river in the area around the Johnson property.

Some people in West Fargo whose past behavior made them worth looking at, had to be eliminated. Neighbors had been interviewed and might be worth another visit. An important avenue of investigation would be learning more about Pollie and her personal life, which could provide a starting point for where to look next. With Pollie, they would want to know about boys interested in her, girls who might have been jealous, what the people did who were in her social crowd—such as marijuana use or anything that might lead to some sort of problem.

Another possibility to be looked into was the rather transient element that made up the clientele of the C&C Market, where she often served customers. Since she was so outgoing and attractive, investigators needed to know whether any suspicious person had been coming in when Pollie worked. They would have to check with the family for any new thoughts they might have had. One obvious thing to consider again was whether Gene had any enemies from enforcing the law. Much of this would be a matter of trying to eliminate everyone who could not possibly have been responsible and seeing who remained.

That much they could map out, but, at the same time, calls were coming in locally with tips and suggestions worth tracking down. The murder had been a big enough story that they were getting frequent contacts from other agencies around the country to pursue. That process could be demanding and possibly require use of a much larger budget, but if they had promise, no cost was spared.

They would just have to keep gathering information and digging through it, plus checking with informants they'd heard from in the past until there was a break or a pattern set them on the course to solving this. It was time to start digging.

On the day of the funeral, Special Agent Olson conducted an interview with a former boyfriend of Pollie's older sister, Carrie. There was nothing that indicated he might be the killer, but it looked like sex could have been the motive for Pollie's murder, and he had an extensive history of sexual misconduct to the point that he was being treated for it at the Southeast Mental Health Center. He was in that category of people investigators thought should be looked at carefully because of his background, plus he knew the Johnson home well. He owned three guns but hadn't known Pollie well. He was open to questions and very cooperative, readily agreeing to take a lie detector test. He had nothing to hide about himself or the day of the murder and seemed an unlikely suspect.

Leads from outside the area were tracked down almost immediately. During the week of the funeral, Larson and a deputy were in Seattle, Washington, interviewing a seventeen-year-old West Fargo boy at 2:00 a.m. in the King's County jail. The young man they were looking at had been charged with burglary after being arrested along with six others, two adults and four juveniles, all from Fargo. They were found with stolen goods in the car in which all were sleeping. What most interested Larson was the .22-caliber rifle also found in the car, which might be the big break in this case. News reports had reported that the murder had been committed by a "small-caliber weapon" without specifying what it was, but the officers had been aware from the beginning that it was a .22 because they had found the shell casing. However, whatever else this youth had done, he had not killed Pollie. The flight to Seattle proved useless other than eliminating someone who hadn't been under serious consideration. The Associated Press said that local authorities claimed this was a "good, solid lead" in the case, but a "dry well" was how Larson characterized it in the continuing report of no progress on the investigation.

While deputies were working on more neighbor interviews and frogmen searched the river around the Johnson residence, a lead came from an unexpected source about the time Larson and a deputy returned from the West Coast. A seasoned older columnist at the major area paper, *The Fargo Forum*, wrote a long story with the title, "Psychic makes predictions about West Fargo murder."

The confused Cal Olson said, "I don't know what to think about it, and I'm not quite sure how to handle it."

An old friend from his goose-hunting days, whom he hadn't seen for fifteen years, had come to his office and asked whether he would be willing to meet his sister-in-law, who was visiting from Los Angeles and was a psychic. Olson said he didn't believe in psychics, but he tried to remain open-minded, and his friend said he and others had been sitting around discussing the murder when his sister-in-law got a message "from the spirit world." Olson's friend then handed him a piece of paper with a physical description and the first initial of a man the woman said had committed the murder. She wanted the police to know. Olson's friend thought he had the connections to get this information checked out.

Olson was introduced to the sister-in-law, Betty, who, he said, was of indeterminate age, smoked three packs of cigarettes a day and was the first person he'd met who drank more coffee than he did. But, "Serene. She came on with this serenity." Born in Wyoming, she had moved to Los Angeles and claimed she had been psychic all her life. She said she got most of her messages clair-audience, like someone talking in her left ear. "This is the voice of my Master Teacher. He is Tis Lama, who was a Tibetan monk in his life on earth. When he comes, I get a ringing in my left ear, and then I go listen. He has a very soft-spoken, loving voice."

The Tibetan monk, Tis Lama, was talking to her? This was all sounding very California to someone who had written for the *Fargo Forum* for so many years, but Olson wrote, "And then, right in the middle of the whole discussion, she leaned forward with her elbows on her knees, and looking directly at me, and, speaking in an intense and concerned tone, she told me something about myself that no one ever has told me. She gave me seventy-five words on my past, present, and future that not even my wife could be expected to come up with. Then we sat back and picked up the conversation and poured some more coffee."

Betty said her predictions might have been clearer if she had some of Pollie's possessions, since the vibrations come through better when she had things to handle. Olson was impressed enough that he headed for the sheriff's office and convinced a deputy to give him Pollie's Social Security card and driver's license. Betty held them and after murmuring and making exclamations for a while, began speaking fast, running together descriptions, concerns, estimates, predictions. Olson ended with twelve pages of notes to deliver to the sheriff's office the following morning. He said some would be libelous to print, but it should be all right to say killer will be caught within two weeks, within the area, and more or less by accident. "The police will fall into it."

Two weeks passed, however, and the police weren't much farther along. The name initial the psychic had provided hadn't panned out. When asked later why they had paid any attention to this, lead investigator Earl Larson said, "They seem to get vibes, or whatever you want to call it, or feelings and some of those things are accurate. Psychics do work sometimes, but in [this] particular case they didn't."

It wasn't unusual for authorities to be contacted by psychics, and he added, "Those people rescued us a couple of cases later, so we better deal with them again. They do hit on certain things and sometimes they're right, but in that case, they weren't. There was a young guy in West Fargo, about Pollie's age, a little older, and we were looking at him. The psychic told another agent that inside the drawer in his apartment (he was living with his parents), 'You're going to find a gun. It's in the junk drawer.'

"So they went to the apartment and looked in the drawer. There was a small caliber .22 in there. So, they do come across things that are accurate sometimes. I'm not a disbeliever and some people want to put everything, trust everything in them."

Talks with Pollie's friends about her life began to bring up more possibilities. Jana Swanson let on that there were different social groups that visited Johnson's, and the groups behaved differently. Marijuana use had made its way into some of the visiting crowd, but the deputies were more interested in some customers at the family store when Pollie was working. One who deserved a look was a high-school student who had been caught stealing by Pollie and became belligerent. He had said he didn't care who her father was. He'd come back and rob the store. Then there were several older customers who went by nicknames. Goldie was the first to be brought up. He would come in on Saturdays beginning in spring and usually just have a bottle of pop and hang around. He wore black leather and blue jeans and had long dark, kinky hair, and wire-rim glasses. He had once taken Pollie on his motorcycle.

Another re-interview with one of Pollie's friends added a few more pieces. She hadn't seen Pollie since two weeks before the murder and that had been at the Moonlite Drive-in Theater after Pollie had suffered some physical abuse from her boyfriend. She talked about Pollie's boyfriend's friends and also about who else came to bother Pollie at C&C Market when she worked and mentioned a man in a black coat and blue jeans with wire-rim glasses and long, kinky hair who would come in during spring on Saturdays and drove a motorcycle. That sounded like a description of Gary Guilbert, also known as "Goldie." There was also a high-school-aged guy who used to come in and ask Pollie to go to dances, but she didn't know who he was. One thing Pollie's friend found strange was how a couple of girls who Pollie didn't like at all were now acting like they had been the best of friends.

Larson and Special Agent Rolle re-interviewed Kelly Rogers. He was very agreeable and cooperative and provided considerable information. Kelly knew the makes of cars people drove and told of a fight that a number of West Fargo boys, himself included, had been involved in at Dunvilla, a resort in the Pelican Rapids, Minnesota, area. Going to the nearby lakes in the "land of 10,000" was common for both adults and teenagers who could drive, especially on weekends during the hot summer months. There had been a fight with a with a group that ran one of the entertainment places after a stranger sat on Carrie Johnson's lap. It had involved four guys, older in some cases, seventeen to twenty-one, and one big guy with shoulder-length hair and a dark beard. Kelly recalled the model of car he drove. The next week when they came to have a keg party, they brought along more friends in case these guys returned. Pollie had been on these outings, which were about a month before her murder.

Locally, there was "Rocky," who might have been attracted to Pollie, but Kelly said he wasn't a candidate, just a shy guy, and Pollie was so friendly to everyone and outgoing. The investigators' early suspects' names were brought up, and Kelly said they called Goldie "Coffee Grounds," because of his shabby beard. There was also "Putts." Goldie and some of his friends had come to the Johnson home in a van once, and an argument ensued between them and Kelly and a bunch of others. One of Kelly's friends pulled a Billie club out of the van Goldie had arrived in. An additional item the investigators asked Kelly about was drugs in West Fargo and who supplied them. He gave them names and again, the cars they drove.

Although Kelly had called in the homicide, taken a polygraph and testified several times, suspicion of him as the murderer didn't vanish. He had police and sheriff's office operatives watching him regularly even though he remained good friends with the Johnsons, who didn't harbor suspicions. They'd taken his boot prints, and he was aware of their surveillance, as he observed, "I knew I was being watched because, I mean, I knew that there were police cars looking when I woke got up in the morning and went to do whatever I would do . . . I knew what cop cars were whether they had a cop light on 'em or not." Kelly found recognizing the sheriff's officers easy because, throughout high school, he'd worked at Sheyenne Lanes, the bowling alley in town, and the sheriff's department had a team in the local league, so when a regular was on duty, another would be in taking his place and Kelly saw them all.

Kim Johnson, another friend of Pollie's, filled in some details. An earlier interviewee had said Kim might know who the "fat guy" was who had tried to get Pollie to go on a date at their store. She said he was known to them as "Chip," and was eighteen or nineteen and worked at Fargo Tank Company. He wasn't a bad guy, and after the murder was discovered and first being investigated, but Kim brought out Chip's continuing attitude about Kelly. Chip had said he was going to get some guys together and beat up Kelly until he admitted to committing the murder.

Kim's father was involved in stock-car racing, and she said the night of the murder she had gone to Grand Forks with her parents for the races, and Chip had come with them to work the repair pits with her dad. Kim also gave the name of one of the local marijuana dealers who was already being investigated by a deputy as a suspect in the case. Her boyfriend's car was beige.

When September arrived and the temperature began to drop, considerable effort had been expended but little progress had been made. Sheriff Dailey said the investigators were still "beating the bushes" for clues. A number of suspects had been interviewed and eliminated and seized items were still under analysis by the FBI, but no warrants had been issued and no arrests were in sight. A reward fund had been established early in the month with a $200 donation from the West Fargo Lions Club, and the donations were being handled by the West Fargo State Bank, and Fargo National Bank was also collecting for the fund. The money collected would be returned if no arrest was made within one year, so names and addresses were requested from anyone wishing to donate. Within days it was over $1,000.

As the weather began to change and the leaves were starting to take on new colors with the yellows and occasional reds that would soon mark what was for many the most pleasant season of the year, other topics were taking on importance. A new flu-like condition had

45

killed twenty-eight Pennsylvania Legionnaires and 180 cases had been discovered in the nation during the past month, bringing on curiosity and concern. Farmers were still harvesting crops, and the eagerly anticipated duck hunting and goose hunting seasons were drawing near. More than anything else, football dominated conversations. "How about them Bizon this year?" The Thundering Herd of North Dakota State University was in Fargo and a leading national football power in Division II. Only someone from some snobby part of the country would pronounce the Bison with an "s." West Fargo had reached a size that meant it would be competing against the larger North Dakota schools of the Eastern Dakota Conference, so things didn't bode well for the Packers.

Negative reminders of the case receding from public attention came in September, and the police took these seriously. Threatening calls to two West Fargo cheerleaders, saying they would "get the same thing as Pollie Johnson" were made and another call was made to cheerleaders at Fargo South High School, also mentioning Pollie's murder.

There was some official deception going on by the sheriff's department, since the press reported that authorities had not been able to tell whether the murder weapon had been a .22 caliber weapon or from similar caliber gun, pistol or rifle. The forensics experts had been able to determine a considerable amount about the shell casing found near Pollie. But eliminating suspects remained the major part of what they could do without more evidence.

Pollie's father, for example, had access and knew she was alone, so that meant he had to be a suspect. A good community man, a law enforcement officer, father of the victim — who wanted to interrogate Gene? They would have to bring up personal and private questions about possible things Gene might have done that could lead to retribution, and those would be very awkward to ask. Someone he barely knew was brought in for the interview. It wasn't pleasant for him, but he had no skeletons in the closet. It was just the idea of people thinking he possibility had been responsible. Still, he knew it was part of the job that had to be done and that they had no solid leads. They had been keeping him informed, but still, he said, "It's kind of tough when they're talking about being involved in something that led to murder of your daughter, like having an affair with some man's wife or something. But I was in law enforcement and I understood they had to eliminate every possibility."

Earl Larson said Gene and his reputation had a special affect on the investigation. So many people admired Gene, including those in the area who had committed crimes in their pasts and felt Gene had treated them fairly, Larson got help from all sorts of unexpected places and unexpected people. Earl put it, "Everybody liked Gene Johnson. I mean, there were guys who normally didn't have much time for cops who would do anything. They would call us with any kind of information. So really, the whole town cared. People, the 'criminal element,' came forward who otherwise would have been uncooperative or disinterested, but they wanted this one solved and were asking, 'How can we help?'"

That had been made very clear to Larson when he answered a phone call from a bar, and the message he received was, "Earl, we been talkin' and if you've got a suspect and you don't think you'll be able to charge him, let us know who it is and we'll take care of it."

He didn't think they were that drunk. They were very serious about it.

The well-liked Gene Johnson was another small-town North Dakota product, born to a farm family in Ypsilanti. It was Depression time, and his father went to California and found a job at a seaside resort where he could send money back to the family. They moved out to California, and his dad worked in the shipyards during World War II. After the war they at returned to Marion, North Dakota, with its population of 215. Gene soon got a job working for a grain elevator as a buyer about the time his dad had a stroke.

The Korean War broke out and Gene was drafted in 1951, and had a year in Japan and another in Korea. After returning, he found a job with an oil company working on farm deliveries. He also found Norma, a farm girl from Grand Rapids who was working at the bank in Marion, and they were married in 1954. In the late fifties, Gene thought he'd try something different and applied for both the Highway Patrol and Border Patrol, willing to accept whichever was first to offer him a job.

The Highway Patrol came through and in 1959, and he began in Cando. In 1964 he was transferred to Devils Lake, and in 1966 to Fargo. In Fargo he and two other officers started a business. They began dealing with Northern Freight Sales, a company that acquired damaged freight, refused goods, and late deliveries that were not accepted. They set up three small stores, and in the early 1970s, split them and each took one. Gene took the C&C Market north of West Fargo and turned it into a convenience store.

Kelly and Pollie both spent a great amount of time at the C&C Market, and it catered to the nearby trailer courts. All of the Johnson kids were expected to work there, just as they were expected to do chores at the farm house. Everyone in the community admired Gene's kind nature, but he wasn't a pushover and expected his children to work. The way to assure that chores at home were completed was to say, "Dad's coming."

Late in September, the team of investigators hit on a theme. Something was noticed in the many investigations going in many directions that offered promise of an area to examine carefully. All the haphazard accumulation of information and analysis might have given them a new motive. Within a ten-mile radius in the five weeks following the homicide at Johnsons' home there had been seven break-ins in similarly isolated rural homes. In some cases the occupants had only left their houses for quite brief periods, so someone apparently had been watching to know when the residents were away. This pattern was being looked at as a possible link to the murder. Lyman and Larson and others knew there had been a sex crime, but this could be looked at as a robbery gone bad, though nothing was taken. There could be a new set of suspects. As the inspectors carried on, the fund grew and topped $4,000 in October with a $1,000 donation from Johnson's colleagues in the State Highway Patrol.

Investigators were now working on the break-in theory, along with looking at all other aspects of Pollie's life. Fall was moving along, and it was getting on to Indian summer, that wonderful time of year after the first frost when high-pressure systems bring clear blue skies, making being outdoors such a pleasure, especially since the warm spell also warned that winter was soon to follow.

Larson received a local tip to check that was off the radar. It showed what an unsolved crime can do when the investigation begins overturning all the rocks in a small community. The desperate search for a murderer exposed the town's secrets and peccadilloes.

Jack Turner, an employee of Fargo City Garbage Utilities, said he had information that could be relevant to this crime. He came to the sheriff's department and told his story. According to Turner, his wife operated a milk-delivery business north of the Fargo-West Fargo area. One of her customers was a neighbor of Gene Johnson. She had been delivering milk there twice a week for years, but for the last six to eight months only once per week. She usually arrived at about 5:00 a.m. On October 18, she saw a woman in the garage doing something with the deep freeze. It surprised her, since she knew there weren't women living there. She took the milk to the house, and the woman called out, saying she wanted some candy bars. That was when Mrs. Turner realized it wasn't a woman. It was the man she had delivered to all those years dressed in women's clothes, wearing a gray wig, nylon stockings and high-heeled shoes. His voice was still his same male voice, and he didn't seem embarrassed or surprised at being seen.

Mrs. Turner saw him in the same clothes the following week, accompanied again by a request for more candy bars. She was a bit frightened and concerned about the possibility that this neighbor had some connection with Pollie's death. She had her husband accompany her on her November 1 visit. When the two of them arrived, the man in high heels and gray wig again requested candy bars and complimented Mrs. Turner on her new vehicle, while Mr. Turner was paying attention to the male voice and the boney legs.

What the investigators knew of this man was that his wife had died of cancer and that he was very "old fashioned" in many ways, doing some of his farming with horses, threshing grain using separators and horse-drawn wagons, keeping old equipment around. He had an absolute hatred of daylight savings time. His old-fashioned ways might have extended to moral feelings about the way the Johnson girls lived, with all the traffic at the residence and its seemingly a hangout or gathering point for young people. It was decided he should be considered a suspect.

Larson called Howard Bud Teton, an instructor at the FBI Academy at Quantico, Virginia. Teton had done a psychology profile on the homicide during a recent North Dakota Peace Officers' Convention. He stated that the "murder of Pollie Johnson was either done by a psychopath or someone who was high on drugs." Johnson contacted Teton a second time in Sioux City, Iowa. Teton said it was possible that, in this man's frame of mind, he could commit this murder. The FBI profiler said they should consider him a prime suspect.

The best people to ride with Mrs. Turner and confront this man would be from the Crime Bureau in Bismarck rather than individuals Larson knew from West Fargo. In the meantime surveillance would be maintained. Soon his relatives were called in and interviewed, but nothing fit for considering him. He was also called in for a hard interview and given a polygraph, which eliminated any doubt. The answer wasn't going to be as easy as finding a sad and suffering man living a secret life in the countryside. This was another dry well.

The high school nurse, who lived in a nearby small town, called to say she had been visited by a book salesman at her home on the afternoon of the murder. He had a Southern accent. Not really a crime.

Norma had questions of her own. Some of it didn't make sense. When she called at 8:30 the night of the murder, she had asked Pollie to check the grocery list in their bedroom, which was in plain sight. Pollie said she couldn't find it, but there was no way she could have gotten to the bedroom and back to the phone in the time it took her to answer. Norma had tested it herself and found it wasn't possible. That, combined with the fact that the dog in the house wasn't barking, which it usually did if there were strangers, didn't add up. They had to put the dog out or away when visitors were over. What had happened to the dog, and who had been there?

By December students were watching the Fonz on *Happy Days* like young people everywhere and going in to Fargo to see Rocky's inspirational heavyweight bout with Apollo Creed at the Fargo Theater. The large team of investigators found many new leads to pursue. On the December 7, they were contacted by the Minnesota Crime Bureau which had been working on a shooting death of a gas station attendant on August 10 and whose path they had traced across the country. They thought he had been involved in a number of homicides across the country. He was in custody in California.

Larson requested shell casings from the weapon used after the test firings. That same day Gene Johnson contacted Larson to tell him that his wife had come across a note in Pollie's belongings that mentioned Todd Ferris aka McLaren. Following up on that was assigned. Two days later, an FBI agent called to say a woman whose son was in grade nine at West Fargo High School had overheard a girl at the school telling three boys she had seen a pickup truck parked near the scene of the Johnson homicide on the day of the murder and knew the driver. The girl's name and the boys she was talking to were all reported and contacted by investigators for more information.

The next day the team received a call from a farmer near Harwood, which was very nearby. He said he was clearing some trees and rubbish with a bulldozer and came upon a .22 rifle. The rifle was brought in and turned over to Deputy Arland Rasmussen for shipment to the FBI lab in Washington, D.C. The weapon looked like it had been out in the weather for several months, and its thin coat of varnish would have deteriorated rapidly under the conditions where it was located.

Three days later, as tips kept coming in, the office was contacted by an anonymous caller who said he possessed information about the case. He told of a seventeen-year-old boy who lived in Brookwood Mobile Homes Park who entered the military immediately after the homicide. He said that things about the boy's family made him suspicious and worth a look. Deputy Lyman was assigned to track this down. He found a boy fitting the description, a recent graduate of the high school, and an older brother who had been a parole violator in Florida. The West Fargo Police caught the brother and returned him to Florida, and the sheriff's office would contact the West Fargo Police for assistance on this lead.

In mid-December Special Agent Rolle visited West Fargo High School, a plain, two-story Depression WPA project, which, with the football field behind it, occupied much of a town's block. A large structure had been needed at the time, since the school district included not only West Fargo, but also the nearby small towns of Harwood and Horace, or as one of the school secretaries liked to say, Whorewood and Hardass. The building was a stone structure that had been painted an unusual light green that led one to suspect there must have been a special on that color at the time the paint was selected.

Rolle was there to interview a girl an FBI agent reported had been talking at school about seeing someone near the Johnson place on the night of the murder. After lunch, prepared by school cooks Helga Benett and Enga Oslo, Rolle located and spoke with the girl. He learned that Becky Erickson had seen a car on the Maple Bridge near the Johnsons' farm home the night of the murder at about 7:30. She and her sister had been driving the family pickup from their residence to another home near the Johnsons to do chores. The car was parked off to the left side of the north-running road by the Maple River Bridge, facing south. It was light tan, and the guy's feet were sticking out. She didn't get a real look at the man but thought he wasn't fat, possibly slim, with dark hair and might have had a beard or moustache.

Rolle next interviewed Erickson's sister. Her recollection matched — that the car was an off-white color and the driver had dark hair. She was shown pictures of suspects being considered and couldn't pick anyone out, but lingered the longest over Goldie.

Other deputies were looking into the possible involvement of boys arrested for rape in recent years who were also being charged by Moorhead police for the robbery and beating of a store owner. They were digging through the town's dirty laundry, looking for suspects to consider, as no leads were obvious. Michael Grey's name came up and on December 20. Larson and Rolle attempted to contact his wife, who was living in Fargo. This turned out to be a challenge, as it was her third marriage. She wasn't with Michael any longer but knew some of his background. She had met him when he was a gas station attendant in Fargo but found he had had a troubled life. Both his father and mother had been married five times, and he had served time in jail for various reasons, including obscene phone calls in Washington. When he was younger, he had been in trouble as a juvenile for breaking into three trailer houses and cutting up the women's clothing in them. There was the time he, "lived in Harvey, North Dakota, with a bunch of hippies." He had been dishonorably discharged from the military because of drug use. Alcohol consumption had become a problem, and he had landed in the Minnesota State Mental Institution in Fergus Falls, a forty-five-minute drive from where they were.

It sounded worth checking out Michael's August 8 whereabouts, so the agents made the drive. They learned that supper was usually served about 5:00 and bed checks at 10:00, though sometimes later. It wasn't impossible he could have made the trip unnoticed, but he was completely willing to take a polygraph concerning the case. The hospital was unwilling to turn over psychologist or counselor reports. There seemed little reason to suspect him unless the polygraph indicated otherwise.

The final day of the year brought another lead to follow. A teletype arrived from Coconino Sheriff's Office in Flagstaff, Arizona, that stated:

> Reference your homicide of highway patrolman's daughter, is your murder weapon a .22 caliber? If so, please contact on possible location of .22 that might have been in possession of Terry Lee Farmer.
>
> Detective Randy Paulson, Flagstaff, Arizona.

Contacting Detective Paulson made this a more interesting development. Farmer was being accompanied by a Larry Hartley and was thought to have stolen a number of cars and committed several homicides while traveling from Texas through the Southwest up north before being stopped in North Dakota. The FBI and several other state agencies were trying to catch them. The renegades apparently stole cars and drove them for a week or two until they wanted to change or needed gas, then stole something different. They picked up hitchhikers, especially young women.

Farmer was thought to have murdered several owners of cars, and a report from Texas told of them leaving a pickup truck deserted, holding several young runaway girls, who had been given guns and told to shoot any police who came along. Farmer's weapons of choice were said to be a .22-caliber pistol and a shotgun. His movements make it appear likely he would have been in the West Fargo area on the date of the murder. Finding a car stolen near that date that matched the description of the one from the Bridge would be worth checking on. They would get shell casings from the .22 in custody in Texas sent to Larson after the test firings.

The next day they did two more interviews with high school girls but gained little new, and the day following that Larson and Rolle drove to Pelican Rapids, Minnesota, to pursue a call from someone who said he had information. After asking around for directions they found the old bachelor who had called them about noon, then listened to his story. He had been visiting his brother-in-law while his nephew's wife had been in the hospital and was contacted to give her children a ride. His nephew used to live in Moorhead and was camping in a tent on a lake nearby when he went to see him. He saw a second unoccupied tent next to his nephew's tent, but there were four people in his nephew's tent, and he believed Pollie Johnson was among the group.

As the conversation continued, this man made it clear that he thought his nephew had been involved in many other crimes in the area and his nephew's criminal activity included homicides, along with dealing in heroin and running with "wild people from Texas." Some time after the conversation they checked with the nephew, Clyde Hagen, who said his uncle's imagination often ran wild, and he remembered camping in late July. His eighteen-year-old wife had been there and her best friend, Peggy Olson, who also had blonde hair and weighed about 100 pounds. She was with someone named Ramsett, but he wasn't sure of the first name.

It was still December 29 when the team heard from the Fargo Police Department that a rifle had been recovered north of Fargo. It had been found in a drainage ditch by a young boy out setting traps for rabbits. The temperature was thirty below zero. Too cold for searching a drainage ditch. The Fargo Police went the next day to look at the location. The gun was identified by Alcohol, Tobacco, and Firearms Division of U.S. Treasury as having been bought new in October in Detroit Lakes, Minnesota.

The year 1976 came to an end with the investigators grasping at straws and hoping for anything to fall in place to solve Pollie's murder.

Things started to look up at the beginning of 1977. January 3 the sheriff's department received a call from a former Fargo resident who had been in Cass County jail with Steve Skar of West Fargo, and claimed that Skar said a person he knew had spoken of going to West Fargo the previous summer to "fix" someone. The caller said he heard two were involved in the murder, and one had fled the country while the other left the area.

When the investigative team finished local interviews related to the tip, they received a call from the Jamestown Sheriff's Office where they were questioning an informant who finally had what appeared to be some very reliable information about the homicide. Officers drove to Jamestown, ninety miles west, to interview Dale Bjerke. Bjerke had been in the State Industrial School, an institution for juvenile offenders, and a friend from the school had visited him recently to spend time driving and talking. His friend, Jerry Swenningson, talked big. He claimed he had just finished a couple of "hit" contracts, one for $10,000 and another for $15,000. Their drive took them to Main Avenue in West Fargo, and he pointed out the C&C Market. He had shot her, Pollie, right in front of the store, he said. That was around the time when he was using a sniper's scope on a rifle to kill a commissioner in Fargo, or maybe it was Bismarck. He'd been paid but went to Seattle, and the people who paid him beat him up and took all the money back. So, he had a tale to tell, but he wasn't a real suspect. Swenningson had already been looked at earlier by the investigators when they visited Seattle.

Within the next two days, the man who had called Johnson's and said, "One down, seven to go" was given a ninety-day jail sentence, and the caller who had threatened Fargo South High School cheerleaders and mentioned Pollie's murder was arrested. Neither was considered to be a suspect.

The communication with Texas and Arizona concerning Terry Lee Farmer wasn't pursued until February, when Larson was contacted by Sheriff Jack Dailey after receiving a call from Sheriff Gordon

56

Taylor of Grand Forks, North Dakota, who said they had people in custody that Larson's investigation would find interesting. Edward Burkowski was being held for shooting into a private home in Grand Forks. Held with him was Ralph Bell, also known as Terry Lee Farmer. A number of associates of theirs were also in custody, and they were traveling carnival people. The carnival hadn't been at the West Fargo Fairgrounds on August 8. Larson went to Grand Forks and interviewed Burkowski. Burkowski's outgoing mail had been censored by Sheriff Taylor, and it mentioned something about Pollie Johnson and the killing possibly involving Farmer and the others. He claimed he had nothing to do with it and had arrived in North Dakota after it took place. Burkowski said he and Farmer did some work together after meeting in Grand Forks. They'd painted a house and stolen jewelry and rings from the owners. They had a grudge against the owners because, after they were caught, they were ordered to pay more than they thought they'd taken was worth, so they shot at the house. They also shot at the Border Patrol.

Burkowski's information showed that an unsavory group of people was likely to have passed through the West Fargo area unnoticed. How often did such things happen? The town was becoming larger and more impersonal, no longer a place where people recognized each other. Strangers were more common. Just how dangerous these people were came out in Burkowski's deposition. His written statement said:

> On or about September 15, 1976 . . . Terry Farmer disclosed. A salesman had given a ride to Terry and another male. Both were hitchhiking. . . . They later stopped in a sparsely populated wooded area. This is where the operator of the car was told he was going to be killed. On his knees Terry Farmer made a statement to him. Do you want to die smiling or frowning? The gentleman started to smile and then Terry Farmer discharged a revolver which was against the man's forehead. The bullet only creased the side of the man's head and did not kill him. His traveling companion then walked over to the body, drew a revolver and fired a couple of

rounds into the man's head . . . his wallet, credit cards, money, etc., were removed. The car was used by Terry. . . . Also briefly (speaking of what Farmer did following that) . . . murder of two hitch-hikers (male and female) . . . were picked up, the woman raped and both of them killed.

The revelation that such malevolence had very likely existed unnoticed in the West Fargo area around the time of Pollie's murder was disconcerting, but known only to a handful of investigators. It added support to Reverend Krangas' prophetic words at Pollie's funeral of the presence of "evil in this world," to which West Fargo was not immune. By the time even the investigators were aware of the people who had been mixing in with them without being recognized, new circumstances had developed that commanded the attention and resources of West Fargo.

Throughout the time from the homicide to early 1977, as the investigation went its many directions without success, the *Fargo Forum* continued to carry stories that invariably ended with "still no definite leads," "No warrants have been issued," "Sheriff's Department reports, 'Nothing new to report,'" or similar disclaimers of progress. The investigation team had learned a lot about what hadn't happened, but not much about what had. The area robbery scheme might have some relation to the murder and many people had been eliminated as suspects, but there was no weapon or apparent motive. No witness seemed to possess key information or have seen anything to make this a case that soon might be closed. They were growing pessimistic about a solution emerging, but determined to keep exploring everything then rethink it and to continue to pursue leads from outside. For the Johnsons' sake and for the community's sake they were not letting up.

5

MURDER OF DIXIE OLSON

J anuary is the harshest month, when the snow crackles under the clumsy steps of red-faced walkers. With the flat land and nothing to slow the prevailing westerly winds, the wind-chill often reaches dangerous levels, where exposed flesh is at risk. When the temperature reaches twenty below zero and the wind is thirty miles per hour, the effective temperature is negative eighty, making outdoor activity hazardous. Over lunch, some without indoor parking start their cars and let them idle so they'll start four or five hours later in time to head home. Scraping the ice off windshields is a morning ritual for those without garages, and owning a good scraper, one with a brush as well as a strong blade is a necessity. Still life goes on and people adapt.

Dixie Olson was trying to adapt. She was a twenty-nine-year-old Catholic woman with light-brown hair who liked country music and country dancing and whose life seemed summarized by country songs commonly heard in West Fargo bars and diners and tuned to on the radio. Waylon Jennings and Willy Nelson could have had her in mind when they sang about a "Good-hearted Woman in Love with a Good Timin' Man," as could, Tammy Wynette, who admonished, "Stand By Your Man." But her husband's recent arrest had pushed her beyond the limit, and she had reached the point where Wynette's "D-I-V-O-R-C-E" finally struck the right chord. She was separated and raising her three children in the house her husband, Gary, had built in West Fargo.

Dixie worked as a waitress at Country Kitchen in the past when Gary had served time for armed robbery. Many of the regional cops stopped there for coffee, so she was familiar to some of them. She had redone her life a bit and was receiving some government assistance through Aid to Dependent Children and had a job as a cleaning woman at South Elementary School in West Fargo that paid about $300 per month. She also took on cleaning work elsewhere to make ends meet, including the cost of a lawyer for the divorce to get away from her husband. Not much time or money remained for pleasure or hobbies, but she had a car and kept the kids entertained, often taking them roller skating.

She had one good girlfriend, Linda Johnson, whom she talked with several times a day, which was a positive element in her life. After spending the day of January 23, 1977, with her kids, she had stopped over in the evening at Linda's nearby apartment where they were going to put a little more excitement in her appearance. Linda frosted Dixie's hair, leaving it with the bleached-blonde ends that were popular. After dinner, Linda came over to Dixie's to comb and style the newly colored hair. The children were in bed when Linda left at 9:30.

On the frigid Monday morning of January 24, Dixie's alarm went off to get her moving so she could make breakfast and organize the children for school. She didn't shut it off. It continued to buzz. Her nine-year-old daughter, Michelle, eventually went in to awaken her mother and turn off the alarm. Michelle walked in to a horrifying sight. Her mother was lying on the bed with her head immersed in a pool of blood and disfigured to a point beyond recognition. There was a second deep pool of blood, and blood saturated the entire surface of the bed.

Michelle awakened her brothers and the older, eleven-year-old David, came in to Dixie's room. He returned to his room and checked the knives he kept there to see whether there was blood on them since he and his mother hadn't been getting along well. He found they were clean and returned to partially cover Dixie's face with a blanket before rushing to the next door neighbor's home to seek help. After repeatedly pounding on the door and ringing the bell, he managed to awaken Larry Toso, who came to the house and called the police and an ambulance, then took the children to his home.

Officer David Weaver arrived first. After a quick look and check to see that rigor mortis had set in, David contacted Chief of Police Kenneth Hansen who arrived in minutes. While waiting, Weaver had made a brief check of the basement, in case the perpetrator happened to still be in the house. Chief Hansen had brought along the Police Department camera, but they found that neither of them knew how to operate it, so they contacted the photographer for the *West Fargo Pioneer* to take photographs. They also got the word to West Fargo Detective Don Jones, and the Police Department contacted Earl Larson at the Sheriff's Department. The photographer arrived and took a series of shots of the victim and her room and other views of conditions in the house that inspectors thought might be of value as evidence. He was careful to get detailed shots of the basement window at the back and the area around it, as all noticed early upon arrival that the window had been tampered with, and the snow around it appeared packed down by boot prints. They looked like they'd come from cowboy boots, commonly worn in the town. It appeared to be the likely point of entry for the assailant.

With photographs taken, the coroner released the body to the ambulance crew that had arrived hours earlier and instructed them to take it to St. John's Hospital in Fargo, where an autopsy would be performed later in the day. Don Jones, a relatively tall, muscular brown-haired man whose glasses and brown mustache gave him a distinguished look, was a conscientious officer who had risen quickly to become West Fargo's only detective. In one of life's whims, the Vietnam vet had completed his tour of duty and had been on his way home, but was bumped off a plane in Alaska. That plane then went down and those onboard died. He returned on another flight and entered law enforcement. Jones took a consuming interest in this case from the moment it began and was in charge of overseeing the investigation.

Yellow tape and black flags surrounded and sealed off the home as a crime scene area, and initial investigation began. The victim was wearing pajamas and her panties were on, which might eliminate possible sex motives. Officers were also checking to see whether Dixie had been shot or beaten. Earl Larson's first reaction was that she had been shot in the head with a large bore riffle, because the head was so distorted and had several gaping holes.

Chief Agent Hilde of the North Dakota Crime Lab, who had arrested Dixie's husband years earlier, assigned Dale Remus and Dick Olson to the case. They headed to West Fargo to collect evidence. Larson, Police Chief Hanson, and Detective Jones were in the department's unmarked car, discussing what had taken place and what procedure to follow in late morning when two cars pulled up to the house. One was a 1966 beige Plymouth, followed by a newer Chrysler.

A man got out of the first car and stood in the street, staring at the scene. The officers recognized him as Gary Dean Olson, Dixie's estranged husband. The three approached him, and he asked what was going on. Detective Jones told him there had been an accident involving his wife, that she was dead, to which he exclaimed, "Oh, no, what happened?"

Jones thought he did appear somewhat upset, but his major concern was his desire to see the children. Jones said that they were fine and he could see them soon, but they would like him to first answer some questions. Olson agreed and went with the officer to a squad car.

Jones read him his Miranda Rights and Olson also consented to a search of his car. Jones then questioned him about his activities of the previous day and heard what would become a familiar story. Olson said he was awakened in his rented room and had come to Dixie's residence around noon to pick up the kids to go roller skating. There was no one home, and he recalled Dixie mentioning possibly going to her parents' home, so he used his key to enter the house and get the dog to take it with him to drive to his sister's home in Enderlin, North Dakota, an hour away. His sister, Gwen Johnson, and her husband didn't find it unusual for Gary to drop in. His mother was staying there as well, and in the afternoon he left to drive to near-by Sheldon, where his brother Orvin, commonly known as "Mick," ran a bar. They played pinochle. Then Gary returned to his sister's home in Enderlin for dinner. He said he fell asleep on the couch short-ly after dinner and woke up about 10:00 p.m. and had a few beers. He turned on the television, but there was nothing on but news, so he shut it off. After reading the paper a bit, he fell asleep until 8:30 or 9:00 that day, just hours ago.

Jones asked him twice whether he had been drinking that morning because he thought he could smell it, and Olson said he hadn't. The question of why he had come to the house came next, and he said his car wasn't running well, so he was going to leave so he could to fix it. He also had to fill out weekly unemployment forms and get them to the Unemployment Office. He gave permission for fingernail scrapings to be taken, so Jones did the procedure and col-leted them and bagged them as possible evidence.

While this interview took place, the other officers were busy. Larson went to the Chrysler that arrived with Olson's car to learn who those people were, and found Gary's sister, Gwendolyn, known as Gwen, and his mother. He told Gwen that her sister-in-law had been murdered, and she went with him to be questioned. She said Gary had stayed at their home on the previous night, as he did quite often. He arrived around dinner time, and she and her husband went to bed at 10:30 or 11:00. Gary had fallen asleep on the couch with the television on, and she came down and turned it off later. There was a bedroom on the ground floor where he slept, and that was where he was in the morning. Her husband was up at 5:30 to go to work that morning, and she was up at 7:45. Gary was still sleeping at the time. She had heard Gary let the dog out of the house shortly before midnight. She was sure of the time because she had a lost a child to crib death recently and taken to watching the clock closely. That was all she heard during the night.

For background, she said Gary spent quite a bit of time at the Town Hall Bar in West Fargo and used to work for Steiger Tractor. He hadn't been paying child support and received $105 or $110 per week unemployment. He was thirty-two and had been married to Dixie for twelve or thirteen years, but they were having problems over Gary's drinking. Gwen said Dixie left the kids home alone from five in the afternoon until ten at night when she was working, and the oldest boy didn't want to live at her home. An episode two days earlier had led to him run away, but Gary brought him back. Their kids had been doing well in school, but Dixie had been screaming at them a lot. Along with a number of negative comments about Dixie as a mother, Gwen brought up that Dixie had been a Catholic, and Gary was Lutheran.

Gwen claimed Gary had been visiting a priest, hoping to get the marriage patched up. The divorce was to be finalized in February. As to why she had followed Gary to his house on this day, she had a doctor's appointment in Fargo, and her mother came along so they could go shopping at the large shopping mall, West Acres. Gary had said he had an appointment for his unemployment and had to be present to sign for it, and, since his car wasn't running well, her following him seemed the reasonable thing to do. Gary hadn't bought gas for the trip back, nor had she. Gwen didn't like Dixie's friend, Linda Johnson.

Chief Hansen was interviewing the Olson children at the Toso home while the others were being questioned. The nine-year-old Shelley Renae Olson, known as Michelle, informed him that since the previous day had been Sunday, they went to Blessed Sacrament Catholic Church, then to the Highway Host for breakfast. They also went roller skating. That evening Linda Johnson had come over and said she was going to dye their mother's hair. She went to bed at 9:00 p.m. and doesn't remember hearing anything during the night. In the morning, she heard her mother's alarm and went in to wake her and found her dead. Eleven-year-old David was interviewed next and mentioned the roller skating and Linda Johnson coming over to dye his mother's hair, as well as running away Saturday and his father returning him. He said he owned a sixteen-gauge shotgun given to him by his father that he kept downstairs, but he didn't have shells for it, and he also told the officers about his knives. One of Gary's friends' names he could come up with was Big Al. There were others who used to come over to play cards.

David said his mother was cleaning for her lawyer who was handling the divorce. Also, they had moved to Milwaukee at one time, and his father left to live with the Indians, but later returned. And the direct question to David: Did he have anything to do with his mother's death? He said he didn't.

Larson then did his own interview of Gary Olson. He asked who Olson's friends or associates were. Olson mentioned a plumber, Ole Olson, and a couple of workers for the City of Fargo, but he made it clear that most of his associates were people who drank at local bars, the Town Hall or the Frontier or Silver Dollar. The Town Hall's owner was one of the people he considered a friend. He played pool and some poker with several of these people. A number, including Al Miller, Donald Surdel, Nick Hennebree, were members of the Grim Reapers, a motorcycle gang Larson would soon learn more about. Olson's children were returned to him, and he was advised not to leave the country.

Dr. Obert called to say the autopsy would be conducted at 2:00 p.m. at St. John's Hospital, and if they wanted to gather anything as evidence, they should meet him at the morgue. By early afternoon Special Agents Olson and Remus were going through Dixie's house, looking for evidence. Remus was a short man and was a stabilizing influence on situations. He had been to the FBI Academy and knew how to collect and handle evidence, so Jones wanted to have him there to see that it was done correctly. He had helped on the evidence with Pollie's homicide, but now the focus was the gruesome evil just committed.

He and Agent Olson collected and bagged blood soaked bed linen, cigarette butts, a .22 casing, hair found in various locations. In the bathroom clothes hamper they found a hand towel that had red spots that appeared to be watered down blood. Blood pools were noted on the mattress in separate spots. The clothing in the drawers appeared to have been strewn on the floor, and the contents of Dixie's purse dumped as well as papers scattered from desk drawers. On the kitchen counter was an envelope sealed with the return address: Gary Dean Olson, 624 5th Court Street, West Fargo, to Employment Security Bureau. There was a fresh stamp on the envelope.

Richard Olson's search of the garbage container in the kitchen yielded an interesting item: an envelope containing a letter in what appeared to be Dixie's handwriting. She had addressed the envelope to herself, and the letter inside said, "Don't know what you find so interesting in my garbage, but when you find it, let me know." Written on the back of the envelope in a different hand was, "Trying to find out who's causing me trouble. When I do watch out."

Agent Remus had a close look at the window that was the apparent point of entry for whoever committed this act. He found that the assumption didn't hold up. The lock was open and nails that at one time had been pounded in and bent forward to hold the window in place had since been bent in the opposite direction. The window had been pried open from the inside to look forced, but the marks on it were small and all interior. The hinge missing on the top right hand side had been unscrewed, not stripped as it would have been if someone had forced the window, and the thread marks could be seen. However, the story that the break-in had come through the window was perpetuated that week by the *West Fargo Pioneer* in its story, "Dixie Olson Murdered; Found Dead Monday," where it was added that burglary was the suspected motive and the basement window had been found pried open. How they came to report such inaccuracies is unclear.

There was a bench below the window where someone might have stood that still was wet from melted snow, and finger prints were found on the window frame, a clear one found on the interior side of the window. In the basement they also found David's shotgun, which had a Federal shotgun shell in the barrel, and there were boxes of pornography hidden away.

While this search had been going on, Jones and Hansen had been to the morgue and taken more photos of the body, then gathered physical evidence. They took two vials of blood and stomach contents, a piece of kidney, and a piece of liver. The blood was for investigative purposes, though far less sophisticated than they became later. Blood types were used as evidence, but the first use of DNA testing was nine years off. The liver, kidney, and stomach contents were for the state toxicologist. West Fargo lacked appropriate storage facilities for such organic evidence, and what they had was turned over to Captain Hewitt of Fargo Police for protection.

In the afternoon Dixie's sisters came to the home to get a dress for the funeral and find a photo for the funeral director to use as guidance when he attempted to reconstruct her face. One of the sisters, Donna, told Larson that Gary would spend his unemployment money on the kids and give Dixie no money for bills, and "this was the reason that he was a good guy and she was the mean old mother." Donna also told of Gary punching a hole through the wall of his and Dixie's house, and sometime around Thanksgiving, attempting to hit Dixie when she was by the car but missing and breaking his hand on the windshield. She said Dixie was especially upset when she ended up with the forty-dollar bill for his medical treatment.

Jones talked to Dixie's parents, who had come in from Dixie's hometown of 251 people, Litchville. They never liked Gary, but didn't see Dixie often. The three Olson brothers turned up fairly often, because the hunting was good in the area. They knew Gary and Dixie had troubles and were three payments of $385 behind on their house, plus were behind on car payments, utilities, and living expenses. They had thought they would probably help, but were anxious to see Dixie out of the relationship, and she wanted out before Gary's upcoming trial. Gary had wanted to get the oldest boy as part of the settlement, but they said that would never happen. They called later to say that Gary had contacted them about Dixie's death, and "Gary said he had not done it and that he had an air-tight alibi."

Larson got a warrant to search Olson's residence in the Grindahl home, where he rented a room. Remus had also instructed him to get hair samples and the clothes Olson had on that day, plus have him do handwriting samples. Olson complied and was getting ready to clear out of the rented room. The sheriff's deputies and police department officials present helped him pack up. Olson was taking his kids to Enderlin to stay at his sister's.

Larson also went to see Dixie's friend, Linda Johnson. She was at work, but her son called her and Larson gave her the news. Someone from her office brought her home because she was distraught and couldn't immediately function. When she had a grip on herself she went through the story of frosting Dixie's hair and calling her later in the evening. They had been friends for about six years and talked on the phone a few times every day. Dixie had talked about getting divorced for quite a few years, and finally got Gary out. They'd tried to make the marriage work in the past by going to group therapy for alcoholics, but Gary quit. Dixie, who didn't drink, went a few more times, then gave up. Dixie didn't have any boyfriends.

Gary had beaten her up before. Dixie told Linda that, when they lived in Milwaukee, Gary beat her up so badly that the neighbor girl didn't recognize her. Gary was jealous and would dig through her garbage, looking for evidence of infidelity.

Gary spent his time at the Town Hall, Silver Dollar, and Frontier. He had been kicked out of Town Hall for some reason. He had a terrible temper, and got mad at Rick Fugere over a pool game, was going to kill him over an argument over a game where Gary lost money. Rick lived near Arthur. Gary had told her he had three on his list he was going to kill.

Linda told Larson that she was afraid of Gary and said she wasn't going to stay at home that night. She would go to Fargo and stay with relatives or friends.

The autopsy report said Dixie Olson died from multiple strikes from a dull instrument that had, in one incidence, broken off skull bone inside of her head. Jones got an industrial tool catalogue and tried to find what type of instrument would leave the sort of marks on her head. Having little luck with that approach, he contacted Ralph Studabaker, whose business was to know tools, and asked him to come to the police station. Jones described the marks he had seen on Dixie's skull, and Studebaker said he was looking for a mechanic's pry bar, probably Pronto or Snap.

Larson learned more than he had expected from Studabaker, who lived very near the Olson house. The previous evening they had guests over and someone thought she heard a scream not long after 11:00 p.m. Dixie had been employed as a janitor at the workplace of Mr. Studabaker, but she had been let go because they didn't feel she did a very thorough job.

Remus and Jones headed to Enderlin in the late afternoon to speak with Dennis Johnson, husband of Gwen and brother-in-law of Gary. They hoped to catch him before he had time to talk with the others in the family, and at 4:55 p.m. when Johnson returned home from work at Melroe Manufacturing in Gwinner, they headed him off. Johnson hadn't heard about Dixie's death, so they were especially interested in hearing his story. He said Gary had spent the previous afternoon in Sheldon, North Dakota, playing cards with a brother, then returned to the Johnson home about 7:00 p.m. He and his wife and children were playing a game in the kitchen, so Gary just stretched out on the couch and watched TV. He was asleep there. It was not uncustomary for them to leave Gary alone on the ground floor, and he oftentimes stayed overnight. Johnson said he personally was a sound sleeper and didn't hear anything during the night. He was up at about 5:00 that morning and noticed that Gary was not on the couch. Since he saw Gary's car was still there, he assumed he was in the ground-floor bedroom. He thought the cause of the divorce would be Gary's drinking, which was substantial. He had never seen Gary physically hostile towards Dixie, and thought he was usually good with their kids.

Johnson suggested that Gary's "avid relationship for hunting" could also have been a festering problem that possibly helped in initiating the divorce. Gary would oftentimes take his eldest son, David, and go hunting and leave the other two children at home.

His analysis of their marriage problems could fit in somewhere, but he seemed to be telling the same story they had heard earlier in the day from Gary and Gwen. They agreed that Gary spent the previous night in Enderlin, while the coroner put the time of death at between 2:00 a.m. and 4:00 a.m. the preceding night.

Johnson took the investigators into his home on Enderlin's Broadway, where they were met by his daughter and a surprise — Gary with his three kids. Olson showed where he had slept the previous night, which had nothing other than a beer can laying about, which wasn't in any way unusual. He was more informal in his new surroundings, asking whether any new leads had turned up. He had one to add, which was that David had forgotten to tell something when he was interviewed in the morning, and he brought David forward.

70

David said he heard footsteps downstairs a few days earlier between 6:30 and 8:00 p.m. He didn't tell anybody, not even his mom, because he thought it was just a squeak in the house or something he was imagining. He also said that, when his mother went out, she didn't get a babysitter, and he took care of the others.

Jones saw another chance for another check on the validity of Olson's alibi and interviewed Bobbie Johnson, age nine, who said Uncle Gary was lying on couch in the living room sound asleep when she went to bed, and she never heard anything the rest of the night. She got up about 6:30 that morning and assumed he was in the bedroom. Once again it seemed they were all in agreement.

Casings had been found in the living room, and Dennis Johnson was asked to produce all the firearms in the house. Sample test firings would need to be done on two .22 rifles. This was prior to seeing the autopsy report, and they did not definitely know the cause of death. Also, both were working on the Pollie Johnson homicide and attempting to retrieve a variety of different casings fired from different brands and models of .22 rifles and hand guns. The casings from two rifles would be sent to the FBI lab for comparison to a casing involving the Johnson homicide.

After returning to the police department in early evening, Jones went back to Dixie's home, where he continued the search and found more hard-core pornography stashed in a box packed away in the work room.

To the investigators, this case seemed solved from the beginning, but everything was circumstantial and the seemingly guilty party had an alibi supported consistently at this point. This was still the first day, but things seemed as if they should get pulled together somehow. The community needed it, and they could barely look beyond Gary Dean Olson, things seemed so transparent. They would begin anew in the morning and see whether other real possibilities existed or whether Olson's story held together outside his own family. With another investigation still ongoing, this would be a good one to crack soon.

The news that day of a second murder in West Fargo in less than six months hit hard. There was an evil lurking beneath the town's surface and it seemed to be sprouting. Was there a killer stalking the town? Nothing would command sympathy and mourning comparable to the murder of the innocent young Pollie, but Dixie's homicide was right in town with neighbors all around, and it brought on more fear. A local resident recalls, "That was a break-in to somebody's house, so you had to lock the house before you went to bed." State's Attorney Mervin Nordeng said, "I think a lot of people started locking their doors."

Larson's view was, "Dixie was more frightening. We figured Gary Dean, but nobody really knew because it happened in the middle of the night in a residential area. I went in in the morning just to have a look at the crime scene to know what was happening. It got to be 10:00 at night, and we were still working on this thing, interviewing neighbors. So I went over and knocked on the door of high school basketball coach, Fritz Fell's home. 'Just a minute,' and I heard the thirty-ought-six cartridge being put in his rifle. Then, 'Come on in,' and that's the way a lot of people felt."

Larson found that he was no different, being involved in both cases and becoming more edgy as his anxiety increased. His brother-in-law had stopped by his home not long after and had left to walk his dog. When he returned and began to open the door without knocking, Larson had his service revolver out in a flash.

6

INVESTIGATION OF DIXIE'S MURDER

There were plenty of places to look and people to check, since Gary Olson's story oozed with unanswered questions and the brutality of the murder required looking not just at Gary, but at Dixie's life, to see whether anything seemed unusual that could present other suspects. Her family and children, friends, and co-workers might be aware of something. Then there was Gary's "air-tight alibi." Few working the case with Jones had believed air wouldn't escape from it. They fanned out to do interviews and redo interviews, seeking to get an understanding of the Olsons and their relationship along with what their lives were like up to the previous day, and soon a more complete picture began to emerge.

A new element was added with the discovery that Dixie had a life insurance policy. Frontier, Inc., where Dixie had previously worked, called Detective Jones to tell him Dixie had a $2,000 double indemnity life insurance policy still carried by their company that paid $4,000, and Gary was sole beneficiary. The policy was scheduled to expire at the end of the month, so it was valid for only six more days. Perhaps a money angle existed for the unemployed Olson. Jones continued to get more of an understanding of Olson, as he continued digging through his basement and found a great amount of hard-core pornography involving sadism, masochism, child nudity. He added that to his growing collection of evidence. He also located a slag hammer that looked like it might have possibly been capable of inflicting the wounds he'd seen on Dixie.

Dixie's sisters provided some information immediately that shed light on the relationships, beginning when one of them, Donna, and her husband, Nolan Monson, came to the West Fargo Police Station the morning after the homicide and told of Gary going through Dixie's garbage, trying to find phone numbers or names of men he suspected her of seeing. That helped make the letter Dixie had written and addressed to herself found earlier understandable. Donna had been receiving phone calls as recently as the previous Friday night at 9:30, and no one was on the other end. Linda Johnson, Dixie's best friend, had been receiving similar calls at the same time. Both assumed they were from Gary, checking up on Dixie.

The Monsons also told about the Saturday three days earlier and what led to David running away from Dixie's home. They had come to West Fargo and picked up Dixie to go to the Bowler in Fargo, well known for its smorgasbord. After eating, they remained for much of the afternoon for a Children's Bureau (CB) meeting, before returning to Dixie's by early evening. The Children's Bureau was an agency that monitored state child welfare services to achieve positive outcomes for the children and families receiving aid. Dixie was receiving aid since Gary hadn't been paying the child support settled on in their separation agreement. At these monthly meetings there was an unfortunately named award, the "Bucketmouth of the Month," perhaps created by a fisherman of prized large-mouthed bass, given to a child who had done something successful.

After they returned to Dixie's, they were discussing the meeting, and Donna mentioned that she wondered whether the boy who won the award was retarded, and David was paying enough attention that he only heard "retarded." He already preferred being with his father, and this was too much. He ran away to Gary's, saying he didn't want to stay with his mother any more because Donna said the kids were "retards." It was an upset Gary who returned his son to Dixie. He took David back, and said to Dixie, "What the hell is going on having people run our kids down?"

Agent Remus went to visit another of Dixie's sister's, and interviewed Lenore Ann (known as Lynn) Klitzke at her home in the Sheyenne Trailer Court south of Lisbon. Lynn had talked to Dixie the day before she was found dead and heard her complain about Gary going through the garbage, even the attic, and about visitation rights. Dixie wasn't going out with anyone else. She feared they would lose the home, which was on the market, and they had agreed to divide the receipts from the sale. Lynn had lived in Fargo for years and seen Dixie black and blue on numerous occasions and said that Gary had told Dixie a number of times that he was going to shoot her, but those were times when he was fairly drunk. Drinking was the big problem, and he started, but dropped out of, AA, which ruined chances of things working out. He was winning the children's favor by spending lavishly on them while Dixie struggled with the bills. Lynn thought Gary killed Dixie.

Lynn had another intriguing story, but it was difficult to see whether or how it was a piece of any puzzle. Back in September, nearly five months earlier, the two families had gone on an outing and been fishing. Gary and her husband had been in one boat. They all drove back to Lisbon, and her husband sent his daughter in their home. He drove off, taking their boat with him, and hadn't been seen since. Numerous attempts had been made to locate him, but he had vanished.

Deputy Arland Rasmussen headed to the West Funeral Home in nearby Casselton and met director William West. In the funeral home morgue he took fingerprints of Dixie that he brought back and turned over to Detective Jones. He then spent time learning more about Gary's behavior and associates by visiting a couple of his favorite hangouts and talking to people Olson had mentioned as friends of his. In the afternoon, he and Deputy Pralguske interviewed Billy Parkhouse, owner of the Town Hall Bar. Parkhouse said Olson didn't talk much about his wife, but talked about being charged with burglary, and claiming he had been in the Town Hall Bar when two guys were chasing him, causing him to run into the Triangle Western store. That was where the police caught him and arrested him for burglary. Parkhouse said he had asked the bouncer, Pete Richardson, if he had seen anybody chasing Olson, and the bouncer hadn't. Parkhouse hadn't seen Dixie much. He didn't recall Olson's arm being broken or notice any personality change recently since Dixie's death. Drinking buddies Van and Gene Johnson (not the Gene Johnson who was Pollie's father) did, though, and thought something was troubling him. Parkhouse said he'd met Olson years before and that he was always clean, wearing nothing fancy, just work clothes.

They were unable to contact any members of the Grim Reapers motorcycle group at that time but had more success at the Frontier Bar. Regulars there said Gary had been drinking heavily lately, and had once said his wife should be dead. His story there for coming in the bar with his arm in a sling after the incident where he hit the windshield swinging at Dixie was that he had hurt it "poking at his old lady." They said it was just after he'd been fired from O'Day Equipment. As far as his social life, one said he thought he might have once been down at the home of a woman they said euphemistically was known for her availability to "get around," but didn't know of girls Gary had gone out with. Bob Goldade spoke up to say that on Friday morning he had seen Gary with two "go-go dancers" from the Town Hall, strippers that one of the others recalled. One was a red-head and the other a blonde. They also said Olson had been wearing new boots lately and that he was a loner. He was all right at pool but rotten at pinochle and liked to gamble. He bet on the games he played, and after sports events he was often really flush or broke.

An old high-school friend of Dixie's, Donnette Klever of Fullerton, called the station to say she had stayed with Dixie two weeks earlier, and she and her husband had known Dixie well for years. She used to double-date with Dixie and Gary many years earlier. Donnette said Gary had talked Dixie out of divorce before by going to AA, but it didn't work and she was fed up. He was always playing up to the children, especially the oldest boy, and said his lawyer told him not to worry about the burglary charges. Gary hadn't changed, and she believed his family would lie for him. She said his mother always bailed him out of trouble. Her husband agreed with her that Olson was capable of having committed this murder.

Another call came in on January 25, this one from Brian Wanzer, who lived near the Olson home. He said that at 1:30 a.m. a snowmobile driving through the drainage ditch north of his residence woke him up, and it idled there for a time. While he was watching, a dark 1967 Chevrolet with wide tires on the back was moving by really slowly, possibly carrying two people. He then noticed that a dark-brown older four-door Ford had been parked by the fence that separated the Olson property from his was parked on the street Saturday night. Whether any of this meant anything, he wasn't speculating, just reporting, since things were different, and it was the critical night.

A third caller that day recommended they contact Marlys Frost, an ex-bartender at the Frontier Bar who had moved to work at Camelot Cleaners. She told them about a conversation that took place between Thanksgiving and Christmas at the Silver Dollar Bar, where she had stopped at about 4:00 to have a drink. Gary had told her he and his wife were getting divorced and said he believed his wife was having an affair. He thought it was with her lawyer, David Overboe. He told Frost he was going to find out for sure, and if it was true, "he was going to kill both of them." Gary had been in prison in the past and it didn't bother him to go back again. Frost had said, "What about your children?" and Olson answered, "I don't care."

More puzzle pieces to consider, but nothing clear to go on. Jones and Remus interviewed Overboe in his Sheyenne Street office, who told them Dixie had first contacted him in April and initiated divorce proceedings, then called them off when Gary began attending Alcoholics Anonymous, but returned November 30 to begin again on the basis of irreconcilable differences. Gary didn't work, and just spent his time drinking and hunting. She didn't have enough money to pay what the attorney charged, which was a flat fee for divorces, and they had worked out an arrangement for her to take care of her bill by cleaning his newly-built house. Gary had also come in for legal aid, and Overboe had said it would be a conflict of interest and directed him to another local lawyer, Leland Hagen. Dixie wanted the divorce over before Gary's upcoming scheduled trial for burglary and had also contacted him the previous week when Gary was taking the kids overnight, since she feared he wouldn't bring them back. The officers found all that helpful, but were especially interested in the relationship that had existed between Dixie and Overboe. He said she had a key to his house and had been over to work a number of times and worked hard. He had been home on several occasions when she was there and had found her, he said, "Very pleasant to get along with," and once prepared her a dinner.

Not all the calls coming in shortly after the homicide were casting aspersions on or reinforcing suspicions of Olson. There was a female who called in to give a statement in support of Gary Olson's good character. She was Trarese Goulette, a go-go dancer at the Town Hall Bar, who wasn't a local, but worked for the Pride Agency of Mason City, Iowa. She informed Jones that Gary had made a date with three of the dancers to go roller skating on Saturday. They were to meet at the Town Hall, but he didn't show up. Tammy Jones was one of the others, and Trarese added that Gary had told her he loved his wife and children very much, and these girls were confident he was of upstanding character. It wasn't convincing enough to slow the investigation, and the callers would be useful later on in learning more about Gary.

Special Agents Olson and Remus did more interviews that day that kept them locked in on Olson. They interviewed David, and heard the story about thinking the kids were being called retarded. He said he thought the back door was locked when he went to get neighbor that morning after seeing his mother. He had left three dollars on kitchen table after going roller skating Sunday. On Monday morning after finding his mother dead, he couldn't find the three one dollar bills on the kitchen table. David knew how to get in and out of the house through the basement window and on one occasion he had sneaked out through it and left home for a while. This was the window allegedly used for entry into the house for the murder. He had seen his father hit his mother on at least one occasion. And what about the divorce; why was that happening? He had a definite answer for that: "David states that he feels the divorce has been caused by Linda Johnson as she is an expert and has been divorced three times."

Greg Warren, who was a new officer at the time, had been assigned to secure the scene in the morning. Like Lyman and Larson, Warren was a graduate of West Fargo High School. At 11:30 that morning, Gary Olson arrived and wanted to get clothing for his children from inside the house. Remus was present investigating and, along with Warren, accompanied Olson to each of the children's bedrooms while he secured clothing. Jones called Warren in mid-afternoon and sent him to secure Olson's apartment and allow no one in until Jones arrived with a search warrant.

Agents Olson and Remus did an interrogation of Gary Dean Olson in the late afternoon at the West Fargo Police Department. He gave his date of birth as April 17, 1944. He was in trouble from that point on, since he was asked whether he was on any medication, and he first said no, then "Oh, yes." He said he was taking Valium and pulled out a vial of prescription five-milligram tablets from his pocket. Agent Olson took the vial and found prescription, dated October 14, 1976, issued to Mrs. Dennis Johnson by Dr. Lewis of Enderlin. His sister had given the pills to him. They told him they were keeping the Valium, which was a controlled substance, and it was a violation of law to be taking someone else's prescription. He admitted to having taken one in the morning and another an hour before the interview. There were other tablets in container Agent Olson took as well.

The questioning carried on, and Gary said the last time he'd been in the basement of the house at 624 Fifth Court Street was over a week earlier, attempting to clean up from a paint fire from the fall, when a lit cigarette hit some paint thinner. The last time he had done any work on the windows was a year earlier when he nailed some shut. The window locks were broken, which is why he had nailed them. The house was usually unlocked during the day, and the kids slept with their doors halfway shut. He admitted he did not give his wife money to pay any of the bills, but said he did buy some groceries occasionally. In the robbery in Marion, North Dakota, that sent him to the State Pen earlier .22 pistols had been used, and he stated it was his brother who hit someone on the head during the crime, and they only got about $200. Presently he was up for a burglary he hadn't committed, although he was caught in the place while the burglary was in progress. He conceded he had a drinking problem and said there were times when he had drunk to the point he couldn't remember anything, which usually took at least a fifth of whiskey. He added he liked beer but loved whiskey.

Gary repeated his version of the events of the previous days and his love of hunting, saying he owned a .22 bolt-action, a 12-gauge pump shotgun, a British .303 rifle, and recently bought his son a 16-gauge shotgun. He and his son David made good hunting partners, he believed. On Saturday he'd been hunting with his boys and his brother Mick then brought them back to West Fargo at 4:00 or 5:00, and saw a note on the table that Dixie was with her sister. He said he walked through the house and found her sleeping, so he left the kids there and went to his apartment. Shortly after, David ran over saying his mother and Donna were talking about them as retards, and he took David back. Dixie said maybe she'd better not let him see the kids anymore. From there he went to his apartment, then to the Town Hall Bar and back to bed. He woke up 8:00 or 9:00 Sunday and went over to pick up the kids, but there was nobody there. He left a note saying he took the dog, Sophie, and went to Enderlin, to his sister's home, the Johnsons. After getting to the Johnsons, he went to Sheldon, where his brother lived. He had several cans of beer there, then returned to Enderlin and fell asleep on the couch. He woke up, had a few more beers, went into the bedroom and slept until 8:30 a.m. In total he had ten to twelve beers on Sunday.

In the morning, he got into his car and was followed by his sister and mother and drove back to Dixie's to leave his car, get his unemployment check and fill out a new application, which was a weekly process. He and Dixie had been married for eleven years, and his drinking problem was something that was apparent when he drank whiskey, which he imbibed like water and got him crazy. In his view beer had no affect on him.

Olson said they had good times during their marriage, and also some arguments, and at times he had slapped her around and backhanded her in the mouth. They had had no intercourse for two months, and he hadn't slept in the main bed of the house since New Year's Eve. He also asserted that he had not touched the basement window since the house was built. He conceded that he was very jealous and admitted he had stated "he would fix her good," if he ever caught her with anyone else. He also admitted to digging through her garbage.

Gary said the last time he'd been in the bedroom was on Saturday and his wife was lying on the bed. He talked to her for a minute, then walked out. In the past three or four weeks, he had probably averaged weekly visits to the house to get clothes from the closet. In a surprisingly interesting comment, he said that for the last three days he had been wearing the same clothes. His clothes were then taken from him by Detective Jones and Remus. Olson's final words on the matter were that he did not kill wife, and to demonstrate that fact, he would consent to taking a polygraph.

Olson voluntarily brought in his firearms to Earl Larson at the sheriff's department. One had been found in the basement. Agent Olson discovered a single shot 16-gauge Springfield shotgun purchased from an employee named Lamont at O'Day Tank approximately two years earlier. He observed, "It should be noted that this weapon was also found in a loaded condition." Agent Burke of the Alcohol, Tobacco, and Firearms Bureau was contacted because Gary Dean Olson was a convicted felon, and possession of firearms was a violation of federal law. He also had a 12-gauge pump shotgun, Enfield 303. The only gun he claimed was purchased from bona fide dealer was the 12-gauge, which came from Scheels Southside in Fargo.

Gary's often told the story that he had borrowed Gwen's car on Sunday because his was in such poor working order. In Jones' opinion the car seemed to run all right but had a very noisy exhaust system, and was just in overall poor shape inside and out. A thorough search of his car revealed "x-rated witchcraft type pornography" and a green club found lying along the left side of driver's seat, but it wasn't the murder weapon. The car also contained whiskey and beer, hunting knives, a large number of tools, hammers, shotgun shells, candy, cigarettes, jumper cables, and junk. Agent Olson confirmed Jones' view of the car, saying, "In the opinion of this agent and five mechanics at the place it was stored, the car had a good running engine." He agreed the exhaust system needed some work.

It was discovered that Gary wasn't the only member of the Olson family to have visited Dixie's house on Saturday. Gary's younger brother Robert, commonly known as Robbie, had also been there. The agents headed to find him in his trailer in Morreton, North

Dakota. Of the four children in the Olson family, Gary was the oldest, followed by Orvin, or Mick, then Gwen, and youngest was Robbie. Unlike his brothers, he had no previous arrests, and Dixie's sister thought he had been kinder to her than the others had been. He still had been there, and they asked why. Robbie said he had come to Fargo twice in the past year and had come in on Saturday, hoping to see the movie *Helter-Skelter*, the story of the Charles Manson cult and its bloody murders of seven victims in 1969. He had stopped at Dixie's to talk and use the phone to call his mother to ask for a loan of $100. Robbie said, "I knew Dixie was going out. Her appearance. I liked her. At least her appearance looked like she was going out. I didn't know if she was or not." He clarified that her kids had said she was going out, as he heard in Enderlin the next day.

He'd been wearing a tan jean jacket and blue bell-bottom pants along with the only pair of shoes he owned, which were work shoes. He ran a punch at an iron bench at Frontier, Incorporated, in Wahpeton and other shoes weren't needed. Robbie said he thought he might have had three beers before getting to Dixie's, and he stayed in the kitchen, where he could use the phone. He left two dollars for his calls and discovered *Helter-Skelter* had been shown on television that week, so he went to see *King Kong*, and then returned home to watch *Hogan's Heroes* on TV. He had no arguments and had never had any romantic involvement with Dixie. They got along.

Robbie admitted that he drank beer continuously and, like Gary, claimed beer's influence was minor, saying, "I drink a lot, but I never get drunk." He said he didn't own any guns and carried some tools in his 1973 Oldsmobile. He was willing to take a polygraph if it wasn't too inconvenient, and was a cooperative subject who allowed his fingerprints to be taken and his vehicle searched.

Earl Larson checked around town, trying to learn more about Dixie and her relationship with Gary. He visited Country Kitchen, where he remembered her as a waitress, but they no longer had a record of her employment. Coworkers from her school job remembered more, and one said Dixie had appeared very pale before Christmas. Another mentioned Gary going through Dixie's garbage and said she thought he had murdered her. He learned her routine, which was to return home from work between 6:00 and 8:00 to make supper and get the children ready for bed, then return to clean the school. He contacted Joni Wich of the Cass County Social Services and learned that Dixie had recently started receiving Aid to Dependent Children, approved December 1, 1976. Her December grant was $389.00. She had applied for welfare because she hadn't received any financial support from her husband and couldn't speak about their divorce or separation without breaking down and crying. Larson also found Pam Bommersbach, who had a room in the same house as Gary, to see whether she had heard anything Saturday night. She hadn't heard anything before midnight, which was all she could account for, and she had known Gary for years, usually seeing him having had too much to drink at the Town Hall or the Nugget Bar.

Three days after the homicide was discovered, Joe Turman, a recently appointed assistant states attorney, contacted Detective Jones to see about including Dixie's skull in the evidence he was putting togher to be sent to the FBI in Washington for testing. Jones called the FBI lab and talked to pathologist Fred Wallace. Wallace said a local pathologist could testify as to a tool used to crush her skull, so it need not be sent, and the funeral parlor took it and began the work of patching the holes in preparation for recreating her appearance.

Detective Jones and Lieutenant Larson went to the Olson residence with Linda Johnson, and she identified the blue slacks, sweater, and blue blouse Dixie had been wearing when she had been with her the previous evening. The clothes were found in the bathroom on top of the bathroom clothes hamper. Jones took them as evidence. She had also offered comments about Gary and Dixie including that, when they were first married, he hit her and grabbed her by the neck. The physical abuse was accompanied by verbal abuse.

84

On the following Saturday afternoon at 4:00 Johnson came in to the West Fargo Police Department to give a written statement. Her nine-page Voluntary Statement told of her frosting Dixie's hair the previous Sunday night and calling her later, but the phone being busy. Two days later, she was coming home from grocery store at 5:10 in the afternoon, when she had encountered Gary's car at a four-way stop. He motioned her to pull over, then came to her car and said "Linda, it's been hell."

Then he proceeded to unload on her. He had just picked up Dixie's car and been questioned, and had admitted to abusing and hitting her on occasions. But, he, "had said he would take a lie detector test and any other kind of tests to prove he didn't do it. He said he loved her and that he couldn't have killed her . . . Dixie's parents and relatives were going to try to get the children." He was pulling them out of the West Fargo schools and enrolling them in Enderlin, and pleading innocent to the current burglary charges against him. Gary asked if Linda would be going to the funeral and also asked directions. Then Olson made a muddled attempt at explaining his feelings. She recalled, "He said he was suspicious and that he knew Dixie had never cheated on him. He said he disliked me because Dixie and I were always talking on the phone and asking each other questions and helping each other. He said it was not me that he disliked, but that he would have disliked any person who was a good friend to her like I was. He also said that he had asked for affection from Dixie and that she was the type of person who couldn't show it."

Linda thought there had been some truth to the affection comment, noting that Dixie had told her Gary had said he wished she would be more affectionate, and do things more like come up and put her arms around him or kiss him. And the side of Gary the investigators were becoming familiar with was clear, with Linda's report, "Gary made the statement to my parents in the early part of December 1973, that his first loves were drinking and gambling and then came his family. . . In Milwaukee he had beat her so badly that her next door friend could hardly recognize her." When she was pregnant and they were walking at the County Fair and he hit her in stomach a few times. He also put his fist through their kitchen wall. His explosive temper and drinking were a bad combination, and "Dixie stated that Gary on occasions after physical or verbal abuse to her stated that he 'said I don't remember doing it.'"

They would follow up on the Milwaukee story by contacting the Milwaukee County Sheriff's Office to see whether records existed of wife-beating by Olson. Jones then interviewed Linda's husband, Lowell Johnson. Lowell said he had known Gary since Olson got out of jail in 1971, but didn't really care for him. It was because Dixie was Linda's friend that he associated with him some, and they used to get together for cards, usually canasta. Gary thought of himself as the world's best pool and card player, but he wasn't actually very good. Jones had heard of an incident where Gary had ended up in a fight and thought Johnson would know about it, since it involved one of his employees from his construction company. Johnson remembered the night well.

It had happened during the previous hot, dry August at the Nugget Bar. Larson had come in for a drink after work with two of his employees, Dennis Littlefield and Tom Johnson. At 5:00 p.m. Gary came in for happy hour, when it was two for one, and was drinking vodka because he didn't think Dixie could smell it. This was still when he was trying to keep life in their marriage. Gary put five dollars on the pool table and said, "That's all the money I have." He and Littlefield began playing pool for five dollars a game and Littlefield paid him thirty dollars after Gary won the first few games. Then Gary started swallowing the vodka fast and started to lose equally fast. During the game, a barmaid came over and asked whose kid was lying down in the hallway. It was his Gary's younger boy, and he left and took the child to his car. While sitting there talking, drinking and playing pool, he would at times go out to the car and check on his kids. During one pool game, Johnson asked if he was worried about them. Olson said, "No, Dixie probably came by and picked them up."

In the meantime, Littlefield was finished and the game stopped. Gary owed Littlefield around eighty dollars, and he wanted to be paid, but Olson wouldn't cover his losses. He eventually took out his checkbook and wrote a check payable to Lowell Johnson, who didn't want to be involved. Olson wrote it anyway, and Johnson endorsed it, then gave it to Littlefield. He tried to cash it at bar, but they wouldn't accept it, since Gary's checks weren't reliable. An argument then began, and suddenly Gary pushed Littlefield backwards over a chair and jumped on him. Littlefield hurt his back enough that an ambulance was called, but it was cancelled when he struggled to his feet. Johnson had separated them by pulling Olson off, grabbing him around neck. When he did, Olson said, "Not you, too, Lowell?"

Once the ruckus was calmed, the bartender came over and kicked Gary out of the bar for being such a troublemaker. He sat in his car and waited for the others to leave, then when they emerged, he sat swearing at them out of his window, finishing with, "Next time I see you, I'll kill you."

Littlefield went over to Olson's car and punched him in the face, and Gary floored his accelerator, spraying gravel all around as he got away. When Lowell returned home, he told Linda of the incident, and she called Dixie, fearing Gary would take it out on her. Instead, Gary had gone to Enderlin, and he later told Dixie that if Lowell Johnson ever set foot on their property, he would blow his head off.

One other story Lowell told that could fit in was that, two days before the homicide, he had met Verne Knodel, a business associate, for drinks at the Hi-Ten Steak House. He called home and asked Linda to join them for dinner, but Linda said she already had arrangements with Dixie to go out for hamburgers. Lowell suggested they both come to the steak house instead, which they did. There was nothing more than that to the situation, but appearances could be enough. Linda received a call with no one at the other end between 8:00 and 9:00 p.m.

Marlys Frost also came in to make a Voluntary Statement and repeated her story of sitting in the Silver Dollar Bar sometime between Thanksgiving and Christmas when Gary came in and sat next to her. He said he'd been sleeping in his car because he couldn't go home, and his wife was divorcing him. He thought there was something going on between Dixie and her lawyer, and she said, "If he found out about it or caught them, he would kill them both, and it didn't make any difference who the guy was." He'd been in the Pen before and even though he had kids, it didn't make any difference.

The funeral for Dixie Olson was held four days after she was found dead, giving the funeral home time to prepare her appearance for the open-casket event Gary insisted upon. That was the extent of his involvement in the planning of funeral arrangements, which some of his own relatives found strange. Linda had told him where the service was to be held and he attended, but there were peculiarities about his presence that raised more questions. On Friday morning in St. Francis Catholic Church at Marion, North Dakota, the service for Dixie was held, and Gary had spent most of the previous week drinking. Since the homicide, he drank heavily and was beginning to behave in ways that frightened those close to him.

During a body viewing, he put a picture of their family in the open casket with Dixie and kissed her. Dixie's brother, Jerome, later called the Police Department to report more taking place than that. He noticed Gary taking several small white pills in the church basement before the funeral and again afterwards at her parents', the Hansen's home in Litchville and had asked them what they were for. Gary had said they were for his nerves. A more serious claim was that Jerome thought the casket had been tampered with between the first and second viewing of the body. He said that the body appeared to have been moved slightly, pulled up where it was strapped in the casket, and believed Gary had disposed of evidence in the casket at that time. He'd seen the Chester Arms .22 single-shot Western style ivory-grip-handled pistol used back in Gary's first felony that was never discovered, and suspected that Gary had slipped it under Dixie in the casket.

Jones and the others thought this might be a bit imaginative but were interested in what Jerome had to say about his sister's hair, and if it appeared accurately colored. He said it looked more red than it should. It definitely didn't look frosted, and was too dark for Dixie's hair, so much so that her daughter wouldn't look at it because she said it "didn't look like mommy."

Jones's interest in the hair had come from a recent call Gary had made to Linda Johnson. Calling Linda was something he was doing more frequently as the days passed, and his drunken confusion mounted. After the funeral, Jones noted, "He also told Linda that he didn't like Dixie's hair after it was frosted." That made Jones wonder when it was that Gary ever saw Dixie with frosted hair. Olson's story was he had left for Enderlin at noon on Sunday and returned to West Fargo along with his sister and mother Monday morning, after the coroner had sent her off for autopsy. Dixie had it dyed Sunday evening when he slept in Enderlin.

By the end of the day of the funeral, Detective Jones had 104 items of evidence that he packed in a foot locker and an additional box and that he sealed and was ready to transport to the FBI lab in Washington, D.C. On the morning of January 31, Jones and Agent Remus were driven to Fargo's Hector Airport by West Fargo Police Chief Hanson to board Northwest flight 336 to Washington. They were cautious with their cargo and spoke with the airport manager and pilot in Fargo before boarding, and stayed with the evidence until it was locked in the cargo compartment of the aircraft. The flight stopped in Minneapolis and they stayed next to the aircraft throughout its time there to prevent any possible tampering. Once in Washington, they were met by two FBI agents and delivered the evidence to the lab directly, receiving receipts for what was transferred. They spent time discussing the evidence at the lab that day and returned for more discussion the following day before heading back.

Upon their arrival they heard from Chief Hanson that the FBI had identified the prints on the basement window as being those of Gary Olson.

That made things a bit awkward for the campaign Gary had begun to mount in his own defense. Twice he had contacted Dixie's mother and stated how strange it was that someone could have gotten in that basement window without breaking it. He also mentioned to her he was to receive a $2,000 life insurance policy payoff, though the amount was $4,000. He told his brother Mick he had heard "the buggers" had gotten in the house through the basement window.

Agent Olson learned about Gary's comments during a visit to Sheldon, to interview Leon Strand, owner of Wonder Bar, Mick's employer. Gary had been in the bar that day about 9:30 a.m. and drank and gambled for about four hours while he left his two sons running around the town's streets. Mick had started drinking more and made statements to Mr. Strand which made him believe Gary might have committed the crime.

By the time a week had passed since the homicide Gary's behavior was becoming bizarre. He called the West Fargo Police Station at 12:30 p.m. and said he wanted to go in the house, which remained sealed off as a crime scene. Chief Hansen said they couldn't send anyone over right then, but he could enter and get what he needed. Olson became very angry, then said fine, he'd go in by himself. He called back four hours later saying he wanted to talk and told the dispatcher he would call again in five minutes, and if no one was there to talk to him, he'd leave. Hansen responded to the next call in which Gary said something was missing, something of Dixie's. Nothing had been taken other than some clothes for the funeral, Hansen replied, and to Olson's insistence something wasn't present, he said, "Your wife is missing." Gary said no, his wife's purse was gone, and was told it had been taken as evidence. Olson added he was sitting on the bed and had turned the mattress over, but hoped to sell the house and get the money.

Fifteen minutes after that call, the department received another call from Linda Johnson, who said Olson had called her at 3:00 p.m. and talked for forty-five minutes. He said he would never get rid of the bed, and told her he had been sitting on the bed talking to God and Dixie. He told her there was blood on the mattress so he turned it over and was just sitting there having a few beers. He was going to keep all her clothes and hang them in the closet next to his, and he'd been on tranquilizers and sleeping pills since it all happened. He'd also had a six-pack in the morning. He complained about the police not giving him any information and spoke of how Billy Parkhouse was looking for the guys who chased him into the Triangle Western the night of the burglary he was charged with, and his attorney was going to get those charges put off for a long time, under the circumstances. He spoke of the skeleton in the Olson family closet and living in a funeral parlor, but she didn't know what he meant. He had lifted Dixie's head in her casket and kissed her, he wanted Linda to know. She managed to get off the phone by asking about David, and he said he'd left him sitting in the car. Linda suggested he might want to get back to him.

The investigators heard there was a rumor around town in Enderlin that Gary had come home drunk and told his mother what he had done and they concocted the story to use. There was another that a barmaid at the Friendly Tavern in Enderlin had heard Gary talk about killing his wife. It took very little time to discover these were the sort of rumors that often proliferated after a heinous crime, when people talked about possibilities and speculated and after their thoughts were repeated several times it began to sound as though there might be truth to them.

After a week of investigating, further proof of Gary's previous treatment of Dixie came in from the office of the sheriff, Milwaukee County in a letter to Lieutenant Earl Larson, that said, "Detectives also investigated an alleged beating by Gary Olson to Dixie where she was beaten to the face to a point of being unrecognizable; this beating occurring sometime in 1969 or 1970. There were indications from your informants, the victim may have received hospitalization at the West Allis Memorial Hospital, Milwaukee County."

Added to that argument within another day was an unexpected visit to police headquarters by Father Moore, the parish priest at Blessed Sacrament Church. He said Dixie had come to him about year earlier looking for advice on whether to get a divorce or try to patch things up. He had taken a strong stance and offered the pragmatic advice that, in her circumstances, it did not appear to be of any use to attempt patching things up, and she would be better off getting a divorce. He hadn't given her that advice the first time she came in, but later on through the year, he had. Father Moore was ahead of the times in his advice, since the Catholic Church's position had been consistent since the Plenary Council of 1884 that if Dixie ever remarried, excommunication was automatic. Pope Paul VI would alter that position later in 1977, but too late for Dixie.

Gary apparently knew she was going to a priest to have meetings, which were generally in the evenings after she had finished work. Since the proceedings began again in November, Gary had come to talk to Father Moore and said he would do anything, including becoming a Catholic, if the priest could keep them together. The priest said that would be out of the question. Father Moore said Gary was a desperate alcoholic who would say anything to get what he wanted. He didn't believe Gary loved Dixie at all, but that she merely served as a sexual object for him.

It was time to look more closely at what the Olson family had to say. Gary's father, Orvin Olson, Sr., said he had heard Gary calling his dog at 4:30 Monday morning. He lived two doors south of the Dennis Johnson residence, and was employed by Soo Line Railroad.

Agent Olson tried Sheldon where Mick and Donna lived. He learned that the four of them, Gary and Dixie, Mick and Donna, had been together in Milwaukee. Donna said Gary was always beating up Dixie. At one time it got so bad Dixie had come to live with them for two or three days, and it was happening out in the open on the street. Recently Gary had said if he ever caught Dixie with another man he would kill them both. On February 1 in the morning, Gary said to her on the telephone that he said he was going to get Dixie's killer and it would all be over in about a week. He advised Donna to keep her doors locked. She had reached the point where she was afraid of Gary and thought he had killed Dixie.

Mick confirmed the story about some railroad worker having heard Gary call his dog at 4:30 on the morning Dixie was killed. After Gary had talked to Donna about keeping the doors locked, Mick had driven to Enderlin to ask him what was going on. Gary had said, "Don't preach to me," and told Mick the same thing about getting Dixie's killer and that they should keep their doors locked. They went into West Fargo after that to go to the house and pick some things up, and during their ride, Gary told Mick he had been lying on the mattress, which was still full of blood, and praying, waiting for Dixie to return. Mick didn't want to believe it but had begun to think his brother killed Dixie.

One thing Mick and Donna were absolutely sure about was that Gary was not wearing the same clothes on Monday that he had on when he came to their home on Sunday. On Sunday he had been wearing a dark red shirt, and plaid pants. Gwen Johnson told Donna she had washed these clothes. On Monday, following the murder, it was lavender pants and a lavender shirt that Gary had said he wore continuously from January 23 through January 25. The lavender combination had been confiscated, so the question became where had those lavender clothes come from? Where had he changed? Gary said he didn't keep any clothes in Enderlin. Agent Olson questioned Gwen, who didn't recall the clothes Gary wore that Sunday, and said she couldn't remember whether he had kept any clothes in Enderlin, but didn't think so.

Larson and Jones went to Gwinner and after that to interview Gwen's husband, Dennis Johnson, and began by reading him his rights. He said that on the Sunday in question they had gone to the Lutheran Church in the morning and Gary had used his wife's car to go to Sheldon. Gary had used his wife's key and returned the car to its original parking position. Gary doesn't get along with his father. Neither did rest of the family, and his mother had remarried. Gary got along with his mother except when she asked him to quit drinking. Johnson didn't think Gary could have slipped out and returned that night. His wife would have heard because she was a light sleeper, but it was possible that he drove away and neither of them heard. Dennis stated that it was his personal opinion that Gary did not commit this homicide, but Jones noted, "However, Mr. Johnson seemed uncertain when he answered this."

Linda Johnson called in during this time to say she had also received another strange call from Gary. It included an allegation that Dixie had been raped when she was thirteen by her brother-in-law, which Linda said was out of the question, and talk of the "cruel bastard" detective who continually interrogated his son. This was followed by an invitation to his house for the next Friday afternoon. There was something about him calling and inviting her over while he was sitting on the blood-soaked mattress where her closest friend had been murdered that felt very wrong. She said she would be unable to attend, and he made the enigmatic reply, "If I don't see you on Friday, or if I don't see you again, good luck."

The time was ripe for the polygraph Olson had consented to previously. On February 4 Detective Jones and Sergeant Whitehead of the West Fargo Police Department picked Olson up in Enderlin at 10:15 in the morning to make the ninety-mile drive to Jamestown, where the polygraph was to be administered. Whitehead was a big man, six-three, 275 pounds, who knew Olson from the past when both had worked at the same construction company. The strategy was for him to keep the conversation light and stick with topics such as hunting and fishing. They were setting up a sort of "good cop-bad cop" approach to Olson, depending on how things developed. By noon they arrived in Jamestown then stopped for something to eat before proceeding to the State Crime Lab Office for the polygraph.

Special Agent Dick Olson formally stated that he, Gary Dean Olson, was taking this test to determine possible involvement in the murder of wife, Dixie Olson. Gary signed the request for the exam and waiver of rights. He was taken to be tested in a private room and, a pretest was done, having Gary tell the story of January 23 and 24 once again. Gary added that he had never actually seen Dixie with another man plus whoever murdered her must have gained entrance through the basement window. He also said that he had not been near the basement in a very long time. The initial question period took place before interrogation began, and the suspect was hooked up to the polygraph machine. It had taken less than ten minutes, including the reading of rights, the explanation of the procedure, and the pretest storytelling. At that point Olson stepped out of room and said he and wanted out. In Whitehead's words he was, "very physically shook up, said his stomach hurt and appeared near tears." He didn't want to or couldn't take the test. The polygraphist noted in his official report that, "During the entire pretest interview, every time the subject was questioned about any relevant fact in the case, he cleared his throat, lit a cigarette and squirmed."

Following that, they return to Enderlin, and Jones was again the driver while Whitehead sat in back with Olson. Before they left, Jones told Whitehead to try to carry on a sympathetic conversation with Olson. Whitehead was successful, and Olson spoke about his jealousy and his view of Linda Johnson, whom he believed was trying to drag his wife down with her as another divorced woman. He listened to Gary's considerable concern over the custody of the children after the divorce was finalized.

Enough of the "good cop." It was time for the "bad cop," or "hard ass," as Whitehead put it, to take over. About halfway between Jamestown and Enderlin Jones pulled the car off to the side of the road and confronted Gary. Jones said he had no doubt Gary was guilty, especially after his refusal to take the polygraph. For over five minutes, Jones was on the attack, saying Olson ruined Dixie's life and had since made a mess of his own. He had to be enough of a man to realize the mistake he'd made and not make it worse by dragging his three children in on it and messing up their lives as well. Jones continued going after Olson, saying the only thing Gary was proving by his behavior was that the homicide wasn't done in the heat of passion, and he was cold blooded for not being able to stand up to his heirs and dragging his children in it the way he had done.

Jones recalled, "He mentioned that the children needed him, and I told him that it appeared to me as if he needed the children worse than they needed him." He had told Jones he'd been drinking continually since the homicide, and had told other people that he had been staying drunk. Jones said his children weren't able to do this to forget, and he was using his children as a crutch. Gary had a choice, he said. He could tell them what really happened or he could wait for the State Crime Bureau agents, whom he didn't like, or the sheriff's department. In addition to his homicide investigation, Jones said he would work on the burglary case that was coming up against Olson, the A.T.F. was going to investigate him because he was a felon owning guns, and if he ever heard of another case of Gary taking kids uptown and leaving them in the car while he was drinking, he would turn him over to Child Welfare.

Olson wouldn't look either officer in the eye from the time this started and both Whitehead and Jones thought there were times when he was on the brink of confession, but pulled back. He went into what seemed to be a state of depression and said nothing in the car for the remainder of the trip back. Olson stared blankly out the window and mumbled.

Upon the return, they dropped Gary off in Enderlin and went to the local police department, where they collected a search warrant, and returned to Gary's sister's home to search the house for clothes matching the description of what Mick and Donna said Gary had been wearing the Sunday prior to the homicide. While the search was taking place, Whitehead had another attempt at talking to Olson, and took him to the sheriff's car so they could sit alone. Whitehead said Gary could try another lie detector test at a later date when he was feeling better, or feeling under less tension. He informed Olson that the questions wouldn't be the same as those he had already heard, so trying to build up resistance to them wasn't likely to be helpful to him. Whitehead recalled, Olson seemed, "quite disappointed" to hear that. He also said that investigators probably had some good leads, if there was this much pressure, and Olson responded, "I don't know what they could be." Whitehead looked him in the eye, and he urged him to get it off his chest, but with no success.

Detective Jones drove to Miller's Service Station four miles west of Enderlin because Gary had told him he had bought ten dollars worth of gas there for his sister's car when he was heading to Sheldon on August 23, but no one remembered him being there. He headed on to Johnson's and kept searching for the clothing, which was appearing to be good evidence to begin making things convincing. Gwen said she didn't remember washing any clothes Gary had worn back then. The closest clothes to Mick and Donna's description they had found during the search warrant executed at Johnsons' were a pair of red-and-white-checkered pants and solid-red pants. He returned to Gary's brother's and they said neither was the correct pair. Jones tried asking Gary, who suggested he look in the laundry room, but the pants were not to be found.

The FBI Lab , Latent Print Division contacted the West Fargo Police with more information, saying there were unidentified prints but also two on the basement window that were identified as being those of Gary Dean Olson as were two on a letter to North Dakota Employment Bureau. There was also one on the basement floor and several were found on the contents of Dixie's purse. The FBI findings as summarized by Detective Don Jones were that one colored hair was found on the west side northwest basement window of the Dixie

Olson house, the window where staged entry occurred, but none of the hair samples submitted were from Gary Dean Olson. None of the victim's hair was found on the white T-shirt, blue jockey shorts, lavender pants, lavender shirt, or white belt taken from Olson, the clothes he says he wore from January 23 through January 25, 1977. The red synthetic fibers in five segments of thread removed from the posterior scalp wound could not be associated with any item of clothing, bedding, or carpet submitted. Unexplained variations in limited comparable known writing samples meant a definite conclusion could not be reached whether the handwriting on the envelope found in the kitchen wastebasket and other notes had been written by Olson. Along with the prints of Gary Olson identified, a print on the cup and the top of the deep freeze belong to Dixie Olson. A total of twenty fingerprints were submitted, and twelve were identified.

Remus, Larson, Hanson, and Jones met with Assistant States Attorney Joe Turman at the Cass County Courthouse and decided Turman would contact Merv Nordeng to discuss the route to take in the apprehension and prosecution of Olson.

Turman requested statements be taken from Gwen Johnson, also from Robert, Orvin, and Donna Olson. Jones did a check with other relatives on Gary's allegation that Dixie had been raped by her brother-in-law and found no support for it.

Gwen came into the station and gave a twenty-six-page statement. It followed the same story line it had since the time she arrived at the home on the day of the murder. Jones tried to pin her down on details about amount of gas in the car and where the keys were along with contradiction in her statement and details she had previously provided. Asked if it was a possibility he had left, she responded, "There is always that possibility, but I think if he would have started the car it would have woke me or the dog would have barked." Her admiration for her older brother was evident in her statement, as she discussed her three brothers, saying, "Gary is the strong one. He is the one that always comes to the house, panels, carpets, does those things for us. You can depend on him where the others you can't." It was in line with her confidence in his innocence, that she stated, "I do not believe my brother killed his wife and the one reason I will give you is because he loves those kids so much and if you could see how close they are I cannot believe that he would do this and let the kids find their mother." Gwen wouldn't commit to taking a polygraph, but gave it a partial, "I think so." She had washed clothes on Tuesday and said she had never seen a pair of plaid white pants.

Jones found a number of problems with this statement. She had stated that Gary had asked her to use her car. She previously had told the police Gary had driven his own car, and the story hadn't changed until February 3. She said she gave Gary ten dollars to fill the tank and said the car was between empty and one-eighth full. Ten dollars would put the tank at about three-quarters. Later in her statement, she was asked whether they ever discussed anything in relation to what to say if questioned about his driving his own car, and her answer was no, then said Gary told her when asked the question she was supposed to tell the truth. Donna Olson had said Gwen told her she washed the clothes Gary wore Sunday. Gwen said she doesn't know about the clothes. Jones also wondered about a statement Gary had made to her on January 27. He had said he didn't know how somebody could have gotten into the basement without breaking the window. How did he know the window was not broken?

Robbie had also been at the Olson home, and to see whether there was reason to consider him a possible suspect, West Fargo asked Lieutenant Harvey Gruel of the Fargo Police Department to run a polygraph on him. Robbie turned up, and Gruel ran the test, his observation being he didn't believe there was any deception, and Jones thought Robbie could safely be eliminated as a suspect in the case.

The Sheriff of Ransom County was concerned by this time about Olson's mental stability. Gathering investigating officers for support, he called the county judge, and the investigators involved in the case presented their views. Jones said that while he had no clear and present danger evidence to present, he thought Gary might present a danger to himself or others and emergency commitment was appropriate. He specified, "The feelings on which I base my feelings are as follows:

That Gary Olson had called the chief of police of the West Fargo Police Department, Kenneth Hansen, and informed him that he had been lying on the mattress on which Dixie was murdered and was talking to God and Dixie and praying for her return. That he had also told Linda Johnson that while he was talking to her he was sitting and/or lying on the bed and talking to Dixie and God. Gary had mentioned to the investigators that he planned to stay drunk 'until the whole thing was over.'"

Jones also told more of Gary's bizarre behavior, including wanting Linda Johnson to come over to house on February 4, and when she said she wasn't available, him wishing her luck if he didn't see her again. He recounted the story he had heard from Sergeant Whitehead about the curse Gary feared since his mother had a dream that three people in the family were dead. Gwen's baby boy had died in a crib death, and Dixie was dead, and he wondered who was next. Dennis Johnson had become concerned about Gary's behavior while he was drinking and was concerned for his family's well-being. Donna Olson, Gary's sister-in-law, had been visiting with Gary on the telephone on February 1 when he said he was going to get Dixie's killer, it would all be over in about a week, and they had better keep their doors locked. Her husband, Mick, confronted Gary about this, and Gary also told him it would all be over in a week, that they'd better keep their doors locked.

The case had been tough on Detective Don Jones. He would sit at the dining room table at his home and stare at the fish tank for hours, an exercise he called his therapy. On February 18, 1977, shortly over three weeks after Dixie's murder, the Sheriff of Ransom County, Lieutenant Larson, Sergeant Whitehead, and Detective Jones signed the complaint, and the Ransom County Judge ordered the emergency commitment of Gary Olson to the North Dakota State Hospital for psychiatric care at Jamestown.

Budd Warren, brother of Greg and another graduate of West Fargo High School, transported Olson then and on a number of occasions. Budd's first job in law had been as a jailer. He said, "It was like a college. If they can't deal with inmates on the inside, they won't be able to deal with them on the outside." Former defensive end #78 for the Packers was physically equipped for handling prisoners, and law enforcement was in the family.

Olson wasn't cooperative about being committed. Warren recalls, "No, what he was doing was trying to run the show. I suspect that, knowing his personality, that's how he was in life. He wanted to run the show, and he wanted things his way. He didn't want to walk into the State Hospital, and he was going to make you do it. We spun him around and leaned him forward and just threw him in my arms and I carried him in. He wasn't very happy about that. But it defeated his purpose of what he was trying to do to us—Okay, if you don't want to walk, we'll carry you. And that's a trick I learned from my dad. He said, just do this, do this, you'll be fine. It's not going to hurt them." Budd's and Greg's father had been a lifetime law enforcement officer who had worked on many crimes and dealt with many criminals, and he passed on practical tips to his sons about how to hold and control belligerent characters like Olson that weren't taught at the Police Academy.

No witness to a crime had been discovered and no murder weapon found, in spite of considerable effort and pressure. But finally Gary Olson was being temporarily removed from the small town societies he corrupted.

7

AHA!

Early on during the investigation of Gary Dean Olson for Dixie's murder, Sheriff Pat Daley had called the investigators working on the Pollie Johnson homicide together for a brain-storming session. Don Jones was present at the gathering and brought up Gary Dean Olson as a possible suspect, saying, "We ought to look at this guy. He's kind of a criminal." Olson's name had never shown up before then, but many things suddenly fell into place and the investigation of Dixie's murder kept adding to the picture of Olson as a prime suspect for both homicides. They had learned quite a bit about Gary in preparing a case to charge him with murdering his wife, but much of that had centered very closely on just his conduct of the day involved. It was basically a circumstantial case, but a strong one, since no witnesses or weapon had yet turned up. They would need to know more to connect him to the murder of Pollie.

Olson was "kind of a criminal," and they were seeing that he lost control easily, and it was in his character to demand getting his way or trouble followed. He wasn't going to be pushed around or admit that he had to accept orders from others. His insubordination had cost him jobs and his possessive and controlling view of his wife were obvious examples of his short fuse and distorted idea of being a Real Man. The picture that had emerged was rather like the "manly" man so successfully marketed at the time by the new green deodorant soap, Irish Spring. In that distorted world between Gary's ears, he was that tough, buff guy with sex appeal, the one who in the popular soap commercial, heard, "It's manly — but I like it too!" from the Irish lass in the cleavage-enhancing bodice. He was the tough guy who bragged around town about shooting a black man when he had lived in Milwaukee, and liked to say he could go over to Dixie's any time and "get a little" even though they were separated. Who could resist such a manly man?

West Fargo Police Officer Roger Whitehead, who had worked with Gary at Kautzman Manufacturing in West Fargo, had heard Olson say many times that he was going to kill their boss. Gary's obsession with possible betrayal by his wife seemed a threat to his manhood, as was apparent after hearing he had abused his wife from time to time and kept close track of her, threatening to kill her if she ever was with anyone else, while he was dating go-go girls and others.

His criminal record dated back seven years to when he and his brother Mick had robbed a store in Marion, North Dakota, and taken $253 from the owner's wallet. Gary's need to show just how tough and defiant he was had been apparent after that, according to one of the officers involved in the investigation and arrest. Theft wasn't enough, but humiliation to show his importance was better, and the owner was made to kneel down and have his hands and knees tied together with his shoelaces, then Olson urinated on him before hitting him on the head with his gun. Gary's lawyer blamed his conduct on his recent loss of his job and on drinking, familiar refrains in his stories.

The officers weren't psychiatrists, and still they had to wonder what made Gary the kind of person he was, and it was a difficult question. He was a small-town North Dakota product, and that had often meant something decent. He had the handyman skills many small-town men possessed and could do a wide variety of construction work, good, honest labor. Somehow something went awry, and planted a seed in him that grew in an ugly direction. Dennis Johnson, his brother-in-law, had provided what could have been a clue when he talked about Gary and his father. He thought the father had believed in "spare the rod, spoil the child," and had physically punished the children, but first-born Gary probably got it worst, and was beaten with a belt.

Dixie's sister Lynn offered her own explanation soon after Dixie's death. She said the behavior stemmed from Gary's eighty-eight-year-old grandmother: "One of the reasons why there is probably problems with Gary's family is that Mrs. Martinson married her cousin." She said Mrs. Martinson's husband was something like Gary and had two children in their sixties still at home. In Gary's home life, as Lynn described it, his original father would try to discipline him but couldn't because his wife would interfere. His father was gone most of the week, working on the railroad. Gary's mother shot her second husband and quit drinking after that, Lynn claimed. Lynn also told Deputy Lyman and Larson something she had learned from the special-education teacher in Lisbon, Mrs. Dobb. Her husband had known Gary when they were young and in school and remembered that, when Gary was about thirteen, he was beaten up really badly, and after it had happened, Gary had said he would kill somebody before he was thirty years old.

How these stories about Gary's background blurred memory, imagination, truth was difficult to judge, but there might well have been some dysfunctional family life and personal humiliation involved out in the North Dakota countryside. It didn't excuse anything, but it might help explain how some of the obstinacy and bullying developed. Gary Olson wasn't a big man. Brother Robert listed his size on his Firearms Transaction Record for purchase of a rifle as height, five feet, five inches, weight, 125 pounds, and Gary was a bit taller but with a similar build. In the land of meat and potatoes this was far from intimidating. Showing he was a tough guy, one who feared no others and that couldn't be push around, his capability to be intimidating came from his unpredictable behavior and short fuse, his rage.

Still, to the time of Dixie's murder and Jones' suggestion, Gary had managed to remain under intense searchlights on the Pollie Johnson homicide. They had taken .22 casings, but the sheriff's office was collecting them everywhere. Now connections and evidence started to mount quickly. Mike Lyman and Earl Larson soon learned that Gary had often gone fishing at Francis Smith's place directly across from the Johnson farmhouse on the Sheyenne River. One summer Dixie and her sister Lynn had spent a considerable amount of time there, and Gary would come out in a separate car. It was a good fishing spot, and Gary was an avid fisherman. That river bank was a place he and Dixie had spent private time together during the better days in their relationship. He had continued to occasionally bring others there. The secluded Johnson home was not an isolated and unknown location for him.

What made the case much more inviting for focus were comments that had been secrets for months. Soon after Dixie's murder, Jones was told by Linda Johnson that Dixie had said to her she had a secret to share, one that Linda should never tell anyone. At the time of Pollie Johnson's death, Gary had come home all muddy. Dixie had asked him where he'd gotten muddy because it hadn't rained in several months. He stated he fell in river while going fishing, and Dixie left it at that.

Larson had also talked to the sheriff of Ransom County who had just interviewed Lynn Klitzke, Dixie's sister. The sheriff had told him that on February 2, Gary had come to Lynn's house to borrow fifty dollars. At this time, according to what he'd been told, "Gary told Lynn that he can still remember Pollie sitting on the counter." The reporting officer wasn't aware of how that had come into the conversation, or what counter Olson was referring to, but Gary had been drinking, and it seemed like a strange topic for him to be discussing within a week of his wife's murder. There were other conversations more directly to the point that put more focus on him, and this looked like it could be the real deal.

When Linda came to the West Fargo Police Department to sign her Voluntary Statement, she requested to speak to Special Agent Remus privately. She said Dixie had talked to her four or five months earlier and said she would tell her something if Linda would never tell anyone else. Linda had agreed, and Remus described Dixie's secret as, "Linda, I have a feeling, but she could not describe it, in regard to Gary, my husband, and the Pollie Johnson girl's death. Dixie stated that Gary used to live by Marion, North Dakota, and knew the Johnsons and, when she was killed, Gary came home all full of mud and stuff on his clothes. Dixie said she asked her husband where he had been and he said fishing. Linda said nothing was ever said about it again, but it was the way Dixie had told this to her and the way Dixie had sounded when she told it to her that Dixie had some type of feeling in regard to her husband and the Johnson girl."

Earl Larson's main focus was the Pollie Johnson case and went with Remus to talk to Mick and Donna Olson about what they knew in early June. Donna told them she had seen Dixie the day following Pollie's murder, and Dixie had asked her if Gary had been in Sheldon the previous night, which was what she had told her. Larson recorded, "Dixie and Donna talked about the possibility of Gary killing Pollie Johnson. Dixie said Gary came home all muddy. At that time Donna knew Gary had been in Sheldon on Friday night. At Gwen Johnson's child's funeral a while back Gary had said, 'It's too bad about that little Johnson girl.' At his wife's funeral Gary said pretty much the same thing."

After the four of them discussed the situation for quite some time, the Olsons asked whether, if they had told what they knew about the night of Pollie's murder sooner, there was a chance Dixie might still be alive. Larson gave it to them straight and said, "We told them we felt this was most certainly true, that Dixie would not have been killed had we been given all the information about Gary."

One of Dixie's sisters, Donna Munson, also stated that on an occasion shortly after Pollie's murder she had heard from Dixie that Gary had been off work on the day of the crime and that he had told her that he was fishing. When Dixie brought this up, she asked Donna whether she thought Gary could have killed Pollie Johnson. This was brought up that one time only and was dropped, but at the time Donna felt Dixie was "very concerned."

An earlier idea showed some promise when a sheriff's office routine stakeout of a downtown Fargo business recovered about $8,000 of items that were thought to have been stolen in a burglary of a secluded rural residence south of Fargo. The targeting of secluded areas by people who were aware of the owner's comings and goings as well as their possessions was showing promise for isolating the criminal involved in the Johnson homicide. Deputy Mike Lyman informed the press that a twenty-year-old and seventeen- and eighteen-year-old rural Fargo males had been apprehended. Family heirlooms, jewelry, cameras, and other "irreplaceable items" had been recovered, and the twenty-year-old remained in custody, while the two juveniles had been released to the custody of their parents. The burglary was one that Cass County authorities had contemplated might be related to the murder of Pollie because of the similar circumstances. Lyman refused to speculate on any connection.

Larson got a tip from Pollie's father, Gene, who had spoken with Robert Nelson, the owner of the Philips 66 Station at Stockyards Corner in West Fargo. Nelson and his wife had gone to the Dairy Queen in town between 7:00 p.m. and 9:00 p.m. on the Sunday evening Pollie was murdered. They had seen a man enter and be waited on down the counter from them. They thought the man had acted as if he knew them, and nodded slightly in their direction. Darlene Nelson remembered him because he used to come in for gas, putting in five dollars worth occasionally. He had three claw marks on one side of his face, like heavy fingernail scratches that ran the full length of his face and a cut in his hairline. It appeared he had received treatment for the cut. He was described as shorter than the five-foot-nine Nelson. When he and Darlene saw Gary Olson's picture in the paper because of Dixie's case, they recognized him as the same person. Their children remembered a light-colored car outside the Dairy Queen with kids in it but couldn't recall the make. Nelson said he had black hair and was kind of small or skinny. Larson had them page through their entire mug shot album, and they stopped at one of the older pictures of Gary Olson, but only for closer scrutiny. When they saw his most recent shot, they immediately made a positive identification.

On June 6 Larson and Agent Remus went to speak with Gary's brother, Mick, at his trailer on the south edge of Sheldon. His testimony about Gary wearing different clothes on the day after Dixie's murder was important to the state's case, which was about to begin. They weren't there to talk to him about that, but about the previous August 8, the night Pollie Johnson was killed. At that point, things finally seemed to be looking up. The unprecedented pressures on local investigators might actually be headed for relief, the "light at the end of the tunnel" in sight. If only life would cooperate. They were starting the trial to put away the man who had shocked the town with the brutality of his crime, and they finally had the solid lead they had been looking for to put an end to the investigation of the crime that had most intensely and personally upset the community, since the victim and the family played important roles in the town and were generally known and recognized. The pressure on solving these crimes had been great and perhaps the reward fund would be going to someone before long in the case of Pollie Johnson, while the case regarding Dixie had yet to be proved, but had reached the courts.

Mick had a story of Gary's involvement, but it wasn't the one they had expected. The "aha" that had them slapping their foreheads after Don Jones brought up Gary's name at the meeting of possible suspects was about to be complicated, and just when there was a feeling of some relief.

Mick told them it was a Friday night, and he had been working behind the bar at the Wonder Bar in Sheldon, and Gary came in about 10:00. Gary said he wanted to talk privately, and they went to the far end of the bar where no one was around. He said he had just been involved in the shooting of a young girl at a rural home near West Fargo. He had been "involved with the Grim Reapers," the motorcycle gang he often tried to associate with, and they had gone to Gene Johnson's to steal guns to sell them. He hadn't been part of it, but through the screen door he watched as the Grim Reapers raped the Johnson girl, then shot her twice in the head. They had used his gun, which he always carried under the seat of his car, and Gary asked Mick where he could get rid of the gun. It was a .22 that his brother, Robert, had bought for him several years earlier, since his criminal record wouldn't allow him to buy firearms through a dealer. Gary also told him that night that the Grim Reapers warned him if he said anything to anyone about what he had seen, they would kill him, but they would start with his family.

Mick said that he told Gary he didn't want to have anything to do with any of it. His guess was Gary probably threw the rifle in one of his usual fishing holes in the Sheldon-Enderlin area. Larsen and Remus asked Mick to ride with them and point out possible spots. No weapon had yet been found for Dixie. Intense efforts had been made to find one for Pollie. This could be extremely valuable. It was a warm day, but Mick appeared very nervous as they drove around, with noticeable goose bumps as he was trembling. He took them to a number of spots, including government lakes, spring-fed sloughs with quick-sand bottoms, the Maple River and the Anderson family's home. There was also a spot on the Maple River at Kramer Implement that remained open in winter where Gary used to do spear fishing.

109

Larson needed to appear in court for Gary's trial regarding Dixie and had to leave, but he thought there was more to be learned and planned to do a re-interview. He noted, "It was apparent that Nick and Donna also fear for their lives from Gary Olson. They are in somewhat of a dilemma as they are also fearful of the Grim Reapers."

It was certainly time to find out more about these Grim Reapers. What the investigators knew was that they were a motorcycle gang, or club. Big guys, many of them were, and some rough characters whose presence was intimidating, unlike the slim Gary. Since they were often in West Fargo bars, it was a vicarious sort of thrill for him to try to hang around with the bikers and feel he was a part of their crowd. They road big bikes, and at times Hell's Angles rode with them, but they were construction workers and others with regular jobs who just liked big bikes and the road, and the camaraderie of getting together. They had an old building that served as their headquarters out on West Main Avenue, near the C&C Market that was owned by the Johnson family. Alcohol and gambling often played a part in things, and for some there was trafficking in some stolen goods, but they didn't terrorize the area. Though their appearance could frighten people, they were law-abiding in most ways. Larson's description was, "They were about six-five, 350 pounds," which was very unlike Gary. Olson was a wannabe who tried to hang around with them, but for the most part, they didn't really notice him or care for him. Bob Fatland, who fit Larson's physical description, didn't remember Olson at all, and as far as their activities, he said, "Ride bikes." Olson didn't have a bike, and the bikers were at the town bars because of the go-go girls. Many had road names, such as "Big Al," "Sausage," "Turtle."

Sergeant Larson headed to O'Day Equipment Company and found Superintendent Roger Holverson. Olson had said this was one of his friends, but Holverson quickly took issue with that claim. He said he had been involved in boy scouts with Olson. He had little to add about Al Miller and the Grim Reapers but knew Miller's address in north Fargo. He also said that he had heard it rumored that Gary had killed Pollie. There was another hint that had been around that the police hadn't known of before. Holverson suggested to Larson that the former superintendent, Palowski, would be a better source for all of this than he was. Larson noted how ill-at-ease Holverson was, and recorded, "It was apparent that Holverson may be more involved with Gary Olson than he cares to remember or talk about."

From there Larson went to O'Day Tank and Steel Equipment on Main, and followed up on Holverson's suggestion. He found Zygmunt Palowski, commonly known as Zyg, who was the former superintendent and now the production manager. He remembered Olson very distinctly and had been his supervisor. He also knew Al Miller, Jr., who had worked their briefly. He pulled out the employment record for both, and that alone made the visit of considerable value to Larson. Gary had begun employment on April 8, 1975, and was discharged November 19, 1976. He had a record for August 8, 1976, which was the date everything now focused on, and it showed Olson took a half day off, starting at noon. He wasn't working that afternoon Ruth Backstrom had watched the car driving back and forth to the Maple River north of town near Johnsons' secluded home. That documented absence on paper from the day was taken and could be another nail in the coffin they were working on for Gary.

Al Miller had started April 28, 1975, and finished in May. Palowski knew Miller was in the Grim Reapers but wasn't aware of whether he and Olson were friends. They were different sorts, as far as employees. Miller was a welder — quiet and very steady on the job — while Olson was temperamental and high-strung, and lost his temper quickly. Olson was a hard worker but undependable, and his alcoholism and absenteeism led to his dismissal. He heard Olson had become friends with someone at AA, but he didn't know whom. It would be worth looking into.

The next stop was the trailer in north Fargo that was home to Al Miller. He said he wasn't a friend of Gary Olson and could barely remember who Olson was. Not much information here. Larson asked

111

him why he had been buying so many guns. He said he had recently received a Federal Firearms license. He recalled drinking beer with Gary occasionally and helping Olson when he built his house.

Larson went to Steiger Tractor Company and talked to general foreman Robert Sedevig. Big Al Miller had worked there. Allen C. Miller, Jr., was a welder and there was a bit of confusion, since they had two different sets of employee records. One showed that on August 2, 1976, Miller had suffered an accident and taken a leave of absence until August 27. Another showed a girlfriend of his called on July 12, 1976, indicating he had been in a car accident and had broken his wrist, and returned to work on September 14. In either case, whichever of the records was the correct story, it seemed clear Miller was not at work when Pollie Johnson was killed.

A number of Grim Reapers were brought in for questioning. Big Al wasn't around long. Larson and Agent Rolle interviewed Donald Surdel, known as "Turtle," a former member of Grim Reapers and said to be an associate of Gary Olson. He said his connection with Olson dated from the previous several years through a friend, "Big Al" Miller. He saw Olson at bars and played poker with him, and they had fished together at Erie Dam. Olson was fair at cards but after a few drinks was more reckless. He was, "Not all that pleasant to be around. They more or less tolerated him because Big Al worked with him at Frontier." They would endure him and put up with him even though they didn't like him as long as he didn't give them a bad time. At times he and Big Al would be in a bar together and would see Gary come in the door, and they would beat it out back door. Neither Big Al nor Turtle was in the Reapers any longer.

They also talked to Bruce Bergson, known as Big Deke. He worked in an upholstery shop. He said Al probably had a shotgun since he was a duck or goose hunter. Gary may have come to their "clubhouse" once when it was behind C&C Market. The last time he had seen him was the winter of 1975-76. It hadn't surprised Bergson when he heard Olson had been accused of killing his wife, as he "wasn't all that sensible" when he was drunk. When confronted about stolen property dealt with by several members, he said Olson wasn't the kind of person you could trust or rely on to sell stolen property or buy anything because he talked too much.

All agreed they had no trouble with Gene Johnson when they had their shop near the C&C Market. Johnson remembered it that way, though he found them a bit unusual at times. While they were a rough group, he recalled a banker was chair of their organization, and they used a barn behind the C&C Market as a hangout on weekends. Especially vivid to him was the recollection of a young woman from the group coming into their store with a dead rat pinned to her vest

Surdel also said he saw no reason Al Miller would have any problem consenting to a polygraph. He said the reason Miller had refused the polygraph request previously was because he was angry at how Remus had talked to him and the others. If they went to Miller and talked to him and treated him decently, he might consent. Larson asked Surdel to pass the message to Miller that they intended to contact him again, and when they did they would treat him decently and ask him to submit to a polygraph.

Miller got the message and the next day he arrived at the Cass County Sheriff's Office, accompanied by his wife. They found his demeanor to be pleasant and agreeable as long as he was spoken to with courtesy, and he consented to take a polygraph. He was told he would be contacted in a week or as soon as it could be arranged.

Larson and Remus decided to hear the story again from Mick and Donna and get them in more imposing circumstances, just to see whether everything was the same, or if anything could be reexamined. They arranged use of a conference room at the Cass County and Emergency Services Building. Mick and Donna remembered Gary wore steel-tip work shoes. Gary had said he parked the car on the road near the Johnson house and walked to a fishing site. He had looked through the screen door at Johnson's and had seen Pollie. Though he usually drank Schlitz or Old Milwaukee when he was fishing, that night he told Mick that he went to Johnsons for water. He claimed to be a buddy of the Grim Reapers, and specifically mentioned Big Al. Again they said Gary usually carried his .22 rifle under his front seat, and he was selling CB radios and other things, stolen property, for the Reapers. Mick said Gary had tried to sell him a CB once.

Gary had told Mick that when he got to the screen door, Pollie was being beaten and raped. The guys who assaulted her walked up to her and shot her in back of the head. They did it because she was screaming. There were three guys he was with, and they all split. One headed to Minneapolis, another set out for Chicago, the third was off to the West Coast. Gary said he had sold a few things for Grim Reapers, and since he witnessed the murder they wouldn't let him quit selling, so he still tried to unload some stolen property.

Mick added that the gun involved in the homicide was possibly the one Gary received from his brother Robert, one a convicted felon couldn't buy. Larson made notes to check on that immediately to locate the sale.

They said Gary spent his time in the West Fargo bars, the Town Hall, the Frontier, the Lariat. He was getting money from his mother during the separation. He wasn't quite like the motorcycle club members with the big bikes, but years earlier he had ridden a small motorcycle. He preferred blondes, and his girlfriend before Dixie had been blonde. He had a young girlfriend in West Fargo they thought was blonde who he described as a "cute little thing," and claimed another girlfriend with small children. He also had a go-go girlfriend who was petite, and he had danced with her on stage at the Lariat. When Dixie was alive, Gary usually visited his girlfriends when she was cleaning at the school. Mick had been in West Fargo at the Town Hall Bar the week after Dixie's death, and there were two girls dancing. Gary had tried to line Mick up with a short black girl named Penny from Minneapolis, and Mick hadn't even wanted to sit next to her. He didn't say it was because she was a black girl, but such an attitude wouldn't have made him exceptional.

The inspectors asked whether the children might have seen Dixie's murder, and Mick replied that David was afraid, but he had said to the others he would tell them about it after their father was convicted. Mick also told them Gary had said to him, "I shouldn't have told you in the first place." He had first instructed Mick to say, if anyone asked, tell them he had been at the Sheldon bar since 8:00. Later he said to say he hadn't been there at all.

Since Dixie's murder, Gary had been drunk most of the time, Mick and Donna added, and he generally ignored his kids before he was locked up. He had previously called Dixie's sister, Lynn Klitzke a bitch and whore, but since Dixie's death and until the time he was committed, he had begun hanging around her place quite a lot. Lynn had told Gary that Dixie was going to run away, and supposedly Dixie overheard that conversation.

What piece of the puzzle it was or whether it fit in, they weren't sure, but Larson and Lyman had found that, at one time, Olson had said he was going to kill Lynn because she and Dixie had been so close. More ominous and clearly related, they discovered he told Lynn after Dixie was killed that, in Lynn's words, "he felt that Linda knew something." That sounded like a possible reference to Linda having heard Dixie talk about him coming home muddy on August 8, since Linda was the one Dixie talked to about everything. The possibility that Gary knew that Dixie suspected he was involved in the murder of Pollie, and that he feared her suspicions and knowledge of his coming home muddy would get out and become known to the sheriff's department was beginning to sound like a potential motive.

More hearsay kept the investigating team thinking it was on the right track. Lyman picked up a tip about Olson's bar talk that had Olson personally making a statement that indirectly tied him to the Johnson homicide. It was from a conversation said to have taken place after Olson had been committed to the state mental hospital but before being charged with murdering his wife. Gary had been allowed back to Enderlin and had gone bowling. When he finished, he had gone across the street to the VFW bar. William Golkowski and several of his friends were at the bar shaking dice for drinks and Olson asked if he could join them. They let him in, and in the course of the conversation that followed, Gary had made a surprising and enigmatic statement, which Golkowski reported as, "When they find the man that killed my wife, they'll find the killer of Pollie Johnson."

The investigation was looking at behavior patterns to see whether anything else in Gary's background fit that could tie him to Pollie's homicide while the case of Dixie moved forward. A story the inspectors heard about an incident involving Gary at a relative's wedding looked like it was worth checking out, as from the little they heard, it offered something that would hint at a pattern in Gary's behavior and attitudes that might relate to the case. Mike Lyman and Larson interviewed Nolan Munson, brother-in-law of Dixie, who lived in Dixie's hometown of Litchville. Nolan and his wife, Donna, offered the information that Gary "had a thing with young girls."

The officers asked about an incident at the wedding dance of Nolan's daughter, Diane Grod. Nolan told them his son, Jerome, had seen Gary "monkeying" with a young girl who was a personal friend of the family, but he didn't want to give her name. He gave some information, including that the girl was fifteen at the time and rather short and lived in Norton, near Harvey. He also said they were frightened of Olson and avoided going anywhere with him. Munson told them he owned three guns, a 12-gauge shotgun, a .22 Winchester repeater, and a pistol. Dixie at one time had a chrome handled automatic pistol, and he had seen Gary with it once.

Lyman and Larson wanted to know more about Gary's interest in young girls and talked to Jerome Hanson. He filled them in. Jerome had been an usher in the summer of 1973 or 1974 at the wedding of his sister, Diane, which was held in Harvey. The wedding dance was in Selz. It was at the dance that he saw Gary fooling around with and attempting to molest Pam Hanson, who was a freshman in high school and about thirteen or fourteen but looked younger. Pam was "kinda cute," with light-brown or blonde hair and was very short. Jerome got suspicious of Gary at the wedding dance when Dixie and the others thought he was outside. He went looking for him, but didn't see him because Gary had gone for walk with Pam Hanson by the railroad depot in Selz. According to Pam, Gary wouldn't leave her alone. Gary started returning to the area regularly to go hunting with Jerome, and when he did, he always wanted to pick up Pam Hanson and Cindy Monson. Cindy Monson was Jerome's sister and Dixie and Gary's niece. Jerome caught Gary in his car alone with Pam one time.

Jerome said Gary always seemed interested in younger girls. He visited Gary in West Fargo in 1973 or 1974, and Gary liked to go to a pizza place where there was a sixteen-year-old girl working. He was always bragging about how that girl wanted to go out with him. Jerome's information seemed consistent with the picture of Olson they were getting elsewhere, which was that he liked hunting and he drank, plus he had an interest in young girls and preferred them blonde or fair-haired. He also thought they couldn't resist him.

It was a pattern worth pursuing farther, and Larson took Deputy Pralguske with him to Valley City to talk to Cynthia Monson, known as Cindy, daughter of Nolan Monson and niece to Dixie and Gary Olson. Her sister's wedding dance, they found, had been June 8, 1973. She was a bridesmaid, and fourteen years old. Gary had been an usher. After the wedding, Gary had been chasing Pam, who was fifteen. There was another girl along with them, LaRae Miedema of Litchfield, and the three girls had a hotel room in Harvey. During the wedding dance, the three girls and Gary had taken a walk around town. Gary said he was going to divorce Dixie and move back to Enderlin. He was really focusing on Pam and told her that he had been "fixed," so she didn't have to worry about anything. Several times during walk, he attempted advances on Pam but was rejected. Later, Gary took Dixie to her folks' home then came over to Cindy

Monson's. She and Pam were the only ones there, and Gary wanted Pam to come along and drink. Gary grabbed Pam at Monson's. He also grabbed Cindy when she was getting out of car.

Gary often visited Litchville after that wedding dance to go hunting, or at least he said that was his reason. At times Pam and Cindy and some other girls would be riding around with Jerome Hansen, their uncle. Gary would usually look them up and try to ride with them. He asked Cindy if she thought Pam would go out with him. Whenever Gary came to the Monson farm, he'd ask about Pam, and whether she was going with anyone. Thirty-two-year-old Gary would show up at parties kids were having around Litchville where Pam was with her friends, all who were eighteen or under.

After one party, Gary gave his niece, Cindy, a ride home. Several miles from her home, he stopped the car and pushed her down on the front seat. She told him she was going to tell her dad, and he let her up and took her right home. Gary told her not to tell Dixie what he had done.

Cindy said Gary always talked to her about girls who were teases or teasing him and bragged about all the young girls he could take out, including young girls in West Fargo. She said it was easy to see if Gary was interested in someone, because he would stare at them.

They asked for physical description of Pam Hanson. Cindy told them Pam was about five-foot, two inches, with light hair, and a fair completion. She was a cheerleader and gymnast, and Cindy thought Pam had been at a state meet in Jamestown, and had also been in competitions in Fargo. Cindy didn't know whether Gary had attended any of these competitions but thought, if he had known about them, he would probably have gone. Cindy graduated in 1976. Pam would have been in these gymnastics meets in 1974 and 1975.

Cindy added that Gary was always drinking beer when he came to town, and he would buy beer for her and her friends. Even if they didn't ask, he would offer to get then some Mogan David wine.

Gary would arrive and drive around Litchville looking for the girls who drove around with Jerome on weekends. When Gary found them, he would stop them and get in the car. At that point the girls would often get out, and since Dixie's murder, Cindy was frightened of him. Gary had shown no interest in the third of the three girls who ran around together, a very attractive girl with somewhat dark skin and dark hair. He was only interested in fair-haired, fair-skinned girls. Cindy was living in Valley City with a roommate and working, and had been at Dixie's funeral. She said that Gary had kissed his dead wife at the funeral home and had "run around her like a little kid at a party, almost."

Larson and Detective Pralguske interviewed Pamela Hanson in Valley City. She told them how she had met Olson at a dance in Selz in June of 1973. She was fifteen at the time and about to be a sophomore in high school, and she hadn't known him before. When she first saw him, "He seemed to stare through her. He had kinda weird eyes."

Cindy introduced Gary to the other girls the night before the wedding. At the dance, when Pam and her friend, LaRae Miedema, went for walk around block, Gary tagged along. He appeared to be trying to act like a teenager that night. He talked about not getting along with Dixie and how he was getting a divorce, and kept bringing up how many good-looking girls there were at the dance. Gary had told her that "there was another girl at the dance that he wanted to 'hustle,' but Jerome Hansen was already after her." They had sat by the railroad tracks briefly, and Gary had pulled Pam down on his lap, but she immediately got up. They continued to walk around a while longer, and he left at that point.

Pam kept a diary and got it out to check the dates on things. The wedding had been June 8, 1973. After they went home from the wedding, she was at Cindy Monson's. Gary came over there by himself. Cindy, Pam, and Gary were the only ones there, and he had asked Cindy if she thought Pam would go with him.

Larson recorded, going to Olson's patterns, "Pam stated that

119

Gary usually came to Litchville after that incident. Gary appeared to be very interested in all the girls, but she did say that he wasn't much interested in the one that was dark and had dark hair." Larson noted the similarities of Gary's preferences with Pollie Johnson and asked Pam about it. He recorded her response as, "Pam stated she went to some gymnastic meets in West Fargo—possibly two years ago. Pam says she remembers meeting Pollie Johnson."

They had established that Gary was familiar with the sheltered area along the Maple River where the Johnson farmhouse was tucked away and had seen enough to say something about Pollie sitting on a counter, perhaps that of the C&C Market. He had a thing for blondes, especially, trim and fit ones, and Pollie had been a very attractive and friendly girl who was both blonde and athletic. His attraction to young girls was documented and something he boasted of, and he talked as though they were equally engrossed with him, though that seemed delusional. Pollie's and her sisters' natures were outgoing and welcoming, and Gary frequented C&C Market. He might have interpreted the pleasantness to him as something more, something to add to his string of boasts.

There were many ways to point a finger at him, but they hadn't found a weapon to match to the shell casing, and Gary had an alibi, again provided by a family member, that he had been a witness and not a criminal. Something of substance would be required before they could consider this a case a prosecutor could prove "beyond reasonable doubt."

Finding the matching weapon could wrap everything up, and they hadn't given up on that. With Gary as the prime suspect in the homicide everyone hoped to be seen solved, no efforts were spared. The river was dammed at Enderlin to make a thorough search of the bottom, but the effort failed to add any new information.

8

THE WHEELS OF JUSTICE IN MOTION

The investigation of Gary Olson for the murder of Pollie Johnson had been carrying on with little fanfare. Investigators had been deflecting attention from the connection and the progress made, and the very public case against the same man for the murder of his wife had been moving along at the same time and was headed towards a climax. On March 22, 1977, Gary Dean Olson was arrested the murder for Dixie Olson. Law enforcement officials stated at the time of the arrest that there was no evidence whatsoever to link the two cases.

Olson's court-appointed second council, the aggressive young Robert Feder, argued for bail of $1,000 on the basis that setting it higher would keep Olson from seeing his children, which would be a punishment to the three young people who had already endured so much suffering. Assistant State's Attorney Cynthia Rothe requested bail of $50,000, but Judge George Duis set it at $100,000, and Olson was jailed. Duis also announced the preliminary hearing for April 14. At that hearing, the prosecution would present evidence to show it had a case worthy of the court's consideration, and the defense would rebut that contention. Preliminary hearings allowed judges to prevent frivolous cases from clogging the system.

The preliminary hearing began on a Thursday with the prosecution going through basic details of the discovery of the body by Dixie's daughter then calling Dr. D.H. Lawrence, the Cass County coroner, to testify on the autopsy and his findings regarding the homicide. Lawrence presented graphic photographs of Dixie's wounds and said her death was caused by hard blows to the head with a blunt object inflicted between 2:00 a.m. and 4:00 a.m. He pointed out two crescent-shaped wounds on her forehead and another near one of her ears along with sharp lacerations to the back of her head and stated that these wounds could have been caused by a tire iron, a metal crowbar used for removing wheel covers and lug nuts when changing tires.

The massive skull fractures and brain hemorrhages resulted in Dixie's death some time after the attack. Blood inhaled into her mouth and airway indicated that the victim was unconscious some time before she died.

Officer David Weaver and West Fargo Police Chief Ken Hanson both testified and told the story of the victim being discovered by her daughter and that the Gary and Dixie were estranged. They described how Dixie had been found in her bedroom where dressers were open and clothes strewn about. They said inspection of the basement showed that the window had apparently been pried open, which first gave rise to burglary as a motive. Their investigators found that the window had been tampered with for what they believed was the purpose of creating the deception that burglary had been the intent. Gary Olson's fingerprints had been found on the window casings.

The court next heard from members of Gary's family. His mother, his children, his sister, and his brother-in-law all spoke in turn. It was an open session, and the reporter for *The Fargo Forum* covering the story recorded Olson's demeanor at the time, as these witnesses formed his key defense, and although he had previously put it otherwise to Linda Johnson's mother, the family spoke at the time of his prime concern. "Olson, stoic throughout the proceedings, wept silently as his mother described his affection for the three children — Michelle, David, eleven, and Keith, seven."

Olson's sister, mother, and brother-in-law all testified that on the night Dixie was murdered, Gary was apparently asleep on the couch in the family's home in Enderlin, North Dakota, when they all went to bed shortly after 9:00 p.m. His sister told of letting Gary use her car for the eight-mile drive to their brother's home and giving him money for gas. Police testing of the car's odometer and fuel remaining on the morning the body was discovered indicated that the car could have been driven considerably farther. The state made the point that Olson had changed clothes between the day of the murder and the following day, and he had no clothes in Enderlin, only in West Fargo. Each of the children testified to having heard nothing in their home the night their mother was killed. David also testified that he had seen a letter that said, "something bad — about daddy." He had told his father that he had seen a secret letter that said, "something bad," about him. The day came to an end, and Olson was allowed a brief visit with his children before being returned to jail.

As the hearing resumed on Friday, a motive was introduced with the testimony of Marlys Frost, who recounted Olson's threats to kill Dixie if she were ever with another man. More evidence for the state came from the testimony of Gary's brother Mick and his wife, Donna, as they swore Gary had on different clothes the day following the murder.

The big surprise came when chief prosecutor States Attorney Mervin Nordeng called a former cellmate of Olson's to testify. Arnold Wayne Neukom had been Olson's cellmate in the Valley City jail after Olson's recent arrest for murdering Dixie. Fargo's jail had been determined to be structurally unsound, so prisoners had been farmed out to North Dakota jails in Valley City, Jamestown, Wahpeton, Grand Forks, and Hillsboro while repairs were being made. Gary had been sent to Valley City. Olson's attorneys objected to allowing the informer to speak, while the prosecution proposed he be allowed to testify anonymously, out of fear of jailhouse reprisal for being labeled a rat. The defendant's objection was based on a Constitutional law argument and the Sixth Amendment, which stated, "In all criminal prosecutions, the accused shall enjoy the right to a speedy and public trial, by an impartial jury of the state . . . and to have the assistance of counsel for his defense." It is this amendment that had led to the requirement of Miranda warnings rights. Olson's attorney's contended that the evidence to be introduced had been unlawfully obtained, since the snitch, Neukom, had made an arrangement with Mike Lyman in exchange for an outstanding Minnesota forgery warrant for his arrest being dropped. After making that arrangement, the defense argued that Neukom was working as an agent for the police when he questioned Olson about the crime. As such an agent, the snitch was required to give Olson the Miranda warning while the two were in jail together, and his failure to do so had violated Olson's constitutional right to assistance of counsel.

Judge Redetzke heard what Neukom had to say about his association with the state, on which the defense based its contention. He had said, "I only had one short conversation with one of the investigators who was handling this particular case. A very brief conversation and most of the conversation was — he just asked certain questions about me. And when he got done discussing myself as a person and background, he told me that, well, you know, what the score is, and let us know when you know something. I told him what information he would need, and I would secure the information if possible."

The judge then questioned Neukom to clarify the situation and the exchange did little to support the defense's agency status claim:

124

Redetzke: "And each time you talked to Mr. Lyman he would send you back to try to secure more information, is that a fair statement?

Neukom: "No. He never sent me back at all."

Redetzke: "I want you to answer the question."

Neukom: "No. He never had me do anything. I acted on my own for my own interests."

Redetzke: "He told you, well, we are interested in learning about a weapon. We are interested in learning about clothing. We are interested in learning about another act — specifics. He never inquired about those things?"

Neukom: "I am telling you he never inquired. I told him what information he would need, and I would secure the information if possible."

Redetzke: "Did Mr. Lyman ever say . . . did he tell you about this thing, that thing, or another thing?"

Neukom: "I related the conversations and the information that I had. They took it down as a matter of record."

Redetzke: "So, you were actually running the ball game, is that right?"

Neukom: "Yes."

The suppression motion was denied. Redetzke ruled that the witness could testify without giving his name. Neukom's testimony on statements Olson had made to him was that Olson never confessed to murdering Dixie but did admit to going to West Fargo after he awoke on his sister's couch in Enderlin. He had gone to her house to search for letters and ransacked her room, then threw the tire iron in an ice-fishing hole in a river. Neukom was cross-examined thoroughly about his relationship with the police, and the defense clearly established that he expected that by being helpful to North Dakota authorities, he would escape facing forgery charges in Minnesota. His dealings on testifying had been arranged by Mike Lyman.

In alignment with Neukom's testimony an affidavit filed earlier from the FBI stated that Gary Olson's fingerprints were on items from the contents of his wife's purse that had been strewn around the workroom. Defense counsel William Yuill challenged it, saying there were many unidentified fingerprints found in the house and Agent Remus had not been able to say when the prints had been left.

The prosecution also introduced into the hearing as evidence, testimony from Pamela Bommersbach, a resident of the house at 102 Second Avenue East where Olson had a sleeping room. She said she had been ill the night of January 23 and had heard someone entering the house early in morning using the stairway to his room.

Judge Redetzke found that ample evidence existed for the case to go to trial, and on April 28 he set the tentative date for the trial of Gary Dean Olson to begin as June 6. He also reduced Olson's bail from $100,000 to $50,000. Olson had maintained throughout the hearing that he was innocent. His attorneys made a pretrial motion to suppress Neukom's testimony and weaken the State's case, but they were unsuccessful in their attempt in Cass County District Court to have it excluded, where the prominent jurist and member of the West Fargo community, Ralph Maxwell, ruled the testimony was admissible.

An arraignment on May 23 made the trial date official, and it was to begin in two weeks. Lester Meddy, who had been an inmate of the Valley City jail along with Olson and Neukom, contacted the prosecutor's office by letter on the last day in May and said he had valuable information to contribute to their case, which was scheduled to begin in one week. On June 4, two days before the trial was to start, the state gave the name of Meddy to the court and the defense and stated its intention to call him as a witness. The prosecution had a case that was largely circumstantial, and had no weapon as well as Gary having an alibi supported by witnesses. But there had been threats and past behavior along with some bits of physical evidence to weigh against his family's testimony. Now they had witnesses to tie Olson to the crime in his own words, not only those from people recalling what Dixie suggested, and Gary's murder threats that Frost had reported. Snitches may not always be the most convincing witnesses, but they supported the prosecution's case. The prosecution felt ready to go ahead, as the evidence seemed compelling. It was time to expose Gary Olson and his flawed ego for what he was and put him away. Bring on June 6.

The parallel investigation regarding Polly had loose ends and still really needed something to tie it all together, since it was much more indirect and supported almost entirely by hearsay. There were conflicting stories about what had happened that night that could cast some doubt, including the one Mick would tell about the Grim Reapers and another told by construction worker Bud Wright. Wright said he had been at the Lariat Bar the night of the Pollie's murder and claimed that three men had come in the bar that August 8 evening and joined him. After some heavy drinking, one said he had killed a kid about six miles north of West Fargo. The two other men had disagreed over the girl's age, but one said she was about sixteen. To get beyond "reasonable doubt," the prosecution needed some lynchpin for their case to attach all the pieces. If only all there searches had led to them finding the weapon involved, but it wasn't for lack of effort.

Mike Lyman came up with an idea. It was born in specialized knowledge, not the sort learned in most criminology courses, but understanding from having the same sorts of experiences as the person one was dealing with. Mike was born on a farm near Lisbon, and his father had been an avid hunter who got him his first .22 rifle when he was seven years old. He liked to go out in the pasture and shoot gophers, since there was a bounty on gophers then, and he also earned money trapping the small creatures. He had moved to West Fargo in 1961 and had been in the Naval Air Force and was attending North Dakota State University in Fargo when he took a job as a jailer with the sheriff's department, then was hired full time. It was his experience as a country boy growing up shooting a .22 that gave him the idea about making a solid case against Olson for murdering Pollie.

There are two ways a .22 could be fired, either rim fire or center fire. With rim fire, the weapon's hammer struck the outer edge of the cartridge casing, and igniting the primer. With center fire, a firing pin struck a primer cap at the cartridge center. The casing found by Pollie's body was center fire, but the strike mark was distorted. Lyman had noticed the mark on the back of the small spent cartridge when he saw the casing at the time it was found on the morning after the homicide. They had a distinct shell casing from the weapon with a partially broken or flawed firing pin. Finding more spent cartridges that had come from a weapon Olson had owned would connect them, if the cartridges had the same flaw. They had been trying to find similar cartridges from the beginning of the investigation, but mainly by test firing weapons.

In talking to people Olson had associated with in West Fargo bars, Lyman had learned that Olson did some target shooting and hunting in the countryside between West Fargo and Enderlin. It was an open area Lyman knew well. His first thought was to try to locate the places where the target shooting had been done, but he thought the possibilities were remote unless someone who had accompanied Olson could guide him. Then he had an imaginative idea that seemed worth pursuing.

It had been a common pastime in his youth to spend time driving around the countryside, shooting his .22 from the driver's side or the passenger's side of cars, aiming at gophers, rabbits, crows, signs. He knew that the spent cartridges, because they were small, accumulated in the vehicle as he drove, between and under the seats, in all sorts of difficult-to-reach places. They could end up going unnoticed permanently, being wedged in locations he didn't check or couldn't reach.

Olson had very likely done the same thing. Lyman thought there might be a way to tie Olson directly to the weapon involved in the homicide by finding casings that matched the one with the flawed pin marking in vehicles Gary had previously owned. Although the vehicles would have changed owners and locations, there might still be casings in unnoticed places. They didn't have the gun to match with them but if these rare and distinctive casings turned up in some of Gary's old cars, that could be the evidence they needed that the weapon used had been Olson's.

The casing hadn't come from the Remington Model 5 bolt action .22 that Gary kept at Dennis Johnson's house in Enderlin, which had been test fired. They needed to find whether he had another .22 rifle, since he had apparently disposed of the weapon used, as his conversation with Mick indicated, or had hidden it very well. Larson and Remus had heard from Mick that Robbie had bought a .22 for Gary. Larson set out to locate the gun and thought he'd begin by contacting the local gun dealers in the Fargo-Moorhead area.

His first call was to Lindgren's Hardware in West Fargo, and the search was over right there. If only investigations would go that way more often. The store reported that a gun had been purchased by a Robert T. Olson. Larson and Remus went over and looked at Federal Firearms form dated January 21, 1973, for a .22 caliber rifle, Winchester model 150. The store's records showed another similar weapon sold locally in June of 1974. They would attempt to get the second weapon for comparison firing. But now it was time to talk to Robert Olson.

Agent Remus advised Robert Olson of his rights before he and Larson began their questioning. Then they reminded him that he had said at the time of Dixie's homicide that he had no guns and had never owned any. He changed that story to owning a .22 rifle and a shotgun that he had loaned to Gary. He rationalized away owning them by saying he, "legally does and morally doesn't." The shotgun had been confiscated during the investigation of the Olson home. Both that and the .22 were purchased at Scheel's Hardware in Fargo, he claimed.

The .22 in question so suited Gary and his world view. He had wanted a lever-action Winchester because it looked like the gun the Rifleman used on TV. The Rifleman had been a popular western from Gary's younger days when westerns dominated black-and-white television. It was the story of a single parent raising his boy on their homestead, a bit like Gary and David, and teaching him his values and to never walk away from a fight. The six-foot, five-inch Chuck Connors with his square jaw and winning smile was the Rifleman. As one of only twelve athletes to have ever played in both the NBA professional basketball and major league baseball leagues, he was a real man's man. A gun like the Rifleman's was just the thing for a tough guy like Gary.

Robert started to get confused and nervous when questions began. The forms from Lindgren's contradicting his story about when and where he had bought the .22 were shown to him, and he admitted that Gary had told him that if anyone asked about the rifle, the .22., he should say Gary had sold it a couple of years earlier. Larson recorded, "He apparently gets mad when he gets into a tight spot and displays the same emotions as Mick and Gary do when they are cornered. . . . Robert stated that Gary had told him he didn't want Robert in trouble. Robert said Gary didn't tell him what to say when we talked to him." It was, "Very apparent he was scared of trouble he might be in for furnishing that rifle to Gary."

Gary had an unaccounted for .22 rifle. The North Dakota Motor Vehicles Department came up with a list of vehicles Olson had previously owned. For Lyman, "Locating each car was an investigation within an investigation." He found a 1961 Rambler Olson had owned at a salvage yard in Valley City, North Dakota, on June 22, 1977, where it had been sitting, never driven since Olson sold it as junk. Another car formerly owned by Olson that Lyman located was a 1970 Hornet that had been purchased by Robert Amundson on July 23, 1976, for his daughter to use at the University of North Dakota.

Lyman's idea turned out to be successful. A careful search of the junked Rambler recovered six .22 casings, and in the second car, the Hornet, they located 106 casings that could not be attributed to its current owner. The Amundsons also told Lyman that when they first received the car from Olson, it had been a mess, so they took it to the gravel alley behind their home and swept it out. Lyman went to the alley with a metal detector, and in the area where they had swept out the garbage from Olson's car he located more .22 casings.

The casings were all sent to the FBI lab in Washington for the most accurate possible evaluation. This could be the evidence to pull everything together if the results came out the way they hoped. From the time Lyman thought to look for the casings until they had authoritative results was going to be a matter of months, but that was the pace of precise collection and processing of information. If they didn't match, then it was back to plodding on and keeping going until something was found or a person with information stepped forward.

The other aspect of the case they looked at was determining just what the motivation for the crime had been. There had been the increase in break-ins into secluded homes, but Larson and Lyman agreed that there was no doubt this had been a sex crime. It might not have started out as one, but it had become one, and Pollie was the victim of a sexual assault. Prosecutor Joe Turman said, "You know, we never got that far. I mean, you don't disrobe someone, the gun in the mouth. We had such a good case."

Judge Cynthia Rothe-Seeger, who at the time was Cynthia Rothe, the second chair to Turman for the prosecution, put it, "Olson sexually assaulted and killed Pollie Johnson. The sexual assault was not charged as a separate crime. It was a horrific crime, and the murder charge was the more serious charge."

Lyman admitted that he was no expert in the field but said that, in his opinion, the gun inserted in her mouth was an extension of his penis. She was shot where her lip met her teeth, as though her mouth had been around the barrel, which was at an angle that the lead slug carried into her brain. The coroner testified that there was no rape, which seemed to contradict their observation, but they did some interviewing that made that understandable. One of Olson's former girlfriends from when he was married told them of his difficulties with impotence. Larson explained, "Although, there was

131

probably an attempt, we found out later that he wasn't able to do that sort of thing anymore." He'd had children, so it hadn't always been the case, and Lyman speculated that Olson's excessive drinking could well have been the cause. Gary still viewed himself as a "man," powerful and magnetic, but the parts weren't reliable, and he lashed out during his own failures so often in life.

Throughout this time, from the first look at Gary Olson as the best candidate for the murder of Pollie Johnson, through the tedious development of the case that had been going on for months, the sheriff's office remained silent on its progress. From the beginning, updating the public had been similar: "No Arrests Imminent in West Fargo Death," "No West Fargo Murder Arrests Are in Sight," "Officials Deny Break in Pollie Johnson Case." They didn't have quite all they needed for reasonable doubt to be overcome.

9

THE TRIAL OF GARY DEAN OLSON
FOR THE MURDER OF DIXIE OLSON

As progress was being made in the Pollie Johnson case, the town's other tragic shock had come to a head. On Monday morning, June 6, 1977, the trial of Gary Dean Olson began in the Cass County District Courthouse in Fargo. Olson was being defended by William Yuill, a man of great presence—flamboyant and handsome and a dominating figure in the courtroom. Leading the prosecution was North Dakota State's Attorney Mervin Nordeng.

Nordeng's route to becoming state's attorney was not a well-planned path. He recalled, "I would have never imagined that I could get up in court. I was never educated in that manner at all. I was a farm boy who became an engineer." He grew up on very small farm outside of Watford City, North Dakota, milking cows and stacking hay. He graduated from eighth grade from the same one-room school his father had graduated from seventh grade. The school's outdoor privies were sometimes an unpleasant experience in winter, but Nordeng received enough education eventually to go to North Dakota State University and get a degree in electrical engineering.

Several years later he went to law school, then worked for the North Dakota Supreme Court. An opening came up for assistant state's attorney. There were only two applicants, and the other didn't want to work full time, while full time was fine with Nordeng. In 1974 he was elected to a two-year term as North Dakota State's Attorney. It was a busy position, and he was preparing to prosecute Gary Olson for the burglary of the Triangle Western Store when the Dixie homicide trial began. He said, "You know, I was the first real full-time state's attorney. Up until that time they were part-timers."

The much-awaited trial for the murder of Dixie Olson began with the *voir dire*, the stage of the trial when the twelve members who were to sit in judgment of the facts of the case were selected from a pool of people called after answering questions from the attorneys and judge. *Voir dire*, often mistakenly said to have come from the French, meaning "to see, to speak," actually had a Medieval origin, and its current meaning, derives from the Anglo-Norman for "to speak the truth." The selection of those who would "speak the truth" in this case began and was a bit contentious, finally being completed by the morning of June 8.

Different attorneys look for different things in potential jurors, and some do studies to find out what they can about the personalities of those who have been called. The defense did studies in this case. Nordeng and the prosecution had general ideas, unrelated to the standard questions on awareness of publicity about the case and speculation or personal connections to the parties involved. It was a time when juries were more apt to acquit than they do presently, and Nordeng found that particularly true among the educated, such as school teachers. Having detail people, probably an engineer was desirable, Teamsters were his ideal, but professors were the greatest challenge, the acquitters.

The panel of twelve jurors selected including nine men and three women. About half an hour after jury empanelment, Judge Redetzke said, "Bearing in mind the court's usual admonition, we

134

will take a recess. . . ." That wouldn't be the end of the story for the *voir dire* of the trial.

After Wednesday noon recess, State's Attorney Mervin Nordeng began his work of convincing all twelve jurors "beyond a reasonable doubt" that Gary had murdered Dixie. His presentation of the case to achieve such persuasion began with a review of the day's events when Dixie was murdered. He hadn't prepped his witnesses, as some attorneys do. He just didn't want to be surprised. His view was, "I was not one who really did that very much. I would go through everything with them so that I knew that if I asked a question I knew what they were going to say. But I didn't say, 'This is the question I'm going to ask you, and then I'm going to ask you this,' because oftentimes when I ask a question, that leads you off on a different path anyway."

He first called Larry Toso, who lived next door to Olsons. Toso said the victim's son, David Olson, had come to his house shortly before 8:00 a.m. on January 24 and asked him to come over to their house because he thought his mother was dead. When he went into their house, he had found Dixie on her bed and immediately called the police. Toso said he noticed the trampled snow by the basement window and thought the window was ajar, so he had thought someone had been in the backyard.

Dixie's young daughter, Michelle, testified that she had been awakened by the noise of her mother's radio alarm. When the alarm continued to sound, she had gone to her mother's room to see what was going on and discovered her mother dead. She said she woke up her brothers after that.

David was on the stand next and said he went into mother's room at his sister's request, and before going to the Toso residence he had partially covered his mother's battered face with a blanket. He told about what he and sisters and brother had done the two days prior to the murder. Both the prosecution and defense asked him about supposed secret letters his mother had hidden and phone calls

135

she received in private. He could only respond that he had some difficulty remembering them. Nordeng then read excerpts from preliminary hearing transcript in which David had said his mother had taken calls in her bedroom after telling the children to leave the room. David also had testified at the pretrial hearing that he had seen a letter saying, "bad things about daddy." It had since become difficult for him to remember such specifics.

David then testified that, when he and father returned to their home some time after his mother's death, they had found clothes that belonged to his mother in the hamper. These were clothes he labeled as "dressy," the sort of thing his mother wouldn't wear even with her closest friend, Linda Johnson. He didn't remember seeing her wear the clothes on the night she was killed. Linda Johnson had been at their home helping his mother bleach her hair that night.

Nordeng called North Dakota Crime Bureau Agent Richard G. Olson to the witness stand to add more to the background. Agent Olson testified that he had spoken to the defendant, who had told him his son had run away from his mother on the Saturday before the murder because of what he had overheard being said. The defendant had said that he had returned his son to his wife's home and told the agent she had said she shouldn't let him see his children again.

Agent Olson also testified that Gary Olson said he spent that night at his sister's in Enderlin. He said the defendant told him he had used his sister's car to return to West Fargo on Sunday afternoon, but didn't find his wife and children at home, so he returned to Enderlin, then went to Sheldon to visit his brother. Olson added that the defendant admitted to being very jealous and suspecting that his wife was having a secret affair. He also put into the record that the defendant had said he would kill his wife if he ever caught her with another man.

With that background introduced, the next point the state attempted to dispose of was the possibility that the killing was the result of a burglary, which was an initial motive considered. First responder David Weaver, a West Fargo patrolman, testified that he saw one of the two basement windows in the Olson home appeared unlocked, but not open. He had noticed that the snow near that window was packed but was dismayed there were no tracks in the yard. He also described the bedroom where he found the body and said dresser drawers were open and some of the contents strewn on the floor. Some drawers in the kitchen were open, and he said he had found Mrs. Olson's purse and its contents, which appeared to have been dumped, in a utility room connected to the kitchen.

West Fargo Chief of Police Kenneth Hanson took the stand and said he also noticed the rear window and packed snow when he arrived. He told of when the defendant arrived at the Olson house sometime before 11:30 a.m., and was informed of his wife's death. At that time Olson agreed to let the detectives search his car.

These first observations about the window, which were made by others as they arrived, had led police to suspect a break-in and burglary had likely occurred and might have gone wrong, ending in the macabre killing. They showed how alert the officers were in immediately seeing the clues and the possible relationship to the outcome, but also the importance in not assuming the first and most obvious answer was necessarily the correct one. That came next when North Dakota Crime Bureau Agent Richard Olson testified that his investigation of the basement window everyone found suspicious revealed some of the bolts had been removed from their hinges. He stated that if anyone had tried to open that window, it would have fallen out of its frame, so it hadn't been opened. He also said the defendant told him that he hadn't touched that window for about a year, when he taped it shut, but no evidence of any tape on or near the window had been found.

Coroner Obert testified that the cause of death had been severe blows to the brain by a blunt instrument that appeared to have had at least one sharp edge. He could not say definitely that only one object had been used and put the time of death at about 2:00 a.m. on

January 24. Pam Bommersback, who lived in a basement apartment in the building where Olson rented a room in West Fargo, next testified to having heard someone walk up the stairs late January 23 or early January 24. Lester Eiltz, another resident at the same location testified to not having heard anything that night.

Saturday's testimony began with the introduction of a motive for the murder, as Marlys Frost was called to the stand. She recalled her conversation with Olson from the Silver Dollar Bar between the past Thanksgiving and Christmas when he had told her he suspected his wife was having an affair and that it was with her attorney, David Overboe. Frost stated that Olson said he would kill his wife if he ever caught her "running around behind his back." Overboe then testified that he had been Dixie Olson's lawyer in the suit she had filed for divorce on November 30, 1976, but had no social relationship with her.

It was time to start hearing from the Olson family. His sister, Gwen Johnson of Enderlin, testified to the familiar summary of Gary having come to their home January 23 and borrowing her car and being told he had driven to Sheldon, eight miles away, to visit their brother. She said she had given him ten dollars for gas. She continued, saying he returned about 7:30 p.m. and watched television on the couch until he fell asleep. He was sleeping on the couch when she and her husband went to bed at about 10:00 p.m. At about midnight she heard him let his dog out. He was sleeping downstairs the next morning when she went down, and after he awoke, he drove his car back to West Fargo, and she followed him in her car. Shortly before holiday recess, Nordeng's questions focused mainly on the mileage on her car. Gwen had testified earlier that she stopped to fill the car in Fargo, even though she had given her brother ten dollars the previous day to buy gas. Police, testing of the car's consumption, had concluded that Olson had driven farther than the sixteen miles to make the trip from Enderlin to Sheldon and back.

State's Attorney Nordeng introduced results of gas consumption tests done on Mrs. Johnson's Chrysler, which she said Gary had

138

borrowed to drive to Sheldon, but defense counsel Yuill objected. He argued that it was prejudicial to introduce the test results into evidence because Nordeng hadn't show the tests were made under the same conditions that existed when Mrs. Johnson drove to West Fargo on January 24. Following that, the trial was adjourned for Sunday, with Gwen's testimony to be completed when the trial resumed.

Monday morning began with Gwen repeating her story of Gary's whereabouts on June 23 as Nording worked to establish his foundation and subtly cast doubt on the credibility of the witness's accounts. Defense counsel Yuill took advantage of Gwen's presence on the stand to establish that Mrs. Johnson was a light sleeper and maintain that she would have heard if her brother had gone and returned during the night. She said the Johnson dog and Olson dog would have barked, but she'd heard nothing. Their dog barked when anyone came to house.

Her husband, Dennis Johnson, was called next and corroborated his wife's testimony, saying Gary was at the Johnson home on the night of January 23. He also supported his wife's statements about the dogs' barking, saying he'd heard nothing.

Olson's mother, Mrs. Doris Johanneson, was called as a witness and said Gary was still at the Johnson home on the evening of January 23 when she went home at 9:20 p.m. She then testified that the following morning she rode to West Fargo with her daughter, Mrs. Johnson, and her granddaughter. They followed her son, Gary, to his wife's house, which was where they learned of Dixie's death. Mrs. Johanneson said they were at the Olson home for about an hour, and then they took Gary to his apartment so he could pick up some snapshots of his wife. They stopped at the police department, then set off to do some of the things they had originally intended to do. They went to the Piggly Wiggly in south Fargo to do some grocery shopping, and Mrs. Johnson took Mrs. Johanneson to her doctor's appointment at the nearby Dakota Clinic. Before they left Fargo, they stopped to get gas.

After the noon recess, West Fargo Detective Donald Jones tes-tified. He spoke about evidence sent to the FBI laboratory in Wash-ington, D.C., but Nordeng was saving the key FBI findings for a later witness. Jones gave evidence on what Olson claimed he had done the night of his wife's murder. He told of his interrogations of Olson, and the familiar story he heard from Gary of how he had gone to his wife's home on the afternoon of January 23 to take kids roller skating. When he found that his wife and children were not home, he had taken his dog and left the children a note, telling them to have their mother take them roller skating. From there he had driven to Sheldon, spent the afternoon with his brother, then headed to Enderlin to his sister's home. He had watched television before falling asleep on the davenport. He woke up about 10:00 p.m., turned the television off, went to kitchen to the read the paper while he drank a few beers. So far there was much repetition and little was being presented that made Olson seem like a legitimate suspect.

Jones then described what Olson was wearing when he saw the defendant in front of his wife's home on the morning following the murder. He had on maroon pants, a lavender shirt, brown cow-boy boots and a windbreaker jacket with pile lining. Olson had stat-ed that he had been wearing the same clothes since January 23, the day before Dixie was killed. Earlier in the trial Gary's sister Gwen had testified that she didn't think her brother had a change of clothes at her Enderlin home.

Jones also testified that he had questioned Olson's brother-in-law, Dennis Johnson, about the possibility of Gary leaving and re-turning without being heard. Jones said his questions dealt with the dogs and whether they would bark if someone came to the door. It had been Johnson's response, Jones stated, that neither dog barked when Olson and his mother arrived on January 23. On the witness stand earlier in the day, Johnson had testified that the dogs would bark whenever someone approached the house, no matter who it was. Defense counsel Yuill had Jones admit that there were fingerprints taken at the Olson residence that hadn't been identified, though Jones hadn't been called as a forensics expert.

North Dakota Crime Bureau Agent Dale Remus was sworn in and corroborated testimony given earlier by Crime Bureau Agent Richard Olson. He described the scene at the Olson home and in addition to finding that the kitchen and bedroom drawers had been opened, there had been spots of a reddish substance on a washcloth in the bathroom sink and in other spots in the bathroom and on two walls and the ceiling in Dixie's bedroom.

Following Remus, Nordeng called Kenneth Gressens of the FBI lab in Washington, D.C. State's Attorney Nordeng introduced fingerprints and hair into evidence. This was the time to introduce expert evidence that indicated the falsehood of Olson's claims about the window. Gressens said that fingerprints found on the basement door and basement window were Gary Olson's. Olson claimed he hadn't touched the window for about a year. Because the basement window showed signs of being pried open, police originally had thought burglary might have been motive. Inspection showed this was a deception. Gressens stated that two unidentified fingerprints were found at the Olson home.

Hair had also been sent to the FBI lab, and FBI Agent Myron T. Schoberg testified that the hair found on the window had not been forcibly removed from a person's head. It had been bleached, but he couldn't say when. It could have been Dixie Olson's, although positive identification of hair was not possible at the time.

The state's case faced collapse on Wednesday, when the defense filed a motion for a mistrial. There was word the jurors had seen a story in *The Fargo Forum* about Olson's cellmate testifying as a witness for the prosecution. The Tuesday, June 14 story was headlined, "Cellmate Testifies in Olson Murder Trial," and the first sentence in the story was, "Today in Cass County District Court defense counsel William Yuill questioned a cellmate's motives for wanting to testify against Gary Dean Olson." The next morning's *Forum* reported, "Earlier Tuesday, defense counsel William Yuill questioned a cell-mate's motives for wanting to testify against the defendant."

This was a problem for more than one reason. The cellmate's testimony was basic to the prosecution's case and clearly implicated Olson, and an impartial jury shouldn't know of it in advance. What was especially strange was that, in both articles, *The Fargo Forum* reported in detail the snitch's testimony and how it was attacked by the defense counsel. The witness had not yet appeared in court and testified. Apparently the court reporter had missed that session and had taken transcripts from the pretrial hearing to use as if it were happening at the trial, but what was reported was a summary of the testimony from the previous April.

Judge Redetzke listened to the mistrial arguments, then examined the jurors. He found that four members, three regular jurors and the alternate had read the story in the newspaper. He then asked them individually by number, "Can you state to the court honestly, sincerely, whether or not that article, had anything . . . had any effect upon your judgment and the fairness in the trial of this case, and did you accept any of the statements contained in that as being relevant to this trial?"

The responses he received were, "No, sir, I did not, absolutely not," "None whatsoever, I'm going just by what I hear here," and two with a simple "No, sir."

Following that, the judge said, "I will ask all of you that I have interrogated, can you state to the court and to the defendant and to counsel, that you can still sit as fair and impartial jurors in this case uninfluenced by this publicity?"

One after another, the jurors responded, "Yes."

Redetzke then asked whether either counsel wished to ask additional question the jurors. Defense counsel Yuill stated, "I think it's not necessary for us to inquire of the jury, Your Honor. I think the court has made all the salient questions to them and received the responses I would wish." The court then denied the motion for mistrial and cautioned the media representatives present that he hoped and trusted that there would not be a repetition. During morning recess, Redetzke made his point clear to reporters as he put thumb and index finger nearly together, leaving a tiny space between them, to illustrate that publicity had come "that far" from causing a mistrial.

Gary Olson's cellmate, Arnold Neukom from the Valley City jail, took the stand for the prosecution, again testifying anonymously for fear of reprisal. Once again Yuill objected to allowing the testimony on Sixth Amendment grounds. Neukom made the same statements about Olson not actually confessing to the murder but said that Olson habitually searched his wife's home after the murder and looked through things he thought she was receiving from a boyfriend, and that he entered the home through the basement window. He had fixed the window so it would open easily and he could get in unnoticed. He had used a tire iron as a weapon that was from his car on the night of the murder and had dropped it down an ice-fishing hole on a river.

The defense focused on Neukom's reason for coming forward with this information. Yuill attempted to establish that the cellmate would have to testify to the state's attorney's satisfaction for a deal on charges being withdrawn in another state to be carried through, giving him incentive to implicate Olson to for his own welfare.

Cass County Deputy Sheriff Mike Lyman testified that an agreement had been made with authorities in Duluth, Minnesota. Lyman said there were seven or eight warrants out for Neukom from four states, including one on a forgery charge from Duluth. He stated that an agreement had been reached whereby Neukom's warrant for arrest in Duluth would be withdrawn if he testified at both the preliminary hearing and the trial. There was no stipulation about what his testimony would involve or instruction concerning what he should say. They were already aware of his knowledge of Olson's conversations before the arrangement was made. Olson's disclosures to Neukom had started when alcohol was smuggled into the jail and Olson became thoroughly intoxicated. Neukom's betrayal of confidences was not solicited by the police

Dixie's closest friend, Linda Johnson, testified on Wednesday of the second week about Dixie's whereabouts the two days before her death. She said Dixie had come over to her home, which was nearby, on January 22 at about 9:30 p.m. and cried for an entire hour. That had been the night David had overheard a conversation Dixie was having with her sister and her sister's husband and thought they were talking about him. This had been mentioned in earlier testimony. David had run away to his father, who returned him to his mother's house. Johnson said that Dixie had called her January 23 and asked if she would bleach her hair. Dixie hadn't treated her hair before in the seven years they had been friends. Dixie had come over to her house about 8:00 p.m., and they started process. Then she went to Olson's until about 9:30.

Questions that came up were that, according to previous testimony, there were dirty pots and pans on the kitchen counter, and the kitchen drawers were pulled out, though the room was not ransacked. What was the condition when she left? Johnson said everything was in its place when she was there the evening of January 23. Nordeng asked about relationships Dixie might have had, and Johnson said Dixie was "totally devoted to her children," and, to her knowledge, never went out with other men.

The prosecution then recalled Agent Remus, first to further attack the option that the crime had been possibly a break-in by an outsider. Nordeng was especially pleased with having Remus on the stand. His style was a product of his FBI Academy training. "He had a different way of testifying, but I think it was very good. It was slow and deliberate, and they could follow everything. You know, when you know all the facts, sometimes you tend to go through it and tend to assume that the people listening to you started out at the same point as you did."

144

Remus was methodical and easy for the jury to understand. He first testified again about the basement window, saying it was partially out of its casing, and the screws were missing from the hinge. He said the nails, which appeared to have been bent over window to hold it in place, were pushed back. If pushed, window would have fallen out. He had examined the window casings with a magnifying glass to see whether there were any scuff marks, but found none. The FBI agent had testified to finding Olson's fingerprints on the window, so Nordeng had Remus testify that Olson said he hadn't touched the window in about a year when he nailed or taped basement windows shut.

Nordeng next questioned Remus about Olson's reasons for driving to his wife's home the morning of January 24. Remus replied that Olson said he drove to leave his car, which wasn't working well and fill out his unemployment application. Remus said he found a sealed, stamped envelope to the Unemployment Bureau with Olson's return address and fingerprint on it on the kitchen table of Dixie's home on the morning of January 24, though Gary hadn't entered the home since Dixie's death was reported.

Nordeng wanted more circumstantial evidence and asked a question to allow Remus to talk about the extent of Olson's jealousy, which was well-captured in the story of Gary looking through Dixie's garbage can for letters and finding one from his wife addressed to him that asked what he found in the garbage that was so interesting. His reply written on the envelope showed his obsession, saying he was looking for who was the cause of his problems.

A late addition to the witness list appeared on Thursday to tell his story. Lester Meddy said he had met Olson while they were being held in Barnes County Jail at Valley City. In March over period of days, Olson allegedly told his cellmate how he'd murdered his wife and disposed of the weapon. According to Meddy, "He said how he went about it, but never came out with the words that he did it."

Meddy then related the story he claimed Olson had told him. He said Olson drove to his wife's home in West Fargo from Enderlin, where he was staying the night of January 23, and entered through one of doors to which he had a key. He had planned to use his son's shotgun to kill his wife, but decided to use a tire iron because it wouldn't make as much noise. Olson told him he then ransacked the house and tampered with the basement window to make it look as if the house had been burglarized.

Meddy said Olson had entered the house several times that way, and still had a key, even though he was supposed to have given it to wife when they separated. Olson told him he went into his wife's bedroom and hit her several times with a tire iron. Meddy had asked why the children didn't hear any noise, and Olson answered that hitting his wife on the head had not made much noise. He got a new tire iron to replace the one he used.

Meddy further testified that the reason Olson gave for killing Dixie was that he had learned that his wife was leaving him the next day, and he didn't want to lose her to another man. He said Olson made a habit of going to wife's home to search for letters that his son David told him his mother received because he suspected she was having an affair. His wife had borrowed some money and supposedly paid some bills and made two house payments, but Olson said when he found she hadn't, he thought she gave the money to her boyfriend. Meddy added that Olson said he searched through his wife's things after he killed her.

Meddy continued. After killing Dixie, Olson drove back to Enderlin, stopping once to drop the tire iron down an ice-fishing hole in the Maple River. He said he washed clothes when he got to Enderlin, but not because he was afraid there might be blood stains on them. Olson hadn't been sure whether he washed them immediately after the return or later.

Olson complained about how domineering his wife was, but said he was content, as long as she would stay and manage his life.

.   When asked why he had decided to step forward with this information at this time, Meddy said he had come forward so he might make a bargain with the police on his behalf. He claimed to have volunteered his information to show authorities he was ready to get out of prison and settle down.

There were now stories about Olson from two snitches, and their testimonies had inconsistencies. One had him entering the home through the basement window, and the other had him using a key. Both had him using a tire iron, but one said he got it from the basement, and the other said he brought it from in from his car. The second witness hadn't been given an incentive to testify like the first had, but his testimony was even more damning. What was the truth in them and who had reported more accurately? Had Olson possibly told them different versions of what happened, or was it all imagination and exploitation? That was for the jury to decide.

For the prosecution, the testimonies supported the image of Gary being portrayed, and there was enough similarity in the stories that matched real evidence being presented that they were effective. Both had Olson confessing to using the basement window, whether to create a false impression of what had happened or as the actual entry point, and his fingerprints supported that, while his denials of having touched the window in the past year didn't. Both had a tire iron as the weapon Olson used, and the coroner reported that the cause of death had been severe blows to the brain by a blunt instrument that fit that description.

Nording wasn't sure how the trial was going, but be was getting a read on some of the jurors. "I was standing up asking questions, and I was pouring water, getting myself a cup of water, and the cup was running over because whatever was coming out was something that didn't make any sense. At least one of the jurors was smiling at me at that point in time. You've got to keep the prosecution human."

The prosecution next called Gary's brother Orvin, known to many as Mick, and followed with his sister-in-law, Donna. While the Olson family had seemed unified in their support for Gary's alibi, the prosecution was about to change that, and the defense counsel was growing increasingly desperate. Nordeng had established through Jones's testimony that Gary had claimed to have not changed clothes from the day before the homicide, when he went to Enderlin and stayed at his sister's home, until the time Jones interviewed him following his being informed that his wife had been murdered. He had also established through the testimony of Gary's sister that he didn't keep clothes in Enderlin. Since the beginning and through many witnesses, it had been made clear that once Gary went to Enderlin on January 23, he borrowed his sister's car and drove to Sheldon to his brother's home. Nordeng's questions to Orvin and Donna were straight forward and dealt with only one topic. What had Gary been wearing when he came to visit on the afternoon of January 23?

Both Donna and Orvin gave the same answer. Gary had been wearing a deep-red shirt and red, white and blue checkered pants. Donna said her brother-in-law had made a point of what he wore by "repeating things as though he wanted us to remember them." Both said he was wearing solid color clothes when they saw him on January 25, the day after the murder.

That testimony was a solid point for the prosecution, since everything Gary said and the basis of his alibi was that he had gone to Enderlin in the afternoon and hadn't returned until the following morning after the murder had been committed. But testimony to that point had indicated that his clothes were in West Fargo. He was wearing something different the morning he showed up at Dixie's and was told of the homicide from what he had on the day he had left town, and he and his Enderlin relatives said he never left.

Defense counsel Robert Feder questioned Donna Olson about the accuracy of her memory of just what Gary was wearing nearly five months earlier. He asked her to tell the court what she or her husband had been wearing at the time when she could recall in such detail the color of the shirt and pattern of the pants Gary had been wearing. She replied she couldn't remember what either of them had worn at the time.

On the morning of Monday, June 20, the prosecution rested the case it had been presenting since the afternoon of June 8. The defense now had its turn. Court appointed lead counsel William Yuill said in his opening statement that he would call witnesses who had been prisoners in jail with Olson, but he lacked the state's attorney's bargaining power to promise them consideration. He also said the defense would show that the key prosecution witness, "Neukom is a pathological liar." He stated his purpose in calling other prisoners to the stand was to help the jury determine the credibility of testimony against Olson made the previous week by prosecution witnesses who had been his client's cellmates.

Yuill's opening claim was that Neukom had told his cellmates that they should make up stories to get Olson convicted if they wanted to do themselves a favor. His witness had agreed to testify in court to having heard that from Neukom. The first witness he called was a prisoner who had been in the Valley City Jail with Olson and Neukom, who had testified against Olson

The witness took the stand but had changed his mind and said he would rather not answer any questions. He refused to identify which officer had brought him from Valley City to Fargo to appear at the trial.

Nordeng then asked Judge Redetzke to order the witness to answer questions, but the witness said he still wouldn't, even if ordered. The witness denied Nordeng's suggestion that he was refusing to speak because of fear of reprisals. Finding the witness in contempt of court was suggested, but Redetzke said contempt wasn't a reasonable remedy, and if he refused to speak, that was how it would be. He explained that the witness was currently serving three consecutive ten-year sentences for burglary, so adding a few years was unlikely to matter.

Defense counsel Robert Feder then took the stand as a witness. Feder was sworn in to testify about what their impeachment witness would have said if he had been willing to answer Yuill's questions.

Nordeng objected. Inadmissible hearsay! A lawyer taking the stand and saying, "I have a witness who was going to swear that . . ."

Redetzke allowed Olson's counsel to testify. Nordeng thinks it was the judge's view that "if he was going to err, he was going to err on their side so that they didn't have appeal issues."

Feder said he and Yuill had a conversation with Olson's cellmate from Barnes County Jail in Valley City who had originally agreed to testify at the trial on Monday. The previous Friday he was frightened and didn't want to get involved, but said he would still come to Fargo to testify. Since he wouldn't speak, Feder said he was relating the prisoner's statement to the court. According to Feder, their witness had told him the prosecution's witness Arnold Neukom was a liar. "Neukom approached him, suggested if he wanted to 'cut myself a fat slice,' I would testify against Olson because all the police have is circumstantial evidence, and they need something to hold the case together," Feder swore to the jury.

Mike Lyman, who brought the prisoners to Fargo in his capacity as deputy sheriff, was then called to the stand and denied threatening the silent witness or telling him not to testify for the defense.

Yuill questioned two more prisoners who were in Barnes County Jail when Olson, Meddy, and Neukom had been there. His purpose was to attack the credibility of Meddy and discredit his testimony against Olson and to overcome the whole snitch aspect that was working against his client. Both said Meddy repeatedly asked them to have their families or friends smuggle in a gun or hacksaw blades to help him escape. Both prisoners also said that Olson told them he hadn't murdered his wife. One quoted Olson as saying, "I just didn't kill her."

That was solid rebuttal that offered enough doubt, they felt, and they had no more witnesses to call. Their alibi witnesses had testified during the prosecution's case, and the defendant was not going to be put on the stand. Nordeng thinks the choice to keep Gary Olson off the witness stand was a wise one, noting, "I think that he would have hung himself. He'd have said something really stupid. Or even possible, you know, a defense lawyer can't put his client on if he knows he's going to lie. I know people don't think that, but ethically he can't."

While the focus had all been on the attorneys and the witness stand—where the action was taking place—the man who had been absolutely obsessed by this case from the beginning was quietly playing a part in seeing it correctly concluded. Don Jones sat directly behind the prosecution and maintained custody of the evidence, so there was always a proper chain of custody, and he looked after it when there were jury breaks or other interruptions. His intensity and determination to see this case solved showed on him physically, as he lost seventeen pounds during the two and a half weeks of the trial

After a day for defense, the attorneys would make their closing arguments to the jury and let justice take its course. State's Attorney Mervin Nordeng knew that his closing was critical, given the circumstantial nature of the prosecution's case. He needed to pull all the pieces together and show how they had proved what they had set out to establish, that without a witness or weapon, the circumstances left no other reasonable conclusion except that Gary Dean Olson had killed Dixie Olson. Nordeng began with a summary and contending that the murder had been a crime of passion. He argued that Olson had been plagued by suspicions that his wife was having an affair, and built up his courage on the night of January 23 by drinking ten to twelve cans of beer. Following that he had driven to his wife's house and confronted her, then killed her. Olson ransacked the house following his homicide to make it appear that a burglary had taken place.

Next he laid out the evidence he said the state had presented in support of his summary. Olson had fallen asleep on his sister's couch before drinking and then slipped away to West Fargo without being seen and had returned to go to sleep in the downstairs bedroom of his sister's house. The coroner said the murder had taken place about 2:00 a.m. Olson told Crime Bureau agents he returned to his wife's home to fill out his unemployment application when he was interviewed on January 24. The stamped sealed envelope with Olson's return address on it and addressed to the Employment Security Bureau in Bismarck had already been found in the Olson home on the morning of January 24, and Olson's fingerprint was on it. Nordeng contended Olson filled out the form when he was there the previous night and killed Dixie.

Gary said he had not been in the basement or touched the window that was surrounded by boot prints, but his fingerprints were on the window. A bleached hair was found between the window and the window frame, and Dixie had bleached her hair that previous evening, and would have had to have gotten up on a bench or ladder to get her head where the hair was found.

Nordeng said the clothes Olson wore were another important contradiction in Olson's claim to have remained in Enderlin throughout the night Dixie was killed. Gary Olson's sister-in-law Donna Olson said when he had come to visit them on January 23 he kept repeating what he was wearing, as though he wanted her and her husband to remember the conversation. Both Donna Olson and Orvin Olson said Gary Olson had been wearing a deep-red shirt and red, white and blue checked pants when he visited on January 23, but had on dark-colored clothes when they next saw him on January 25. Gary said he hadn't changed clothes and he only had different clothes in his West Fargo apartment.

A friend of Gary Olson's, Marlys Frost of West Fargo, had established a motive. She said Olson was very jealous of his wife and suspected she was having an affair, and that he had said he would kill her and her lover if he ever caught them.

Arnold Neucom and Lester Meddy, two prisoners who were held with Olson in Barnes County Jail in Valley City, had testified how Olson told them he'd killed his wife and disposed of the weapon, a tire iron. Their testimonies weren't completely identical, but Nordeng said that Neucom and Meddy knew details about the case they could not have learned from watching television or reading the newspapers.

A convincing case, Nording surmised, and with that information before them, the jury must do its duty and find Gary Dean Olson guilty of the murder of his wife.

Yuill began the defense's closing with a clear reminder to the jury that it must find Olson guilty "beyond a reasonable doubt," or acquit him. He said the prosecution had not presented any hard evidence, only assumptions. He criticized the police for "leaping at the first suspect" they had, and for the introduction of almost seventy exhibits into evidence, "many of them questionable at best." He said he didn't know why many of the exhibits had been introduced because they weren't important to the case, and he couldn't refute their validity because none was given. The prosecution's assault was, he said, like "trying to swat a fly with a howitzer." He criticized the police for not identifying the reddish stain on walls and ceiling of Dixie's bedroom and for not finding the murder weapon. He contended that the envelope found addressed to the Employment Security Bureau was insignificant because it hadn't been opened and no one knew what was in it.

Yuill continued his argument by analogy as he compared the state's attorney's case to a stone bridge across a river. The keystone on which Nordeng had based his case was Neukom, he said, and Neukom admitted to being a con man and jailhouse lawyer. Take the unreliable snitches out and the state's case collapsed.

Yuill claimed that Olson knew nothing of his wife's murder, and that an unknown killer was still at large. He also suggested this killer might have also committed some of the other unsolved homicides in the area. Yuill concluded by taking the position that the police, in their haste to make sure Dixie Olson's murder wouldn't be one of the unsolved cases, arrested the first suspect, Gary Olson, and did no further investigation. Reasonable doubt about what happened existed, and, with reasonable doubt, his client must be acquitted.

On Thursday, June 21, closings had been delivered in the early afternoon and the case was turned over to the jury. Deliberations took about six hours. Shortly after 10:00 p.m., a verdict was returned in Cass County District Court. Gary Dean Olson was found guilty of murdering his wife, twenty-nine-year-old Dixie. Judge Redetzke would set sentencing at a later date, and Olson was returned to custody. It was three days short of five months after the event had taken place.

The state had effectively prosecuted Olson, but there was more to be learned about motive.

10

AND THEN THERE WERE TWO

W hile the agents and the community awaited the sentencing of Gary Olson, investigation into the emotion-ridden
homicide that had preceded it carried on. August came—a year had
passed since Pollie Johnson's murder. That brought up the issue of the
reward fund in Pollie's case and what would become of it. It contained
over $6,000, but the terms under which it was established said that the
money would be returned if no arrest had been made within a year.
Don Witham and the West Fargo Lions Club, who had originally organized the reward fund, decided to continue it. They said that anyone
who wished to could withdraw his or her contribution, but that didn't
happen. This was still North Dakota when it came to supporting the
Johnson family. A grateful Deputy Sheriff Lyman said the fund was
valuable for providing incentive and renewed optimism.

At this time, the strange story of Willard Klitze was pursued.
Klitze, married to Dixie's sister, had been Gary's frequent fishing com-
panion. A month after the Johnson homicide, the Olson and Klitze families were together for an outing and fishing, but once they returned to

the Klitze home, Willard dropped his daughter off, then left, and it had been nearly a year since his disappearance. His family had never heard a word from him. Earl Larson believed Willard had been with Gary Olson the day Pollie was murdered. The timing of it all and his association with Olson made Larson think it was worth a serious attempt to discover Klitze's whereabouts and hear his story.

During that first anniversary week of Pollie's death in August, Larson and Lyman went to Lisbon and Enderlin to look around. At the time, "Lynn Klitzke stated that Dixie always was worried that Gary would do something spectacular—commit some kind of big crime and get them all in big trouble." In the nation's most church going state, church ties remain a common connection, and the investigators discovered was that Lynn had learned that, while there had been no communication with the family, Willard had visited a Lutheran Church in Grand Forks and signed in as guest. He listed as his home their family's former Fargo address. Authorities soon found that Willard had used that address on some car loan correspondence for a Chrysler they had bought.

Larson went to Fargo National Bank and talked to loan officer, Jeff Hanson, who told him the bank had repossessed the Chrysler in the fall after Willard had run off. By winter Larson discovered that Willard Klitzke had been working at a sugar beet plant in Grand Forks. In June, when Gary's trial had begun, Klitzke paid off the car and some other Fargo National Bank obligations, and had apparently been given a loan from a bank in Minnesota that was cosigned by a relative. Hanson had a letter from Klitzke dated June 19, 1977, with an address, Twenty-Five South Lakeshore, Glenwood, Minnesota. He had heard in February that Klitzke had been with Jacobson-Cohen of Bismarck, building a grain elevator in Minnesota, and in March, he had been working in a grain elevator in Gibbon, Minnesota. The bank kept close track of people with financial obligations.

On August 11, Larson returned to the sheriff's office and contacted the Glenwood, Minnesota, Police Department. Glenwood

Officer Terry Mays said the address for Klitzke was an apartment. Along with Special Agent Richard Rolle, Larson made the drive to Glenwood and located the address. It was clear they were on the right track. He recorded that it was a, "large, brown two and one-half story house next to the lake. There was a mailbox—there were three mailboxes—on the front of the house, and one of these had the name 'Willard Klitzke' on it. In the mailbox was a *Fargo Forum* newspaper of Wednesday, August 10th, and also a letter from the State Bank of Glenwood. We checked all of the apartments and found the one that Willard Klitzke was occupying. However, the door was locked. We then drove to the bank in Glenwood, where officer Mays checked and found out that Willard Klitzke was working at a business place called the Glendarosa."

They were off to Glendarosa, a manufacturing plant that made hog-feeding equipment and buildings. The manager told them they were too late, since Klitzke had left the plant a week or two earlier. Larson checked, and it had been July 20 between 7:00 and 9:00 a.m. that Klitzke had come in the spring of 1977 and applied for work but didn't show. After he was hired, it hadn't worked out so well. When he first applied, he had claimed he could read blueprints, set up production, do layouts for manufacturing, but that was all talk. He had arguments over his time and expenses. Klitzke gave the foreman a false address on where to find his keys, if that were ever necessary. The Glendarosa foreman said, "It was apparent that Klitzke was trying to avoid any contact with anyone who might give away his hiding place."

They did get some useful information. Willard drove a dark green, four-door Chrysler, and the last word was he worked at a potato warehouse near Brooter, a nearby Minnesota town. The quest continued. It was on to Brooter. A mile north of town, they found the potato warehouse, an imposing three-quarters-completed structure two blocks long and a block wide. Agent Rolle's sharp eyes noticed a green Chrysler parked at considerable distance near the back end.

They drove to it and while they were copying its license, workers in great numbers began to emerge from a large door. A big man headed to the Chrysler, and they got out and identified themselves. "Mr. Klitzke was more than surprised—he was visibly upset," noted Larson.

They asked him to come to their car for an interview, and he agreed and got in the back seat. Larson recalled, "He was wearing a set of coveralls, insulated coveralls, working at a potato warehouse down in Brooton. And we were just talking, and he was calm, and when I turned the attention to Gary Dean Olson and the murder of Pollie Johnson, I could see his heart beat through his coveralls. He was really jumpy." They began with asking why left his wife, his kids, and his home without contacting anyone, but weren't finding his answers really convincing. He said he did it because of his wife's, Lynn's, excessive spending habits. He liked his kids and got along with them and didn't mind married life, but Lynn's spending habits were getting them farther and farther in debt. They had discussions and arguments, but she just kept on spending, and their debt kept growing. Willard said on Labor Day, he and Gary and the children had gone fishing on Lake Ashtabula in Willard's boat while the women had gone to Valley City to visit some friends. He and Gary had not argued that day and hadn't talked at all about the Pollie Johnson murder.

Larson's notes from the time said, "Willard seemed very calm when we were talking to him about his own personal problems and why he'd ran away and so on. Whenever we would mention the Pollie Johnson homicide, he would show a physical reaction, and his chest would pound or he would exhale and inhale rapidly. He said he knew nothing about the Pollie Johnson homicide nor had Gary ever discussed it with him, but whenever we would swing the conversation back to the homicide, he would react."

He seemed very cooperative, saying he would consent to a polygraph and would be glad to come to Fargo for it. A Friday would be best for him. When it came around to having him come in, it was a different story. On October 13, Lyman and Larson returned to interview Willard and set up the polygraph date, but he said he was starting a new job and would prefer to wait a couple of weeks until he was settled and work was underway. Two weeks later, Larson received a letter from Willard that said, "Would appreciate it if you could set it up after I have chance to talk to my attorney."

They tried to get a subpoena and talked to Minnesota about subpoenaing him, but it was for nothing. He apparently learned what he wanted to know from his attorney. Klitsky found that the only state that didn't honor an out-of-state subpoena was Colorado, and he was off once again, Colorado-bound, and couldn't be subpoenaed to testify. What Willard knew will never be known, as he passed away in the summer of 2007, but it seemed apparent that the large man was afraid to speak out, and there was something he didn't want to talk about.

During this fruitless quest, on September 13, the court announced that sentencing for Gary Dean Olson's June 21 conviction for murder of his wife would be at 9:30 a.m. on September 26 in Cass County District Court, with Judge Roy Redetzke presiding. North Dakota law had an unusual provision that the maximum sentence that could be given for any crime was twenty years in prison. The only exceptions that could be made to this occurred if the court declared the convicted person a "special dangerous offender." If given such a designation, the offender's sentence could be as long as life imprisonment. The state had requested a dangerous offender designation, and the maximum sentence for Olson, Judge Redetzke said, and arguments regarding sentencing and designation would both be made on that day.

Some West Fargoans of Olson's generation were mourning another death before the sentencing and dangerous offender arguments were presented in Redetzke's court. The "king" had died. Forty-two-year-old Elvis Presley's life came to an end at his

Graceland mansion on August 16. He had been the voice of a life-style of freedom and sexuality that the transient community identified with or was comfortable with in blue-collar West Fargo, as in much of America.

When September 26 came, arguments were first on the dangerous offender designation, since that decision was necessary before a sentencing decision could be made. Nording, arguing for the state, said previous convictions, mental condition, any acts of violence used during the crime could be included when determining the defendant's special status. He also said that the type of weapon used could be a factor, and the coroner's testimony in court had been that the victim had been struck a number of times by a blunt instrument that may have been a tire iron. The court could consider the weapon to have been a bludgeon, which would qualify it as a dangerous weapon, and Olson's status as a user of it fit the statute's intent.

Yuill's response, as Olson's representative, was that the statute providing for the special dangerous offender designation was unconstitutional. It was double jeopardy. Olson would be punished twice for the same crime, being punished again for the violence involved in a previous crime he had served time for that was actually committed by his accomplice, his brother.

Redetzke said this was "not a case for the court to be shooting from the hip," and he would take it under advisement and read the materials each side had prepared in support of its case. He would announce his decision at a time following that, and Olson was returned to prison.

With Gary's case concerning Dixie so close to a final wrap-up, Larson's investigators were pursing the missing scraps to close what they hoped would be their case regarding Pollie. Results from Lyman's recovery of casing evidence weren't back from the FBI yet and they still hoped to somehow find the weapon, but while they waited for one good piece of solid evidence, there was still plenty to do. They were not having a difficult time coming up with more incriminating character commentary about Olson. People Gary had worked with when he had a job were interviewed.

Robert Radner came to the sheriff's office to be interviewed by Larson and Lyman about their time at O'Day Equipment. Radner said they had worked together closely, and Olson's drinking problem interfered with his work and outside life. He said Olson was very resentful of his wife and beat her up when he was drunk. He had told Olson that he would turn him in to the police if he found out he had hurt Dixie. Radner said Gary would play five-card draw or five-card stud with workers, and sometimes he got so mad he would throw down the cards and walk off in a huff. Gary played cards with the workers in bars, and sometimes they would let him win a bit when he got ninety or one hundred dollars down so he wouldn't owe so much, otherwise he wouldn't pay. He added that what he, "noticed most about Gary was his whole life centered around drinking, chasing women, and raising hell. Gary was the kind who had to win, no matter what the game or what the stakes or what was going on. If he couldn't win, he would get completely mad."

Curt Bloomnard was another O'Day worker, and he'd had a bachelor's party at Spec's Bar in Fargo where there was gambling. Dennis Littlefield, known as "half pint," was there and Olson lost about a hundred dollars to him. He paid, but then he hit Littlefield over the head with a pool cue and put him in the hospital for a "couple months."

Lyman and Larson interviewed Orville Kautz of Fargo in the sheriff's office. This was a prize interview for summing up Olson's personality. Kautz was a painter-contractor, self-employed as a home decorator. He'd previously been a farmer, then had worked at Frontier, Inc., and was overall shop manager when Olson worked under him as a production supervisor. They had desks in same room, and he had known Gary for about five years. His opinion of Gary Olson was clear. Olson defied orders, always wanted to drink, raised hell, and took out women on the side. Kautz was responsible to see that state and federal safety regulations were set up and followed, and one required there be no glass bottles in the production area. Olson drank about six cokes a day and left the bottles around anywhere, so they had encounters. His evaluation of Olson's morals was "zero." He didn't like Gary, finding him to be a very gross man who was uncouth, misbehaving constantly and obsessed by sex. Olson was suspicious and possessive and had said, "If he ever caught his wife with somebody, he would kill her and cut out her cunt."

Kautz offered a telling anecdote from the past. Years earlier there had been a Frontier, Inc., company family picnic. Gary was there and was wrestling with the younger kids, ages ten to twelve. Tough man Gary was becoming a bit mean with one of Kautz's boys. Kautz's oldest son, who was thirteen and large for his age, was watching and became irritated. He grabbed Olson, threw him to the ground and told him to leave the kids alone. Kautz continued, "At that point, Gary didn't attempt to fight the thirteen-year-old, but unzipped his pants and exposed himself to the women at the picnic."

There was Gary, the sex magnet. He was his own greatest fan, living in his fantasy world, as he told Kautz stories about having sex with step-sisters and half-sisters. He also told of all the teenaged girls who couldn't resist him, how he was getting "some young stuff."

Kautz believed Olson stole many things while at Frontier but he was apparently hired on a vocational rehab program as an ex-con and management was embarrassed to admit they had hired the wrong person. He boasted about conning his parole agents and taking advantage of programs and told Kautz that if he ever got him in trouble, he would kill him. Olson carried large amounts of cash on him, but didn't earn much. He bragged to Kautz that there wasn't a place in Enderlin or Sheldon he hadn't been in or couldn't get in, and the same was true in the West Fargo area.

Olson told Kautz he knew Gene Johnson, his occupation, and where he was from. He bragged about the robbery in Marion that had put him in jail and said he'd do it again. Larson recorded that Olson "told Kautz that after they had knocked out the grocer, they urinated on him. He thought this was quite funny."

Kautz and his wife got along with Dixie but not Gary, who used to go to the Zephyr and some other rougher bars on N.P. Avenue in Fargo, and talked about being a great pool player and winning pool tournaments.

This interview could be important if they charged Olson because it showed a number of things. Gary admitted going after young girls, threatened to use violence to get whatever he wanted, and the sexual nature of the threat to kill his wife if found in a compromising situation. Kautz was a good one to recommend for the witness list if they could get the evidence for charges against Olson on killing Pollie. He would make an excellent witness, being positive in his statements and supporting them with facts.

The problems they could see were other stories that surfaced. Mick had told his version about Gary being a witness rather than a participant in the murder. Another issue to work on before any case against Gary Olson could be presented for a prosecutor was that Oliver "Bud" Wright had presented a story that offered an alternative to Gary's about the murder, and again, there was the chance of "reasonable doubt" when witnesses testified to conflicting versions of what took place. Wright was a construction worker who said he had been in the Lariat Bar after work the night of August 8, and three men had come into the bar and asked to join him. After drinking for some time, one said they had just killed a kid about six miles north of West Fargo, and there was a dispute about her age, but one said she was about sixteen. Whether this was the same story Mick was telling about three people being involved that Gary had witnessed or a new story, they didn't know. They had to get some background before things could move forward.

Larson and Lyman began checking Wright's story by going to talk to Del Hofer, who Wright named as one of the three who had come to the bar. Del Hofer owned a Harley Davidson Motorcycle

Shop by the interstate highway and said he didn't know Harold Hofer, whose name Wright also brought up as being at the Lariat, and he didn't hang out with the biker crowd. He had a motorcycle business, and he did business with them. As to the Grim Reapers who had been in the previous year around the homicide, he remembered Bruce Brinkhause, whom he described as having a full beard of pure black, some gray hair, over six feet tall, and about 280 pounds. He was with a good-looking blonde with shoulder-length hair, between nineteen and twenty-four years of age. His sales records showed Brinkhaus had bought a chain and had a bike common to the Grim Reapers', a Harley Davidson 1947 model 74. He thought the man worked as a welder or common laborer and was working with sheet metal at some place like Fargo Iron or Dakota Tank. His hangout was Diemert's Bar in Moorhead. Another member of the Reapers he could recall was Bob Anderson, known as "Link." Link drove trucks, hauled grain and cement.

Lyman and Larson then went to Grand Forks in search of the next man on the list, Harold Hofer. By this point, they had found that Hofer and some of the people he was related to and associated with came from an unusual background. They were about to be exposed to a small segment of the population that existed largely unnoticed but had found a location on the Northern Plains a century earlier where they could practice their beliefs. These were the Hutterites, followers of the Anabaptist Jokob Hutter, who died in 1536 and was a contemporary of Martin Luther when the Protestant Reformation was in its early stages. Hutter had been burned alive for his religious beliefs, which included nonviolence, community ownership of property, and baptism of adults.

The much-persecuted Hutterites survived in communes and maintained their own dialect of German as they were forced to move from place to place in Eastern Europe. Their strict refusal to wear uniforms led them to seek a new home in the 1870s when Russia revised military service regulations. After sending scouts to North America with similarly persecuted Anabaptist Mennonites, the Hutterites began to migrate and first settled in Dakota Territory. They expanded and established colonies in Montana and Minnesota and more in Western Canada. Wherever they went, they split into communes, or colonies as their population grew, and each colony maintained the traditional Hutterite communal lifestyle. The Schmiedeleut colonies in North Dakota carried on life in simple ways. They continued speaking a dialect of German that dated back to earlier times. Men wore suspenders and usually black or dark trousers with any kind of buttoned shirt. Married men traditionally wore beards. Women wore below-knee-length dresses and younger women and girls wore brighter-colored dresses than older women. Women also wore a *kupfti'echle*, a black, polka-dot-peppered head covering. Girls between the ages of three to about ten wore a bonnet called a *mitz*. No TVs were allowed. Their communes had never become tourist attractions, like the third of the Anabaptist groups that had come to the United States earlier, the Amish. Like the Amish, they didn't allow themselves to be photographed and saw it as a violation of the Second Commandment's prohibition against false idols. They often owned large tracts of land that they farmed together with community-owned equipment and had moved into some other areas of economic activity, including weaving.

Hofer and some of the people he was related to and associated with had come from Hutterite colonies in South Dakota, and were associated with the Weivoda Carpet Company. He was possibly living west of Grand Forks, where Weivoda had a new store. Lyman and Larson checked out the store and talked with Weivoda and several others, but they didn't find Hofer. There was a young man named Wipf from the Hutterite colony at Graceville, Minnesota, who raised their suspicions, because he was hanging around in the background and seemed worried. What they were told by several people was they thought Hofer was at the Hutterite Colony at Flandreau, South Dakota.

The next day Larson and Lyman went to Fargo Tank Company and interviewed a Hofer not implicated in the murder, Michael M. Hofer, Jr. It was very difficult to understand what he was saying because of his extreme German accent. His not having lived in ordinary society except for the last couple of years also made normal interaction awkward. Michael was the brother of Harold and Tim, and he said both were currently living on a Hutterite farm called Pleasant Valley Colony, run by Peter, at Flandreau, South Dakota. Harold had married, and his wife, Lena's, maiden name was Tschetter. Harold had worked for B.C.M. and Ryder trucking in Moorhead, hauling machinery and lumber. Occasionally he went to the Town Hall Bar. When they lived in West Fargo, Harold had a girlfriend named Janie, who was twenty-five or twenty-six and blonde, and Mike thought she looked kind of like a boy. Mike Hofer was open with them and appeared to have no knowledge of Pollie Johnson's murder nor was he hiding anything.

Larson and Deputy Marvin Hanson of the Clay County Sheriff's Office went to Silverline Products to interview the woman Mike Hofer had named as a girlfriend, who was very cooperative. She said she knew all three Hofers, Mike, Harold, and Tim. Mike and Tim had worked with her at Weivoda Carpet in Dilworth, and she thought Harold seemed to be interested in her. He drove a semi for B.C.M., hauling "stuff" from Georgia to Moorhead. He was thirty or thirty-one, and had a wife in the colony at Graceville, Minnesota. The only friend she could think of that Harold had was a thirty-five to thirty-six-year-old trucker named Verne, from Fargo. Verne had five kids, but was dating a girlfriend of hers from West Fargo.

The Hofers usually drank at Town Hall and pretty much kept to themselves. Harold had a big Honda, and Mike had a medium bike, a Honda 350. Harold once got into a fight at the Roundup Bar in Fargo and was hit by a beer bottle. She doubted the Hofers would be involved in anything regarding Pollie Johnson.

They interviewed the girl Vern was dating. She was divorced with several children and remembered the Hofers, mentioning that

Harold and Verne Fevig were friends. Harold and others went to Lorney's, the Town Hall, and the Silver Dollar. A friend of Verne's who would also know them was Bob Stetz. She said the Hofers were heavy drinkers. They drank homemade booze that they brought along from the colony and really liked drinking beer. Harold had cut hair some during his years at colony, but not seriously. She also doubted they would have had any involvement in Pollie's murder. All had a difficult time communicating with most people and fitting in because of their heavy German accents and lack of sophistication.

Larson and Lyman also interviewed Bob Stetz in the sheriff's office to get another view of the Hofers and their adjustment to West Fargo life. Stetz knew the Hofers and remembered Harry had broken his arm in a motorcycle accident. In August of 1976 Stetz had been driving a gravel truck, hauling gravel for Northern Improvement. He said he knew Bud Wright from years earlier when Wright worked at E.W. Wylie Company. He thought Wright was a trouble maker and had left after some sort of disagreement. Stetz hadn't been in the Lariat for six or seven years.

Larson thought they had looked long enough at the Hofers and that Wright's story lacked support. It was just that, a story.

ON NOVEMBER 3, REDETZKE RULED on the motion made by the state to name Gary Olson a special dangerous offender. He agreed with the request. Thirteen days later, he handed down his sentence, as he said to Olson, "This was a brutal killing inflicted upon the mother of your children," that showed he was a special dangerous offender. Redetzke said the violent nature of the murder and Olson's previous criminal record warranted a life sentence, and Olson was sentenced to life in prison. Olson made his first statement since legal proceedings began. He addressed the court and stated, "I will start out by saying that I didn't kill my wife, and I will maintain my innocence . . . I don't think I can get a fair trial in this county." He criticized his lawyer, William Yuill, saying, "I had evidence and witnesses that should have been brought up that weren't." Olson claimed the jury would not have found him guilty if these witnesses had been called and said he would appeal the conviction and wanted a new lawyer appointed.

Redetzke said he was satisfied with Yuill's handling of the case, and called him a learned criminal lawyer. Law enforcement officials asked at the time said they had no idea what witnesses, if any, Olson could have used in his defense. Olson was to be transported to the State Penitentiary in Bismarck, and the court-appointed Yuill said he would ask to be taken off the case after sentencing. Olson had ten days within which to file an appeal with the court about Redetze's decisions.

The month after the decision, Bill Yuill and Merve Nording talked about the case. Yuill had been an assistant state's attorney before he had become a defense attorney and was a friend of Gene Johnson. He was feeling upset about the final outcome of the case. He had hoped to get something better for Olson on the sentencing and felt he didn't do a good enough job for his client. Nordeng said, "Bill, if it will make you feel any better, we're going to charge him with murdering Pollie Johnson this afternoon."

That may have reduced Yuill's sympathy for his client's long sentence, but it was a shock and moral dilemma, as Nordeng recalls, "So that kind of, I mean, totally knocked him over. With his representing the guy we were going to charge with killing his friend's daughter."

The critical news for the Pollie Johnson homicide investigation had arrived. The FBI had looked at all the .22 shell casings that Mike Lyman had collected from cars previously owned by Gary Dean Olson, and the results they reported were the lynchpin for the case that the investigators had been seeking for over a year. In both cars there had been casings found that matched the one that was next to Pollie's foot when she was found murdered. The casings from the alley where one of the cars had been swept out that Lyman found with a metal detector also matched. It wasn't quite as if the gun with the broken firing pin was in Gary's home, but it was close enough. The FBI said by examining the shell casings of the bullets fired that were in the cars and the casing of the bullet found at the crime scene, it could identify they had been fired by the same weapon "to the exclusion of any other firearm in the world."

The scurry of activity attracted attention and the standard denial. The *Forum* ran a story on December 2 entitled "Officials Deny Break in Pollie Johnson Case," where they told of the frustrations being felt by various investigating agencies that had come together for what was described as having been a routine meeting. Lyman was quoted as saying, "There won't be anything today, tomorrow — maybe in a few weeks, I don't know."

It was exactly two weeks later in Friday's *Fargo Forum* that the headline appeared that so many had beginning to give up hope of ever seeing: "Gary Dean Olson Charged in Slaying of Pollie Johnson." Cass County deputies had traveled to the state penitentiary in Bismarck on the previous day and served the murder warrant on Olson, and had planned to return him to Fargo that day for arraignment, but they didn't arrive until late the next day because freezing rain had glazed the roads between the cities and made travel impossible.

The newspaper story made it clear this was the same Gary Olson who had recently been convicted of, and was serving a life sentence for murdering his wife at in West Fargo. It summarized that case, saying testimony had revealed he had bludgeoned her to death, but the weapon was never found, and he had attempted to make the murder appear to have been a burglary. Judge Roy K. Redetzke had used the dangerous offender act of state law so the sentence could be longer than the maximum twenty years allowed under state statutes.

A considerable number of affidavits on the Pollie Johnson homicide had been filed at the Cass County Courthouse that outlined and made public the case put together to prosecute Olson. An affidavit of probable cause had been filed to show they had reason to suspect Olson since a state's attorney's inquest attorney held in Fargo July 6. At that hearing, Gary's brother Orvin testified that Gary had told him he had seen a girl killed on the night of August 8. Orvin also said Gary admitted his gun was used in the killing, and the girl was shot twice. Gary said he had gotten rid of the gun. The affidavit stated that Gary told Orvin to say that Gary had been at the Wonder Bar in Sheldon, North Dakota, between 7:30 and 8:00 p.m. on the night of the murder.

Gary claimed he had gone fishing that day, according to an affidavit. Another affidavit had statements of witnesses who were interviewed and said a car matching a description of Olson's was spotted near the Johnson home on the night of the murder. Also, witnesses told authorities Gary Olson used to fish regularly on the Scheyenne River directly across river from the Johnson home.

An affidavit connected Olson with the shell casings found on the floor near Pollie's body. Two cars previously owned by Olson contained many .22 caliber casings. One sold to a Valley City man as junk had not been driven since Olson sold it, according to the witness named in the affidavit. All six casings found in that car were matched by the FBI lab to the weapon that killed Pollie. The other car had 106 casings not attributed to the new owner. Of them, the FBI lab matched twenty-one to the shell casing found near the body.

The complaint filed was: Olson had been in the area on the day of the murder, entered the Johnson home as burglar when he a came upon Pollie.

The deputies managed to make the trip with the icy conditions and get Olson back to Fargo late Friday. When they arrived, he was formally charged with murder in Cass County Court before Judge Duis. Assistant State's Attorney Joe Truman presented affidavits supporting the charge. The judge said the court would appoint an attorney and no bail was necessary, since Olson was already in prison. With the holiday season festivities and activities such a time-consuming part of people's lives, Turman requested that Olson's next court appearance, his preliminary hearing, be set after January 1. After conferring with the attorney, Duis told Olson he would be sent back to penitentiary until his preliminary hearing.

The recipient of the $6,500 reward fund was left up to the sheriff's department by the fund organizers. They didn't award the money, but retained it for award after a successful prosecution.

Olson had been returned to the state penitentiary for a month before prosecution got underway. A new year had been ushered in, and Olson's wife's murder was a week short of a year in the past when he was returned to Cass County Court House for the preliminary hearing facing charges of second-degree murder. It was second degree since he wasn't accused of acting with forethought, or premeditation. He was being charged that "acting alone or with others" he had been responsible for the homicide "as part of a burglary." Selection of the charge had been carefully made, and the lawyers thought burglary had been the intent.

Testimony in the two-day hearing began January 17, 1978, before Judge Duis, and the state filed an affidavit with the court completed by Earl Larson, the chief investigating officer in case. The affidavit contained a summary of evidence gathered and statements taken that linked Olson with the homicide to show that on August 8, 1976, Olson had gone fishing near the Johnson residence, and had crossed the river to their property to burglarize the home. It presented the evidence the state expected to use in proving its case and the names of the witnesses. The first witness called at the hearing was Pollie Lynn Johnson's father, Gene, who had been one of the first two law officers on the scene, along with a fellow Highway Patrolman, Lyle Marcus. Kelly Rogers, who had discovered the body, testified next. He had found the victim dead between 9:50 p.m. and 10:00 p.m. on August 8, 1976. Cass Coroner D.H. Lawrence said Pollie had been shot twice in the head at close range. Lynn Klitzke, Olson's former sister-in-law, said Gary and Dixie had often fished with her family near Francis Smith's property opposite the Johnson farmhouse on the Sheyenne River.

Witnesses established that a .22 caliber weapon belonged to Olson. Cass County deputies and crime laboratory officials testified that a total of 106 .22 shells and shell casings had been found in cars previously owned by Olson. Aaron Rasch, the supervisor of the crime laboratory at the North Dakota Laboratory in Bismarck said FBI analysis matched at least twenty-two shell casings found in those cars to the one found at the murder scene.

Michael McGuire, Olson's court-appointed attorney, had Olson's brother Orvin testify that he had been working at the Wonder Tavern in Sheldon, North Dakota, on the night of August 8, and Gary showed up at the bar around 10:00 p.m. Orvin said Gary told him he had gone fishing near the Johnson residence and visited the Johnson's looking for a drink of water. It was then, through the outside screen door of the Johnson home, he had observed Pollie being raped and murdered. There had been three men involved, and he had had nothing to do with it, but they had used his gun. They also threatened him after the murder, saying if he said anything about the killing, his family would be killed.

Prosecutor Joseph Turman, assistant state's attorney in the State's Attorney Office during the homicide trial regarding Dixie Olson but not directly involved in that case, challenged the validity of Olson's story on several points. He said Olson claimed he had sold his gun before the murder, but he had gone to see his brother to find where he could get rid of his gun. He claimed he had witnessed Pollie being raped, but although she had been found naked from the waste down, the coroner had testified that no rape had taken place. He knew there were two shots, but the shot through the roof of the mouth was discovered only during the autopsy.

McGuire's counter was that Olson had happened upon a crime and was threatened, told that his family would be killed if he said anything. In a matter of months, on January 24, his wife had been killed. He also attacked the use of the affidavit submitted by the prosecution.

172

At that point Judge Duis called a conference of the attorneys and said questions concerning the affidavit Larson presented outlining the state's case would not continue. McGuire said that since the affidavit was available to the press, it would prevent his client from being tried by an impartial jury. He would ask for a change of venue after Olson was arraigned in district court.

The defense did file for a change of venue on July 11, based on the affidavit presenting the state's case and how the news media had used information in the affidavit to cover Olson's arrest. They filed a motion to move the trial from the First Judicial District in Fargo to the Fifth Judicial District in Minot in the west of North Dakota, making the argument that there existed in the First Judicial District of North Dakota "so great a prejudice against the defendant that he cannot obtain a fair and impartial trial." The court faced a common question of the public's "right to know" versus individual rights.

To support their claim that they couldn't get a fair trial in Fargo, the defense submitted evidence to the Third Judicial District in Wahpeton of the public use of the affidavit of the state's evidence in area media. They had affidavits from the news directors and scripts of broadcasts from the three network television stations, KTHI, WDAY, and KCJB. They also had an affidavit from the librarian of *The Fargo Forum* and copies of articles about Olson that included both the murder of his wife and of Pollie Johnson. Many of the articles and stories discussed and compared the new charges against Olson with his prior conviction for the murder of Dixie. Some articles referred to the fact that he had been found to be a special dangerous offender and sentenced to life in prison for the murder of his wife. Another point made was that some of the information in the affidavit was hearsay, and would be inadmissible at trial, although the public was hearing it and being influenced by it. In summary, they argued, the prosecution had been responsible for making information available to the news media that had been prejudicial to Olson's right to a fair trial. Ward County in the western half of the state would provide a less biased jury pool.

173

Turman, for the state, objected to the motion, saying little of the publicity about Olson was recent, and most dealt with the murder of his wife, not Pollie Johnson. He also contended that the information the media obtained from the affidavit the prosecution had filed with the complaint charging Olson with murder hadn't made the state guilty of improperly releasing information. That material was substantiated during Olson's preliminary hearing.

The defendant's counsels had other motions for the court to consider along with the venue change. John Rowell, who had been officially appointed to lead Olson's defense by Judge Eckert, filed a motion that the court hire a public opinion research expert to evaluate the awareness and attitudes the population held about his client, since the cases were so unusually high profile and emotionally charged. Rowell was a local, a Fargo native and graduate of Shanley, the Catholic high school best known for its nearly unbeatable football teams and as the alma mater of Roger Maris, who had broken Babe Ruth's long-standing home run record in 1961. He introduced a motion that the state pay for a polygraph for Olson with regard to this case. There was also a series of motions introduced by Rowell to require the prosecution to make its evidence available to the defense under the rules of criminal procedure.

Rowell also introduced a motion to suppress the foundation of the state's case, and have the shell casings found in cars previously owned by Olson be ruled out as evidence the prosecution could introduce. His argument for the suppression of the shell casing evidence was that the cars they had been found in were not searched until nearly a year after the homicide, which left open the possibility they had been planted as evidence against his client. Lyman had anticipated this, and the casings found in the alley by metal detector were not included in the state's evidence. They were available to counter the charge of a plant of evidence if the issue were pursued, since the Amundsons had directed Lyman to the otherwise unknown location for the search of what had been swept from the vehicle.

Judge Eckert granted the defense motions requiring prosecution to make its evidence available to defense and told the opposing parties to confer on the polygraph and let the court know of their decision. On the other motions he said he would take them under advisement.

Two weeks later, Robert Eckert denied the motion for the change of venue to Ward County and for the state-financed opinion research expert to determine existing bias. He did order a change of venue from Fargo in Cass County to Wahpeton in Richland County. The defense then submitted a motion for a change from Richland County to Ward County, arguing that the Wahpeton area was within the Fargo media network. Eckhert was the third judge hearing the case. District Judges Roy Redetzke of Fargo and A.C. Bakken of Grand Forks had resigned from the case after defense objections. Judge Eckert had been assigned to it by the Supreme Court, and the defense had also sought to have him removed.

Regarding the affidavit Earl Larson had prepared and submitted when Olson was originally charged, Eckert said it had been, "Nothing more or less than what it should have been—a bare-bones recital of the state's case sufficient to conclude that there was probable cause for the issuance of a warrant of arrest." He said some time had passed since the murders, and public passions had subsided, and he noted that in many news reports it was Olson's possible innocence rather than his guilt that was the theme. Eckert had filed a Memorandum in Cass County District Court that made his view of the impact of the media on Gary Olson's situation absolutely clear, which was, "There have been no expressions of opinion by any of the news media as to the guilt or innocence of the defendant. The news media, if anything, appeared to be attempting to act as a moderating influence upon the passions of the community."

He ruled that the state's attorney could not question Olson about the murder of his wife, but could ask about his armed robbery conviction that had put him in prison before. And most important, the casings evidence was in.

The next court date was August 18 for a conference on pre-trial motions, and Eckert expected the trial to begin by mid-September. Three days before the final formalities, Olson's attorneys filed another motion to move the trial from Wahpeton in Richland County, to Minot in Ward County. They also re-filed their motion to hire, at state expense, a public opinion research expert to lay further foundation for their change-of-venue motion. Affidavits were submitted to show that the coverage area of the Fargo news media included Richland County, where they claimed their client could not receive the fair trial that is his right. Everything was resolved but the defense obstinacy over "where."

11

MURDER MOST FOUL

West Fargo's residents were relieved by Eckert's August words that the trial should be starting soon, and it appeared the town was headed toward putting the aberrations of 1976 and 1977 in its past, but there were exceptions. Bette Wolf and her husband were concerned about their son's whereabouts. Billy, the second oldest of their four children, had gone to West Fargo High School several years before Pollie, and had more recently been working at his father's West Fargo business, Bill Wolf and Son Mobile Home Service. Together they set, serviced and repaired mobile homes, and Billy normally called to see whether his help was needed. He had moved out of the family's double-wide trailer and taken a room of his own in Fargo. Bette Wolf hadn't seen her son since August 15 and on Thursday, the 18th she filed a missing persons report with area police. There had yet to be a response.

August 21, 1978, was a Sunday, and while there were fleeting clouds and a slight breeze for occasional relief, the heat was still oppressive. The dog days of summer were ending, and there were signs in the air of the changes about to come. A hint of color in some of the leaves, and darkness creeping in from both sides of the day indicated that the long summer sun of the northern plains was shortening and fall approaching. But it was still summer, and many people continued to escape to nearby lakes for a quick break, getting ready to close down their cabins. Others were finding diversions closer to home.

David Wambach of Fargo was one who had gone away from his Fargo home but not far, and was out for a relaxing solitary Sunday. He paddled his canoe and followed the dark, slow moving waters of the north-flowing Red River on its journey to Lake Winnipeg in Manitoba, Canada. The river formed the boundary between North Dakota and Minnesota and was high, since there had been flooding that summer. A fortunate sighting on such a relaxed outing would be a beaver, but in the early afternoon, when Wabmbach had reached a point about ten miles north of Fargo-Moorhead, something else caught his eye. Stuck in the exposed roots of a dead tree on the Minnesota side of the river was a green garbage bag. As he approached, he thought it must contain a mannequin, since from it there appeared to be feet protruding. Wambach then saw a second green bag snagged in a tree trunk upstream on the North Dakota side of the river and thought something just didn't seem right.

Rather than dig into the bags himself, he looked to see whether anyone was around, then pulled off on the Minnesota side of the river and located a phone at a nearby residence. He called the Clay County Sheriff's Department and told them he had happened on something in the river, but wasn't sure what. The sheriff's office received the call at 1:29 p.m. and said they would send someone out to check on it.

Two officers soon arrived, and they were in for a shock. Larry Costello, known as "Wopper" to his close friends because of his Italian heritage, was the first to look in one of the bags. He recalled,

"I remember, me and another deputy went out in a canoe, and it was just the most freaky thing I'd ever seen in my life. Then I remember we went back to shore and realized we had a body cut in two, and bags in two different locations on the river, and we went back to, back to land, and we called the State Crime Bureau, the Crime Lab. Oh, it was just unbelievable. I'd never seen a body cut in half and feet were sticking up out of one of the bags, wrapped around some, uh, twigs, sticking up in the air. So, it was pretty bizarre."

The body was not removed until 9:30 p.m. since the medical examiner they called had had a stroke, and also they waited for the arrival of the specialists from the Minnesota Bureau of Criminal Apprehension to arrive and see the scene. The State Crime Bureau sent a lab team with five lab people to look at evidence. It had rained, so things were even more of a mess. In the meantime the word was out about what had been found, and curiosity plus jurisdiction questions overlapped. The arrival on the location of local, county and state officials from two states made gathering and preserving evidence a problem. On a muddy area to begin with and with no actual crime scene, the organizations were operating semi-independently in gathering evidence and, if it existed, possibly obliterating it. The canoeist had seen strange cars, and there were some footprints, though the rain had rendered them very imprecise, but gathering evidence carefully and cataloguing it was difficult.

Since the body halves had been found on opposite sides of the Red River, they had been found in different states, and there were questions of who would have jurisdiction in the case and what factors determined it.

Minnesota authorities of Clay County announced they would be, "handling the investigation until jurisdiction is determined." Larry Costello, the Italian fire plug, was senior investigator for Clay County and named to head the investigation. Final jurisdiction remained uncertain, but Costello released information about the case, saying the victim was a male Caucasian with reddish-brown hair, age twenty-five to thirty, about six feet, and 210 pounds. He had apparently been murdered by a long gash across his face that sliced his jugular vein and had been dead for about three days when he was discovered. Stories that he had been alive when he was being cut in half, and that was how he was murdered would soon be circulated, adding to the terror of the incident. Speculation about the event was rampant.

Clay County was swamped with calls after they released information on the incident and provided some details. The announcements stated that the body had been found in a tan T shirt, jeans, and work boots, which was unwelcome news to Bette Wolf, and she called to say that those clothes matched what was last seen worn by her son when she had filed the missing persons report. The victim was soon identified definitely as Billy Wolf, who should have graduated from West Fargo High School in 1975, but wasn't the best student in the class and ended up a bit short on credits. He had gone to the adult community education center to finish his high school education and received his diploma in 1977.

People were really wondering what was happening in their safest of states and small towns. Costello said, "Oh, I think it was the biggest thing to make the news since Pollie. But I think this became so traumatic to the community because the guy was, you know, cut in two and dumped in the river. It made people more fearful. It's a pretty bizarre crime when you find a body cut in half floating in the river. I mean, you don't expect that one to be a suicide. So it's obviously foul play. And so that was a weird crime. That would be weird not just here, but anywhere. So I think the community reaction was that everybody was pretty concerned at what happened . . . at just what must have happened there. And I think law enforcement was appropriately concerned to put resources on it."

The community was not comforted by Costello's statement three days after Billy's body had been found that it "had to be done with some type of a band saw or something that made one swatch when it went through."

Fargo patrolman, Pete Grabner, was one of those who became involved in the investigation. He said, "There was a lot of press pressure, and there was a lot of pressure from the public. It was a real high-profile thing and it had our community scared to death. There's this big monster walking around out there that cuts people in half. So, they needed to do something and they needed to do it quick. I think at the time it threw a blanket of fear over the community, but you know how Americans are. They remember about one week and then it's over with."

Mike Lyman worked on the case and also saw the body. Billy was still in the bags when he was brought over to Hanson-Runsvoldt Funeral Home. Lyman recalled, "It was pretty gross. But the thing that struck me was how a person would be able to cut a body in half like that with probably a knife or some sharp instrument and be able to go through the spinal cord and everything and get everything halved. It just amazed me you'd be able to do that somewhere. You know, we never found a large volume of blood somewhere, and there certainly [had to have been]. So it wasn't in the vehicle, it wasn't in the house, it wasn't anywhere near the Wolf family. So it had to be out and about somewhere. So you assume you go out in some field, you know, after dark, cut somebody in half like that. The cutting was rough. It wasn't a sharp, sharp butcher knife. It was something like a box cutter, a carpet knife, something like that. The first thing that struck me after they took the bags off the body was just how would you be able to do that? I've shot deer before and quartered deer out and packed them out of the brush and that's not easy to find those spots where you can cut through the bone and joints. And somebody did it in the lower lumbar area of the spine. You know, that always struck me as somebody who knew a little bit about anatomy to be able to do that, because a normal person wouldn't be able to do it, I don't think. You'd have that body all hacked up."

Lyman continued. "Billy Wolf . . . it was a gross . . . it was a gross . . . it was the grossest case you've ever seen. Everything about that case was just somewhat bizarre. I mean, how do you have that much blood and not have a crime scene somewhere? But that happened. Somebody lugs two halves of the body to the river and dumps them in the river?"

Billy Wolf's murder hit the communities and brought out a mixture of fear, confusion, curiosity, and much speculation about what could have happened. What could there possibly be about Billy that could have led to such a horrendous conclusion? While there was great shock and even more profound concern about what was taking place, the incident never evoked the great sympathy as the murder of Pollie two years earlier. No one doubted Pollie had been an innocent victim. For the killers to have gone to such extremes in the murder of Billy made some wonder whether there was something about his life that was less innocent, and put him in less savory company and made him seem less of a victim. This impressed people as something that involved drugs, or, as in another story that quickly emerged, the speculation that he had been an informer who had been found out.

And while there may have been nothing fair about it, Billy was a less attractive member of the community, being a large, somewhat awkward young man who smiled and seemed cheerful, but was deficient in some areas. He had made attempts to get involved when he was in high school, participating in wrestling and as a thrower on the track team, but his father conceded, "He was not really good at either, just average." He spent four years in the school choir and did some yearbook photos when he was in the camera club. Extending himself more, he had played a minor role in the school's production of *Harvey*. In all, it was a fairly diverse record of school participation. But the press and community picked up on the people being interviewed and taking polygraphs, and it was apparent that the investigation focused on possible involvement with a less desirable element of the community than the innocent Pollie, who was the classic victim, caught alone in the secluded home by a sinister predator.

182

While Billy's murder never attracted the public's sympathy the way Pollie's did, his story commanded the attention of the community while Gary Olson's lawyer's continued to make motions to keep Gary from going to trial for Pollie's murder. As the Wolf story was emerging, a less noticed item appeared in the news in the second week of September, when Olson's attorney, John Rowell, petitioned the Richland County Court for a psychiatric examination of Gary Olson by Dr. David Sharbo of Fargo to determine whether Gary was capable of assisting in his own defense in a court trial.

Having jurisdiction in the Wolf homicide was debated briefly, but why either side desired it was less clear. It was a very high-profile case with no apparent direction to follow to solve, and pressure for answers to assure public safety in the area was strong. Federal Prosecutor Gary Annear said the joke in Minnesota soon became that they should have pushed the bag from their side over to the North Dakota side. Jokes weren't common at the time, given the nature of the homicide.

It ended up as a Minnesota case because the man who was canoeing went to the Minnesota side of the river to call authorities. Lead investigator Costello said, "Actually, this should have been a North Dakota case because [the man] was from West Fargo, and everything that initially led up to this activity [happened] in Fargo and West Fargo."

It was all that first phone call, though eventually the case would come to involve nine agencies and twenty-seven investigators at every level of government. Costello explained that originally, "It was between two states in the river. Actually, if the guy had went over to the North Dakota side, they would have got the case originally, but then it became an issue between Minnesota and North Dakota over who had jurisdiction because of the river. And we didn't know where the crime scene was so, our county attorney at the time, Paul Grinelle, said, you know, that we could venue it in Minnesota regardless of where he was killed because of our laws compared to North

Dakota laws. So that's how we ended up being the lead agency. Ninety-nine percent of the work we did was in Fargo and West Fargo on it."

Four agencies were working on the Wolf case in the beginning. In Minnesota it was Clay County with Costello in the lead and Assistant County Attorney Ed Klinger, the prosecutor in charge, along with the city of Moorhead, for which this was the first murder case in thirty-eight years. On the North Dakota side, Cass County and the city of Fargo were involved. Within days Fargo invited the FBI to participate, since nobody could establish where the crime had taken place and because other charges—federal ones—including kidnapping, could have been involved.

The investigation went in many different directions, and the different agencies had meetings where they shared information, but each had its own agendas. Keeping up with what was being learned was a difficult matter with the information technology at its 1978 level and more and more people gathering bits in different or overlapping directions. Though people were personally cooperative, they couldn't keep track of all the information gathered and share it equally. Lyman was originally on the task force put together to exchange information among agencies. He said that, at their biweekly or bimonthly meetings, "We shared information. Then I thought the information exchange was good. I think as soon as that dissolved the information got hither and yon."

The investigation went many directions, one of the first being trying to discover Billy's location on the last day he was thought to have been seen, August 18. A reward fund was established by Minnesota crime agencies that they hoped would bring out some leads, since it was over $25,000. Costello said their investigations included many different possibilities, including drug-related crime, though there had never been a drug-related homicide in North Dakota up to that time, which was where they were looking—a crime of passion, murder with a message, even something involving the

Mafia. The message could have involved undercover work as an informer, and they were checking every possible agency. They had done hundreds of interviews and many polygraphs and consulted a psychic, but they couldn't name any real possible suspects and had no real leads.

The parents, Bill, Sr., and Bette, complained openly about Costello and how the investigation was being run in an interview entitled, "West Fargoans Puzzle Over Son's Murder" that was in the September 24, 1978, *Fargo Forum*. In the story, Bill, Sr., faulted Costello for not taking plaster castes of the footprints near the riverbank where his son's body had been found, and his wife complained of the many rumors and of sympathy cards stuffed with religious tracks. Her husband spoke strongly to refute rumors that his son had been an informer responsible for a big drug raid in Wahpeton the previous month. It was mentioned in the article that a car Billy had owned had been repossessed and a small amount of marijuana had been found in it.

Assistant Clay County Attorney Ed Klinger found it objectionable that the newspaper included in its report William Wolf, Sr.'s, criticism of Costello's handling of the crime scene investigation and not making castes of the footprints. The Minnesota Crime Lab had handled the investigation and found that most of the footprints at the two locations near the river had come from two barefooted young boys and a dog. The boys had been investigated, but other footprints in the muddy area "did not have enough details to warrant casts being made." It was unusual for Klinger to say anything about the case to reporters.

While the Wolfs were expressing their concern about the investigation, the investigators had been focusing more directly on the Wolf family. Costello discussed what had led to that, saying, "Well, the fact they had a huge argument a couple days before [Billy] disappeared. And his dad had been working within six miles of the location where we found the body. And just a lot of other things. Not one thing in particular, but a bunch of them all added up. We weren't getting any cooperation out of his sisters, which really, you know, bothered us a lot. And anybody who has a family member killed is going to want to get to the bottom of it as quickly as possible. And in this case, his sisters were not cooperative with us at all. And the fact that, you know, eighty-five percent of the homicides are committed by a family member or close acquaintance, you know. Obviously, it's even higher than that. We were hearing all those different things, too."

Those "different things" included some that had said Billy threatened to make known certain facts to the public. An FBI psychological profiler said, beyond a criminal mind, they were leaning toward a relative or a close family member as the killer.

Billy's dad wasn't really big, not his son's size, but he had the kind of tools to accomplish what had been done to Billy. Something Lyman noticed was, "The one thing that struck me in that case that I'll never forget: I think the Wolfs gave us permission to search the house. We didn't get a warrant. I recall they lived in a mobile home, and in one room, I think it was their bedroom, they had a book case. That book case was solidly mystery novels. I thought at that time, and I can't remember who the authors were, whether it was Chandler or who it was back in the 1970s, but my thought was that if we could read all these books, this case is in one of those books. Severing the body and cutting the body in half, you know, it was in one of those books. But we never took that direction. Nobody read all those books. Back then it would have been a six-month job."

The more they questioned William Wolf, Sr., the more suspicious they became. He kept telling them what they saw as outrageous and unbelievable stories that he claimed his son had told him. Billy, according to his father, had been abducted, and a couple of people had taken him out on a gravel road and threatened him at gunpoint then had beaten him up. When they finished, they had put him in the trunk of a car, taken him someplace else in the countryside and dropped him off. Billy had also told his father, so his father claimed, that he had been run off the road by some people and shot at. The investigating team's reaction to these sagas of strangers scaring Billy was that his father was trying to outsmart them, to put distract them away from examining the Wolf family by giving them fase leads to pursue. The investigators were reluctant to let Bill, Sr., slip away since they couldn't account for some of his time on the day Billy actually disappeared.

While this investigation continued, John Rowell and his associates met with Gary Dean Olson. Their first meeting took place in the state penitentiary, and they held a second meeting at the Cass County Jail. The Georgetown Law School graduate and his colleagues had little in common with their client and were billing the taxpayers by the tenth of an hour, so small talk was minimal, but Gary stated he hadn't killed Pollie and was cooperative in accepting their ideas on how he could put up a robust defense. The prosecution had been in complete compliance in providing all information to them in a timely manner so there were no surprises. Rowell presented Olson with the list of what the prosecution would argue, and they discussed what they had to counter. They discussed whether Olson should take the stand, and Gary agreed with Rowell that it would be unwise.

Olson's attorneys appealed directly to the North Dakota Supreme Court at that time, applying for a supervisory writ directing the district court judge to move the trial of their client from Wahpeton, in eastern North Dakota, to Minot, in western Ward County. Eight days later, on October 12, Olson won his first court victory, as the Supreme Court granted the venue change. In *Gary Dean Olson, Petitioner v. North Dakota* District Court Richland County, Third Judicial District Respondent, Justice Paul Sand wrote the court's opinion, with considerable explanation and citation that summarized the court's reasoning and many of Olson's arguments:

"The defendant, Gary Dean Olson . . . is charged with the murder of a West Fargo girl named Pollie Johnson. He filed a motion for a change of venue from the First Judicial District, Fargo, to the Fifth Judicial District, Minot, on the grounds that there existed in the First Judicial District of North Dakota so great a prejudice against the defendant that he cannot obtain a fair and impartial trial. . . . Public interest, sparked by the brutal nature of the crimes and the rarity of such crimes in the community, caused considerable news coverage to be given to each slaying . . . there are instances when an appeal from a conviction is an inadequate remedy and the invocation of this Court's original jurisdiction is required to protect the defendant's fundamental right to a fair trial . . . as a result of pretrial publicity a strong nexus has been created between the two crimes involving Gary Dean Olson such as present a reasonable likelihood that Olson cannot get a fair and impartial trial in Cass County, Fargo . . . We agree with Judge Eckert's finding that a reasonable likelihood existed that Olson could not get a fair and impartial trial in Cass County, although we disagree with his decision to deny Olson's motion that the trial be moved to Ward County . . .

"The First Judicial District Court is ordered to vacate its order changing the venue of petitioner's trial from Cass County to Richland County, and further to grant petitioner's motion for a change of venue to a suitable facility in Ward County, Minot, North Dakota."

Six days after the decision was released, Judge Eckert announced that the trial of Gary Dean Olson for the murder of Pollie Johnson would begin on November 13 at Ward County Court House in Minot.

The Wolf investigation had been making quiet progress. On November 11, two days before Olson's trial was to start, *The Fargo Forum* informed the public that, on November 27, following the Thanksgiving holidays, a grand jury would be convened on the order of Judge Gaylord Saetre of Clay County. The grand jury would be looking into the Billy Wolf homicide, but prosecutor Klinger offered no information on whether there were any suspects or whether they had knowledge of when or where the murder had occurred. Klinger did say that this notice would be the last public statement on the matter until the grand jury either indicted someone or there was a "bill of particulars" against a person or persons. A bill of particulars was a detailing of the prosecution's claims submitted to the defendant to provide the facts alleged in the complaint or the indictment that related to the commission of the crime. A "no bill" from this jury was another possibility and would allow for another grand jury, and, under Minnesota law, a grand jury was required if the punishment for the offense could be life imprisonment.

12

JURIES OF THEIR PEERS

I t had been two years and three months since Pollie Johnson's murder, but the trial for that murder commenced in Minot on Monday, November 13, and the *voir dire* began, as prosecution and defense attorneys interviewed seven prospective jurors, seeking out possible bias or knowledge they might possess that would make them helpful or harmful to their planned cases. The process continued the next day, as nine more potential jurors were interviewed. The original estimate of two days for jury selection was giving way to a considerably more adversarial process that could extend through the first week.

Rowell, Gary Olson's counsel, typically began with, "Have you ever heard of a person being wrongfully convicted of murder?" After Wednesday's session when about thirty people had been questioned, Judge Eckert said he expected the jury to be empanelled by Friday so that opening statements could begin the following Monday. He anticipated a trial of two to three weeks after that. By the end of Friday's session, more than fifty people had been interviewed but the standards were very stringent in the high-profile case, and finding twelve acceptable individuals for the jury was proving difficult, even after moving the trial twice to get an unbiased jury pool. They would resume after the weekend.

National news of the next day when the jury pool was off was dominated by a grotesque story coming from Jonestown, Guyana. Nine-hundred followers of the Reverend Jim Jones, members of his San Francisco-based People's Temple, followed Jones's directions and committed mass suicide by consuming a concoction of Kool-Aid and cyanide. It was a weird world out there.

On Monday jury selection resumed. Eckert requested that the local attorneys contact the media and ask them to use caution in the material they reported from the trial. The following day there were problems when two potential jurors were heard speculating over whether the accused could be the same man who had murdered his wife some time ago, and the defense moved for immediate mistrial. The motion was denied, and they demanded that an entirely new jury be selected, which Eckert also denied.

After more than seventy-five people had been considered, a panel of twelve jurors was empanelled. This included seven men and five women. One of the women was breastfeeding her child, and arrangements were agreed on that there would be breaks taken to accommodate her.

Wednesday was a big day. In Minot the prosecution finally began to present its case in the most sensitive of all West Fargo tragedies, while 265 miles to the east action was beginning on the most gruesome and bizarre of those tragedies. In the Clay County Court House in Moorhead, Minnesota, thirty-five people were called to form the pool from which twenty-three grand jury members would be selected to look at the evidence authorities possessed in the Billy Wolf homicide and determine whether it warranted proceeding with a case against someone. The timing wasn't ideal, as the next day was Thanksgiving, which meant there would be a four-day break, right when things were starting to happen.

In Minot the prosecution made a start, and Assistant Cass County Attorney Joseph Turman told the jury that the prosecution was going to introduce evidence to prove that Gary Olson had shot and killed Pollie Johnson during a burglary. Kelly Rogers testified about hearing her sluggish breathing on the phone and discovering her body in the kitchen soon after. He said they had intended to do something together that evening, and he had called her at around 9:00 p.m. Special Agent Rolle testified about the condition of Pollie's body when he found her and examined the scene.

Following the Thanksgiving break, the case moved along more quickly, as Jerard Obert, the Fargo pathologist who performed the autopsy on Pollie, testified and said she had died from a gunshot inside her upper lip, and she had been shot in the right side of the forehead. There was testimony from the Butler girls from West Fargo High School who had seen a car parked near the Maple River Dam on the night of the shooting, but, their statements about the color of the car were inconsistent and neither could identify the driver.

Ruth Backstrom took the stand and told of a light-colored car driving past her home several times while she had been doing chores in her farmyard. She described the driver as having shoulder-length or collar-length curly hair and a mustache and wearing sunglasses, and having seemed to stare at her each time he passed by. She said she and her husband had seen the same car later in the evening parked by the Maple River Dam and Bridge. The two of them had given investigators a description from which a composite sketch had been developed, and under cross-examination she said they saw other drawings later that were closer to a likeness of the car's driver.

Testimony on the car continued. Special Agent Dale Remus took the stand, Turman introduced into evidence the title to a light-blue station wagon that Olson had owned between April 1976 and April 1977.

Debra Butler had testified the previous day that she and her sister saw a light-blue car parked near the Johnson house the night of the murder.

192

Defense counsel asked, "The Butler girls described the car as a sedan, not as a station wagon?"

"That's correct," said Remus.

The prosecution continued to call witnesses and introduce depositions to link Olson to the crime. Gary's brother Orvin "Mick" Olson testified about the night of the shooting and Gary telling him he had witnessed the murder through a screen door. He still maintained that Gary had been an innocent bystander and that the three who allegedly killed Pollie had threatened to kill him and his family if he went to the authorities. Mick said, "I asked him point blank if he had been directly involved in the shooting, and he said 'no' straight out."

Defense established that Olson contended that he had gone fishing nearby and went to the Johnson home for a drink of water. Why the prosecution was introducing Gary's alibi at this point was a bit unclear, but it established that he was aware of the shooting before it was public information.

On Wednesday Robert and Darlene Nelson testified to having seen someone at the Dairy Queen on the night of the murder matching Olson's appearance with claw marks down his face that looked like they could have from fingernails.

The prosecution felt things were going as they should, but heard that the story wasn't being perceived that way. "The press kept telling it worse than what it was. We were sitting out there in Minot, and I would talk to people back here in Fargo and would hear that we were really getting beat up here in court," Turman said.

A big link developed in the prosecution's case when they called on Steven Skar, an inmate from the North Dakota State Penitentiary. Skar's testimony was devastating, as he said that, during a conversation at lunchtime on February 7, 1978, "Gary said he killed Pollie Johnson." Skar testified that Olson also said that he had sold the gun he had used and said, "to find a conviction in this case, they'll have to dig up the gun."

Skar was from West Fargo and had been in school with Johnson family members. He was in the penitentiary for armed robbery and tampering with a witness.

Under cross examination by Irvin Nodland, Skar conceded he knew Pollie and was aware of the $6,500 reward fund involved in the case. He said he had never been offered any promises of money or anything else in exchange for his testimony. Skar did almost get something out of his continuing testimony, however, which was more trouble. Nodland got him to admit to using heroin, crystal meth, angel dust, and speed and to selling drugs. He also said he smoked marijuana and sniffed lacquer thinner at the penitentiary, but at that point Eckert stopped the proceedings. He advised Skar he had a right to remain silent and not give self-incriminating testimony.

That Steve Skar did things that weren't clever wasn't new, as the crime that got him incarcerated demonstrated. He was a friendly sort, but weak in judgment. His luck hadn't been so good either. While living in West Fargo, he had gone to Bernie's Package Store, a liquor store at a small strip mall in south Fargo that seemed like an out-of-the-way place for an easy robbery. There was an off duty policeman sitting in his car across the street, reading a paper. The policeman looked at Bernie's Package Store and noticed that all the people inside were standing with their hands up. He drove over, jumped out of his car with a shotgun and waited until a guy came walking out with a nylon stocking over his head, a bag of money in one hand, and a gun in the other. That was Steve, and his plea of "not guilty" was very difficult to accept.

How reliable of a witness did the state really have, when this was a key element in its case? Being the guy on the inside who testifies against another inmate, knowing that informers weren't well-liked in the prison, Skar again wasn't making great choices. He hadn't even had charges outstanding somewhere to make it worth something to him to trade for being a snitch. Earl Larson viewed this as an example of just how much this case and the Johnsons meant to West

Fargo, commenting, "If there was one time in his life he told the truth, that was it. People felt so strongly about that murder, some pretty hard-nosed guys came forward and said they would work on it to help us with it. They did, with nothing to gain from it. Even Steve Skar. He didn't get anything out of it."

Wednesday was also a big day in Clay County Court in Moorhead. After two and a half days of closed proceedings where the grand jury heard from between twenty-five and thirty-five witnesses, they had reached a decision. Little had been reported during the time the session was taking place, as prosecuting attorney Ed Klinger's only response to any question throughout the period was "no comment." He explained his secretiveness as, "When you go before a grand jury, you don't want to pollute what a grand jury hears. The grand jury and the deliberations and the grand jury evidence before the grand jury is really sacred." His awareness of the problems with publicity that had led to change-of-venue problems with the Pollie Johnson case, "may have had something to do with it, but my style was never to try and generate publicity."

The case they had heard had been fairly convincing, as the deliberations of the twenty-three grand jury members lasted less than three hours. They had begun deliberating at 3:00 p.m. on Tuesday and reconvened Wednesday morning shortly after 11:00 a.m. They had informed Klinger of their decisions. Billy's father, William Wolf, Sr., was indicted for the murder of William Patrick Wolf. The indictments were for murder in the first degree, second degree, and third degree, and manslaughter in the first degree.

At 4:30 William Wolf and his attorney, Wayne Anderson of Fargo, appeared at the Clay County Court House. The forty-four-year-old Wolf was a trim, dark-haired man with strong, appealing features, and his son had born little resemblance to him. He made a dapper appearance in his navy-blue suit and white shirt with blue tie, and his demeanor remained calm during the court proceedings. The indictment stated that the killing occurred on August 15 at an unknown place by stabbing and slashing with a sharp object. The inclusion of so many different charges allowed for determination of the degree of intent to be established as the case progressed.

Judge Saetre asked Wolf if he was in good mental and physical health, and he replied, "As far as I know." Saetre then read the indictment and asked Wolf if he understood the charges, and Wolf responded, "Not really." Satre called a five-minute recess for Wolf to confer with his attorney to have the charges clarified, then read the charges to Wolf on all indictments. Following each charge, Wolf was asked his plea, and he consistently responded, "No plea at this time." He was then released on $25,000 bail.

The arrest of Billy's father for his son's murder didn't shock everyone, since it was one of several common rumors that had been circulating since the body was discovered.

The day after Wolf was indicted, the prosecution completed its case in the Pollie Johnson homicide trial. They had saved what they considered to be their most persuasive evidence for the end. This was the evidence gathered by Mike Lyman that tied the shell casing to Olson. On December 1, FBI ballistics expert, Robert W. Seibert, testified that thirty-seven empty .22 caliber cartridges recovered from different cars that had been owned by Olson had been fired from one gun, the same gun that had fired the round that left a shell casing found next to the victim at the scene of the shooting. That was the most compelling evidence directly tying the weapon to Gary Dean Olson and was the mortar holding together the remainder of the prosecution's case. The defense had hired its own ballistics expert to conduct tests on the cartridges in a state-financed attempt to counter this evidence, but the results had been the same. Tactically, the defense didn't spend its time challenging the evidence because the FBI witness was clearly a veteran at testifying and wasn't going to be thrown off. The longer they allowed him on the stand, the more the jury heard this evidence repeated. The prosecution rested its case and turned the court over to the defense.

13

DECISION, FOR NOW

The defense began to present its case on Thursday, the final day of November. The prosecution had the burden to prove the guilt of the accused person "beyond a reasonable doubt." The defense had to show that even if the case had sounded possible, room for "reasonable doubt" existed. The prosecution had produced no eye witnesses, and, though they had come up with evidence on the weapon used, they had never found the actual gun, nor could they put it directly in Gary Olson's hands. Raising questions in the minds of jurors by offering alternate theories of what happened that contradicted some of the circumstantial evidence and testimony they had heard presented the defense with its plan of attack.

They first recalled Mick to remind the jury of his story that Gary had told him of witnessing the murder through a screen door, which along with a rape, was carried out by three men. They next put Oliver "Bud" Wright, on the stand, to offer something that sounded a bit like corroboration of the story Gary had told Mick. Defense attorney John Rowell thought this was the strongest piece of their case in establishing reasonable doubt. He had prepared Wright before his testimony by going over the sworn statement the Fargo construction worker had previously written, then telling him the questions he would be asked. Rowell didn't want any surprises on this, as it was critical to offer an alternative set of events the jury could see as having possibly taken place.

Wright testified that he was at the Lariat Bar in West Fargo drinking on night of August 6, 1976, sitting alone at a table. Three other men came in and sat down at his table at about 9:30 p.m. and one of the men pulled a knife on him, but put it away when Wright bought a round of drinks. The man who had pulled the knife, Wright testified, "said he had killed a little kid about six miles north of West Fargo." One of his associates disagreed with the "little kid" comment and had said, "No, she was about sixteen years old." Write continued, saying that one man also claimed he had a gun in his car outside the bar, but he couldn't remember the identities of the men. Wright's testimony was that the men appeared to be on drugs and were told to leave the bar later after they began harassing a dancer. When he heard about Pollie Johnson's murder, Write said he contacted Cass County Sheriff's Department with this testimony.

Earl Larson testified about Wright's story, saying he didn't believe it. He had interviewed Wright a number of times and said that each time new details were added that could not be verified. The defense requested that a video tape of an interview Larson or Lyman had originally conducted with Wright at the sheriff's department be played for the jury. Eckhart denied the request, but said his decision was not final.

Deborah Feil, a waitress at the Lariat Bar on the night of shooting was called, but she provided little to enhance Wright's story. She testified that two or possible three men had been at the bar that night and were "hassling" an older man, in an effort to get him to pay for their drinks. Under cross examination, she said she was unable to hear their conversation and hadn't attempted to, but she couldn't offer any support for the story about discussions concerning murder and a rifle being in a car outside at that time.

The matter of the cuts that had been described as having been seen on Gary Olson's face the night of the murder that looked like claw marks, or more like fingernail scratches received possibly from a desperate girl's fighting to defend herself was a topic the defense moved to next. Don and Taeko Schmidt of Fargo testified that they had gone fishing with Gary and Dixie Olson on the weekend immediately following Pollie's shooting. They said Gary had no facial cuts such as those described in Wednesday's testimony by the Nelsons, the couple who had said they had seen Olson on Friday, August 8. Rowell then called as a witness a Minot physician. Olson's counsel had only spoken with him briefly before he took the stand. Dr. R.W. Pierson testified that Olson had the type of skin that scarred easily and if there had been cuts like those described, they would leave visible marks. He proceeded to say that he had examined Gary Olson twenty minutes before court convened that very day and could find no traces of facial scars. Dr. Pierson said that if Olson had suffered cuts similar to those described by the two prosecution witnesses, the scarring would still be evident. According to prosecution testimony, Olson not only had scars on the side of his face, but also a cut on his head and his scalp had been stitched.

The mishandling of evidence by the sheriff's department was raised as an issue, as a carpet sample taken from the home and used as evidence had been stored with other fabric samples. Rowell asked a witness whether fibers in fabric ever led to convictions. The response was positive. Fibers weren't anything essential to the prosecution's case, but anything to instill doubt in jurors minds about how things were handled by the investigation worked in favor of the defendant.

The defense next set out to impeach the harmful testimony that had come from Steve Skar. They had several witnesses lined up for this. First was Kevin Swalley, who was a Wahpeton jailer. Swalley gave helpful, but inadequate testimony that while Olson had been jailed in Wahpeton, he told his jailer he didn't shoot Johnson. Leslie Johnson of West Fargo, who was on parole, had been an inmate of the North Dakota State Penitentiary along with both Skar and Olson. He testified that he was at the lunch meeting at which Skar alleged that Olson said he had killed Pollie. He said he did not recall Olson making any statements to implicate himself in the shooting.

The defense had saved its most direct impeachment witnesses for its finish, and bought out current state penitentiary inmates. Defense attorney John Rowell was going to demonstrate that Steve Skar had committed perjury in his testimony, and he began with the testimony of Bruce Wrolstad. On the stand Wrolstad said that Skar frequently said he would do anything to get out of prison, and had asked him to support Skar's testimony about Olson's admission of guilt. He claimed that, in return, Skar had said he could get Wrolstad released from prison. Marvin Coughlin, another West Fargo native who had been in school with both Skar and the Johnsons, was in the state penitentiary and described his conversations with Steven Skar.

Marvin was serving time for forgery, which seemed an unlikely choice of crimes for him to have become involved in, given how little he bothered with writing or much else when he had been in school. The forgery was of prescriptions, which ended him in serious trouble. He claimed that Skar told him that Cass County Deputy Earl Larson had offered him both his freedom and the $6,500 reward money if he would testify against Olson. Coughlin said, "He told me he didn't want to do the four years he had to do in the penitentiary and was going to fabricate the story."

Larson was called and denied making any promises to Skar or arrangements with other witnesses. The defense had planted about all the seeds of doubt it could, but whether any of them had sounded convincing remained to be seen.

And Marvin, unfortunately, didn't learn from his incarceration. A slightly off-balanced, gangly-looking boy with a certain social

200

appeal, after his release Marvin returned to the behavior that had landed him in trouble in the past. He married, and there was a domestic disturbance call answered by Pete Graber and Paul Laney. Paul was a younger West Fargo graduate who entered law enforcement and advanced through the county ranks, eventually becoming Sheriff of Cass County. When they arrived at the scene, Marvin swallowed an "eight ball" of cocaine, or 3.5 grams. Although there was no generally accepted number on what constituted a fatal dose of orally consumed cocaine, and factors like purity and what was ingested along with it mattered, the Pharmacogenetics and Pharmacogenomics Knowledge Base of Stanford University puts the fatal dose at 1.2 grams, and Marvin gulped down about three times that amount. Laney recalled what happened next: "He went berserk the second he saw us walk in. I was trying to get him in the handcuffs because he was going so crazy and then, all of the sudden, he quit breathing. And the firemen and everyone were right there. We ripped the handcuffs off him and tried to revive him, and he died in my hands." They had called for emergency medical services immediately and done what they could to keep him alive, but the amount of drugs was too great for his young system to handle for even a short time.

The defense rested its case and closing statements were made on Monday, December 4. Joseph Turman summarized the prosecution's case that Olson, acting alone or with others, had murdered Pollie Johnson while fleeing from an attempted burglary of the Johnson home. He dismissed Olson's contention about watching as three other men shot Pollie with his gun and threatened his life and his family if he told the authorities. "Wouldn't it be more logical to assume anybody stumbling on that scene would get out of there as quickly as he could for his own safety?" Turman asked the jurors.

John Rowell for the defense contended that in many areas doubt existed. Because Wright's testimony substantiated the statement Gary Olson had given his brother, that the murder was committed by three other men, the evidence indicated that Olson was an unwitting witness accidentally present at the scene and whose gun was used against his consent. He had been forced to dispose of the gun out of fear that revenge would be taken against his family and himself. The prosecution had offered one view, but these witnesses offered a separate and more probable view that couldn't be ignored. The case was speculation and circumstantial evidence, which was often contradicted, and the prosecution hadn't met its burden for criminal cases and eliminated all reasonable doubt. That meant it was the jury's obligation to acquit their client.

Once again Gary never said a word in his own defense. Why hadn't Rowell put him on the stand? He said because, "The first prosecution question would have been, 'Is it true that you are serving a life sentence for the murder of your wife?'"

The prosecution had not been able to introduce that glaring fact in testimony about Gary, and Turman didn't want there to be any way around the agreed conditions that the jury not hear it.

At 2:22 p.m. Monday afternoon, the case went to jury, and they continued their deliberations for nearly eight hours, adjourning at 10:00 p.m. The jury was sequestered in a Minot hotel and resumed deliberations Tuesday morning.

After fifteen hours of deliberations, the jury returned a verdict at 5:20 p.m. That was a nail-biter for all, but Turman heard it was not as divided as the length indicated. He said, "I learned later from talking to my brother who lived in Minot at the time that there was one juror who wanted to vote for acquittal, and it was eleven to one throughout the deliberations, from the first vote until they finally beat her down. I don't remember who told me this, but the reason they decided to come back with the verdict was that the judge put them up in this old hotel in Minot, and they were afraid he was going to put them up for a second night. I did hear it was eleven to one both throughout the first night and then the second day."

Judge Eckert had all stand as jury foreman Harold Aleshire prepared to read the verdict. Gary Olson, who was thirty-four by then, showed little emotion but hung his head and shook it slowly as he listened, while Aleshire said the jury had found him "guilty." Eckert polled the jury members to see that the decision was unanimous.

Olson and his attorneys met briefly in a private room, where his emotions hadn't held up as stoically as in court. He eyes were red-rimmed, and he was clearly shaken. First his attorney said, "All I have to say is we're deeply shocked." To this day, Rowell contends, "I think there was room for a reasonable doubt." Not long after the decision, when Olson was asked for a comment, he made his only statement on the case, which was, "Only that they (the jurors) were wrong."

Investigators Larson and Lyman along with the prosecutors who shared in all the details didn't feel there was room for doubt. It had been long and tedious, but the right man had been located and convicted. Turman soon asked for a pre-sentence investigative report once again to designate Olson as a dangerous offender. When asked about his case and why his side won, he said it "was made up of a lot of circumstances, and it would be the totality of the case that would be responsible for the verdict." Lyman had done "a good piece of work" that tied his circumstantial case together.

Reporters questioned the defense about their case and lead counsel Rowell's decision to not put Olson on the stand. He said at the time it wasn't because they feared Olson would incriminate himself, but because of threats that Olson contended had been made against him and his family. Most observers agreed his failure to identify the men he said he saw commit the murder as well as the lack of identities for the men alleged to have spoken about the murder at the Lariat Bar were major weaknesses in the defendant's case.

Pollie's father, Gene Johnson, said, "It's a complete relief that it's over." He thought the investigation had been well-run, but highlighted later, "If it hadn't been for Mike," it might not have been solved.

The same day Gary Olson's conviction for the murder of Pollie Johnson had been announced, the North Dakota Supreme Court released its decision rejecting all his applications for a new trial for the murder of his wife, Dixie, and his challenge to the dangerous offenders statute, which Olson unsuccessfully contended was unconstitutional. They said Olson hadn't received a perfect trial in his wife's homicide case but had received a fair trial. The news coverage several read about testimony reported as having happened before it had been given was apparent to those who read it and while it raised questions about whether they could make fair judgment, the defense counsel had been satisfied at the time. Cellmate Neukom, who spoke with Mike Lyman, was acting in his own self-interest and was not a state agent. His disclosures had apparently begun at a time when alcohol had been smuggled into the jail, and Olson was thoroughly intoxicated. The second inmate, Lester Meddy had been added late but within the rules of procedure.

The calendar turned to a new year, 1979, and while some West Fargo students enjoyed National Lampoon's *Animal House* in the theater, many were staying home to see what would happen next to J.R. on *Dallas*. The news might not have all been great for the country, with statistics saying average marriages lasted 6.6 years, but in West Fargo there was considerable comfort, knowing two homicides had been solved. The money from the fund established for information leading to the arrest and conviction in Pollie's case had come to $6,864.23. It was turned over to the Cass County Attorney's office. As far as where it went after that, States Attorney Cynthia Rothe said, "That information is confidential and will never be released."

At the end of January, William L. Wolf, Billy's father, pleaded innocent in Judge Saetre's chambers in Clay County District Court to having committed the heinous act of murdering his son. Saetre set a tentative date of February 26 for the omnibus hearing for considering inadmissibility of evidence and other pretrial motions from attorneys. Judge Donald Gray would preside. Wolf, who was represented by

Fargo attorneys, waived his right to an earlier omnibus hearing and agreed that forty-five days be allowed after the hearing to prepare for the trial.

While Wolf was just beginning legal proceedings, Gary Olson had been convicted of his second murder and was still working on getting out of the first conviction. His attorney filed a motion in Cass County District Court asking for new trial because of new evidence. The motion was filed by the Bismarck attorney representing Olson, Irvin B. Nodlack, concerning a man with whom Olson had shared a cell in Valley City who turned out to be a snitch and testified against him. Arnold Wayne Neukom had testified about Olson using a tire iron and entering the house the night his wife was murdered. The new evidence was that Neukom admitted that he had perjured himself when testifying in a similar case "in return for consideration."

Neukom, so Nodlack contended, was the "key element" of the prosecution's case and was a "vital factor" in the jury reaching its verdict of guilty. Nordlack argued that if the jury had known Neukon's tendency for "intentionally giving perjured testimony in return for favors," his credibility would have been destroyed, and Olson would have been acquitted. A date for a hearing on the motion was to be set later.

The omnibus hearing date arrived in the case of the Billy Wolf homicide, and, at 1:30 on Monday, February 26, the parties gathered at Clay County District Court House. In a shocking move, prosecutor Edward Klinger said that the charges against William Wolf, Sr., were being dropped, and Judge Gray dismissed the indictment the grand jury had drawn up against him. Klinger said the Wolf case had "no particular suspect" and a good case against William Wolf could not be made, given the evidence and new information developed from the investigation. He also said that they wanted to dismiss the case at the moment in the event a case against Wolf could be made at a later date. They would risk double jeopardy by going forward with the weak information they had. The investigation initiated by the county attorney's office tended to demonstrate Wolf's innocence.

Klinger said he discussed the motion to dismiss with the grand jury, but the decision was his, since new evidence contradicted the findings of the grand jury and suggested other conclusions. Klinger described it as a straight-forward decision, saying, "Some other facts had come to light, and reevaluation of it indicated it would be best not to proceed at that time. One reason was that we felt there was not sufficient evidence to convict. A second reason was that if more evidence came in later that led us to re-indict, we could always do that. And I think we were all pretty well convinced by that time that the father had not done it."

Two weeks later on March 15, Gary Dean Olson was given his sentence for the murder of Pollie Johnson. Richland County District Court Judge Robert Eckert first again declared Olson to be a dangerous offender, so the maximum twenty-year sentence was no longer a restriction. Gary received life imprisonment in the North Dakota State Penitentiary to be served, not concurrent with his present sentence, but as a consecutive sentence.

With the proceedings for the two murders by Gary Olson finalized and the community breathing easier, though permanently altered, a connection was becoming more openly recognized. The motive not introduced at the first trial that many main figures involved with the Dixie Olson homicide believe had led to Dixie's death had finally emerged. While Gary's jealous rage satisfied the jury and could have led to the violent conclusion, it was thought that his motive was something that couldn't have been used at the trial for his wife's murder, since it was only a suspicion by that time.

What those closest to the case believed was the motivation for the Dixie Olson homicide was her belief that Gary had been responsible for Pollie's death, and she could testify to his coming home wet and muddy during the driest summer since the 1930s. Linda Johnson had told Agent Remus that Dixie had expressed her concerns to her about Gary being involved in the Johnson homicide, and Mick's wife, Donna, had said Dixie had asked her whether she thought Gary could have killed Pollie. There were Gary's ominous words that he thought "Linda knew something." But only Dixie could testify to his muddy condition that night.

Turman, who worked in the state's attorney's office while Dixie's case was being litigated and who prosecuted Olson for Pollie's murder said, "Yeah, probably. I think the fact that [Dixie] had put two and two together, I think that was certainly a factor."

Lyman was unequivocal, and put it, "Absolutely." He thought Dixie confronted Gary over his clothes and that made her dangerous to him.

Earl Larson was most explicit, commenting, "Yeah. Dixie had found out that he came home all muddy, and I've never seen such dry weather, and because the river was almost dry. There were places in Fargo and around here that doorways had settled away from buildings, they had to adjust doors, building's side rocks were caving in because of this extreme dryness. The only way he could have gotten that muddy was to have gone in the river. She was working at the South School, and she was working for the attorney, and I suppose if you look at it from Gary Dean's point of view, he wouldn't have had a Chinaman's chance with her working for an attorney, and he was suspicious of her. But the main thing is, I think, that she could testify that he came home muddy that night. That was the feeling I got from talking to Linda, that [Dixie] had confronted Gary Dean about it. . . . Yeah, you know how it is . . . you're the hunted."

14

"I Don't Want to Be Here"

Gary Olson had never admitted to having done anything wrong, and he faced two consecutive lives in prison. A rather dismal future to consider, but little sympathy was being expressed. He and his attorneys, acting on their own, were looking at whatever they could in the cases to fight the institutional time that lay ahead.

That fight began on the day Olson's sentence was handed down in the case for Pollie's murder, as Judge Roy K. Redetzke reentered Olson's life. Olson hadn't been very successful with Judge Redetzke when his legal proceedings began in March of 1977 with the pretrial hearing concerning the murder of Dixie. Two years later Redetzke again had Gary's fate in his hands in Cass County, as proceedings were initiated to have a second chance in the Dixie trial and get an acquittal. Numerous reasons for retrial were filed, including that it was improper to have allowed either cellmate to testify.

Redetzke took the motion filed by Olson's attorney asking for a new trial in the homicide of Dixie Olson under advisement to delib-

208

erate on the matter further before making a ruling. Redetzke wanted more time to consider the many complaints thrown together in the motion, with each complaint contending it alone warranted a new trial. Olson's attorney, Irv Nodland, had filed a separate motion of his own, presenting the argument that Olson should be acquitted in Dixie's case because the jury had been influenced to an overwhelming degree by the testimony of one of Olson's former cell mates who had later confessed to committing perjury in a similar case "in return for consideration." This witness had testified that Olson admitted to having killed his wife, and his testimony would not have been credible if the jury had known how little concern he had for the truth and how he understood that he could use the system to further his own cause. Redetzke didn't announce a date for his ruling on the motions.

As the conclusion of the Pollie Johnson trial had neared, John Rowell, Olson's attorney in Ward County, had suggested to Olson that he request a new attorney after the verdict and appeal, arguing "ineffectiveness of council." Olson rejected the idea, and Rowell filed the initial appeal. Two days following the end of the trial and the Redetke decision to take the motion for a retrial on Dixie Olson under advisement, Rowell filed a motion with Ward County District Court in Minot for the acquittal of Gary Olson in Pollie's case. The motion filed by Rowell was somewhat of a technicality, but technicalities had put many people back on the streets, and this was real.

Rowell didn't say Gary Olson was innocent in this motion, but contended the state made an error when it charged his client. It could have charged him under the subsection of state murder statute that related to intentionally causing someone's death. That had been the case the state actually presented during the trial, and the jury had been convinced it was true. But the state charged Olson under a different subsection. The subsection named in the charges required proof that Olson did more than what the state ever contended he did. The charge had been felony murder. Turman had contended that the state would prove that Olson murdered Pollie Johnson as he was escaping from an attempted burglary of the Johnson home. Rowell said, "The state elected to charge him under the so-called felony murder statute which requires that they show the murder took place during the course of a burglary. Our contention is that the evidence does not show that a burglary took place at the time Pollie Johnson was killed."

No evidence had been introduced that there had been a burglary, and nothing had been reported missing from the Johnson home. Sloppy work on the part of the state, or was there some reason they used the questionable charge? Had Pollie's surprise appearance when a burglary was intended to take place prevented it, and Gary Olson had been correctly charged? The witnesses who could really say whether a burglary was in progress weren't going to, since they were Pollie and Gary. During the trial, Olson's attorneys had made a number of other motions that had been denied, and these they were also appealing. All would present reversible or mistrial arguments.

By March 17, Gary had judges in separate counties hearing arguments or reading and thinking about making decisions that left open a wide range of possible outcomes. He could retain his two consecutive life sentences, or it was possible there could be one new trial. It was even within speculation that he might have a new trial about Dixie with no snitches and his conviction for killing Pollie could be tossed out, so perhaps soon he would soon walking the streets, a free man. With technicalities and the questionable reliability of snitches, though walking free wasn't always ideal for society, it was the American Dream of the inmate.

Judge Redetzke quashed those hopes, at least for the time being, when three weeks later he announced that there was to be no new trial for Olson for the murder of his wife. He had decided that on its face, the motion failed because it didn't meet state guidelines for filing for a new trial. Such a motion had to be made within thirty days of getting new evidence, and Nodland had failed to file the motion in a timely manner. Redetzke had taken more than the rules into account in his decision, and emphasized the point that the defense was asking for a new trial on the basis of one copy of an article that had appeared in a newspaper, the *Minneapolis Star*, that made no reference to the trial of Gary Olson. There were no other supporting affidavits, and there had been a second cellmate who had also testified and whose credibility the defense had not challenged. To say Neukom's testimony had been the key and if the jury had known to question his credibility, Olson would have been acquitted was not a convincing view.

It took five months for the challenge to Redetzke's decision to reach the North Dakota Supreme Court. By the time it did, Olson was represented by a different attorney, Robert Snyder of Bismarck. Snyder told the court the that evidence discovered after Olson's trial showing that a witness had perjured himself in a similar Minnesota trial should have required a new trial for his client, and he asked the Supreme Court to overturn the lower court's ruling in the name of justice.

Snyder presented the newspaper clipping that had been introduced earlier in which Neukom admitted to lying on the stand in a different case because he had been promised benefits for doing so. He said Redetzke had described Neukom's testimony against Olson as, "the mortar that held the bricks of the case together."

That being the case, Snyder contended, "If the defense had been armed with the [new] evidence . . . I think that would have produced a profound effect on the jury." He admitted he had made no attempt to contact the *Star* reporter to get an affidavit to support the story he had written on Neukom. Chief Justice Ralph Erickstad was less than impressed with the petitioner's evidence and effort, commenting, "So you are relying on this court to rely on a newspaper clipping you haven't searched out at all?"

Mervin Nordeng argued the state's case, and said that Olson's request had been filed too late after the new evidence was discovered, as Redetzke had noted. He further contended that the newspaper article would be inadmissible, since it was intended to impeach Neukom's credibility as a witness. Confronting Neukom on his testimony if this were admitted would involve "some logistical problems." That was so because, "Since Neukom is dead — that is a verified fact — I don't think there is any more evidence that could be produced at a new trial." Nordeng contended that there had been other testimony to corroborate Neukom's, which wouldn't change even if there were a new trial, and Neukom's statements were disqualified. The court took the case under advisement, but soon rejected the appeal.

Olson appealed his December 5 conviction for the murder of Pollie Johnson on a number of grounds. Olson, who was thirty-five by then, had his case reach the Supreme Court in slightly over a month, where a new decade had begun, and on January 11, 1980, the court heard arguments from the two sides. John Rowell, appointed representative of Olson, argued that Steve Skar's testimony that Gary had admitted murdering Pollie was perjury and should not have been allowed in evidence. He pointed out that two impeaching witnesses had contradicted it and claimed that Skar was promised sentence reduction to say what he had said.

Rowell also contended that the circumstances of the case indicated Olson's innocence gather than guilt. The secluded location of the Johnson home and the murderer having been known to the victim and admitted to the house didn't fit with Gary Olson. He said, "The home is located at the end of a private, winding, gravel road. It is difficult to find . . . that would make one believe that it was someone who knew the family, had some prior acquaintance." The family dog had been found in the bedroom, and that was where the Johnsons put the dog when they had guests in the house because it was a nuisance. The appellants found it difficult to believe it was reasonable to accept that Olson would have been admitted as a guest. Rowell noted that Pollie's father had parked his highway patrol car outside the house that night, although he wasn't home, and, added somewhat cryptically, "We draw some inferences from that."

212

Cass County attorney Rothe countered the reference to the patrol car by saying that Olson could have been watching the house and known that Pollie's father was not in the home. She also told the court that Olson knew enough details of the killing to tell them to his brother within hours of it happening.

The court took the case under advisement, but Shakespeare could have been speaking to Gary Olson when he had the soothsayer in the first act of *Julius Caesar* warn Caesar, "Beware the Ides of March." It had been March 15, 1979, when Olson had been sentenced to his second consecutive life sentence for murdering Pollie, and it was March 15, 1980, when announcement of the court's ruling on his challenge to that conviction was made public. The unanimous ruling written by Justice Gerald VandeWalle found that District Court Judge Eckert had been correct in rejecting Olson's motions for mistrial in each of three areas.

The first issue was, "Did the district court err in refusing to grant Olson's motion for mistrial because of the misconduct of potential jurors?" The *voir dire* had been thorough and conducted over several days, and the trial judge had granted the defense request that the object was to find jurors without knowledge of Olson's previous conviction for the murder of his wife. The judge had consistently admonished potential jurors to refrain from discussing the case with each other. "It came to the attention of the trial court and counsel during the examination of a potential juror that, contrary to the trial court's instructions, certain other potential jurors awaiting examination were talking about an ex-wife being killed, and they asked if it was the same person, and I said I didn't know. So they were just trying to see, put two and two together. Upon hearing that statement, Olson's counsel moved for a mistrial and challenged the entire jury panel."

It nearly happened, but the court wrote, "After considerable discussion as to the effect of a mistrial, including the attendant publicity which would be generated by the reasons for a mistrial and including a refusal by Olson to waive his right to a speedy trial, the

213

trial court denied the motion for a mistrial and the challenge to the entire jury panel. In an attempt to purge from the jury anyone who had overheard the discussion in the jury room, the trial court excused all persons within possible earshot of the conversation. An examination of the record in this instance revealed that the trial court was extremely careful to prevent any person from serving on the jury who had any knowledge of Olson's previous conviction of murder." The trial court had been "extremely careful" in selecting a jury without prior knowledge, which is what Olson's attorneys claimed they sought. That wasn't their objection. The fact that it wasn't made this a complaint with a different twist that found little favor with the court.

What the court found untenable was that the appeal's objection to the jury selection was not based on there being a jury with a prejudice against Olson. The defense had done studies on the individuals called for the jury pool, and the two involved in the discussion, both of whom were excluded, had been among those they considered more likely to be favorable to them. After the court had denied their motion for mistrial and the challenge to the entire jury panel, the state moved to excuse for cause the two potential jurors who had been speculating on Olson's conviction regarding Dixie and two other potential jurors who might have overheard their conversation.

Olson's chief counsel, Irvin Nodland, was asked at the time whether the defense had any objection to excluding the tainted jury pool members, and he had responded, "Well, we're put in a quandary. In terms of ideas. The correct way for me to say this would be [that] we are being asked now to participate in the selection of a fair jury from what we see as being an unfair process, and that's an impossible quandary. All I'm doing, for the record, I want the record to show that these three jurors, assuming they're not tainted, were among our highest — or three of those — were among the highest that we had evaluated, and we made evaluations independently, and then put them together and that was true for all three of us."

214

While the trial judge went through elaborate measures to empanel a fair and impartial jury, "Olson's argument presumes that he is entitled to a jury panel composed of specific persons he believes might be favorable to him." The court did not agree.

The second motion ruled on was, "Did the district court err in denying Olson's motion to preclude the state from eliciting testimony from Steven Skar concerning alleged admissions made by Olson?" The trial court had noted that Skar's testimony was important. In part that was not only because of Olson's actual admission of having committed the crime that he testified to, but also because Skar was from the West Fargo area and knew Pollie Johnson's family. Those connections could have given him more reason to step forward and tell the truth. Olson's side argued that Skar was inherently untrustworthy and lacked credibility as a witness. The defense was forced to put two rebuttal witnesses on the stand, revealing the conversation that had taken place in the state penitentiary and prejudicing the jury against the defendant by making them aware that Olson was an inmate. There was nothing to indicate the nature of the offence for which Olson had been incarcerated, and both violent and nonviolent offenders were in the penitentiary. Olson could have been there awaiting trial in the Pollie Johnson case. By prior agreement, no questions were asked by the prosecution about where the conversation took place. The trial court judge did not abuse his authority in allowing the testimony, as it was his decision to see that the jury heard all the necessary evidence to make an informed decision and jurors could determine the veracity of the witnesses' testimony for themselves.

The third motion ruled on had been filed by the defense after Pollie's conviction: "Was the evidence at trial sufficient to support a verdict of guilty of the crime charged?"

Olson's defense team argued that the evidence presented at the trial had not been adequate for a logical conclusion to have been reached that their client was guilty of the crime beyond a reasonable doubt.

215

Before responding to the question the court made a brief, but important statement about its function, which was that of an appellate court. VandeWalle wrote, "on the appellate court level the role of the Supreme Court is to merely review the record to determine if there is competent evidence for a jury to have reached its decision. They do not substitute their judgment for that of the trial court or jury." The truth, he said, was better be determined by allowing direct confrontation of the testimony of witnesses appearing in court than by the review of transcripts submitted to appellate courts, where the opportunity to confront the witness did not exist. The appellate court would not retry the case, but would consider whether evidence had been presented that could have reasonably allowed for a verdict of guilty.

The court conceded that the evidence upon which the jury had based its guilty verdict had been mainly circumstantial but stated that a verdict based on circumstantial evidence had the same presumption of correctness as did other verdicts they reviewed. The circumstantial evidence needed to be so strong that a court could say the defendant was guilty beyond a reasonable doubt. "At the trial court level, circumstantial evidence must be conclusive and must exclude every reasonable hypothesis of innocence, but on the appellate court level, the role of the Supreme Court is merely to review the record to determine if there is competent evidence that allowed the jury to draw an inference reasonably tending to prove guilt and fairly warranting a conviction."

The court then looked at the case presented by the prosecution regarding Pollie Lynn Johnson to determine whether the evidence offered would reasonably support the jury's verdict that Gary Dean Olson was guilty of her murder. Their fact summary was that Kelly Rogers had called Pollie on August 6, 1976, and then gone to the Johnson home and found Pollie's body lying in the kitchen with a substantial amount of blood around the head, after which he called Pollie's father. Gene Johnson, a Highway Patrolman, soon arrived as did an ambulance and the sheriff's office. There had been nothing

216

taken, although a substantial number of firearms and some cash had been in the house, and there was no sign of disturbance other than in the kitchen. Medical examination revealed that Pollie had defensive wounds, and there was no evidence of sexual contact. An autopsy determined that she had died of two gunshot wounds to the head. A spent cartridge was found lying on the floor near Pollie's body. After an extensive investigation that lasted for months and involved many suspects, Gary Dean Olson was charged with Pollie Johnson's murder on December 15, 1977.

The evidence tying Olson to the homicide introduced at trial included that on August 6, 1976, the day of the murder, Olson left his employment at O'Day Equipment Company early. A number of people testified to having seen a car parked near the Maple River Bridge nearby during the afternoon and evening hours of that day. The testimony as to the exact color and make of car was inconsistent, but the general description was similar to Olson's 1966 tan Plymouth. Footprints were found near a tree that had fallen across the river west of the Johnson home. Most compelling was, "Significantly, a firearms expert testified that the cartridge recovered at the scene of the murder was fired by the same weapon, to the exclusion of all other weapons," as spent cartridges found in cars previously owned by Olson. Gary's brother Robert testified that he purchased a .22-caliber rifle in 1973, and shortly thereafter lent it to Gary, who kept the rifle in his possession. Robert recalled hunting with Gary from one of the cars.

The court described Mick (Orvin) Olson's testimony about Gary coming to the Wonder Bar and telling Mick he had seen three men attack and kill Pollie as he watched through the screen door and that they had used his gun, which he had under the seat of his car. They also reviewed Bud Wright's story of three men coming to the Lariat Saloon in West Fargo that same evening and one saying he had killed a kid about six miles north of town. Steve Skar had said that Gary Olson confessed to having done it, but there were witnesses who challenged that testimony.

217

Olson's legal team argued that the Wright connection with Mick Olson's testimony that the murder was committed by three other men, was a more probable explanation and that Gary was framed because of the threats against his family.

The court pointed out that the defense had made that argument in the trial by both the evidence and in its counsel's closing statement. It was the jury's function to determine the credibility of witnesses and determine matters of fact. That was what they had done. "Although all the evidence in a case is circumstantial, the state is not obliged to negate every reasonable theory consistent with the defendant's innocence." The jury believed the evidence introduced by the state and "it is not our prerogative to resolve conflicts in the evidence, pass on the credibility of the witnesses, or weigh the evidence." Another motion denied.

This left one sticky item—the charge. This was one where interpretation of a single word or the failure of having one obvious sentence said by a single witness could mean a life sentence or throwing out the trial. It is one of those necessary things about criminal procedure and the law that led to frustration and injustice at times. The exactness was required because of the long tradition of misuse and abuse, but when a guilty man walked the streets because of a tiny slipup on some matter of procedure or some minute mistake in witness preparation, the public felt both threatened and outraged. The other side of the coin was the number of innocent victims who had ended up in prison or worse because their rights had been ignored or hadn't been protected.

Olson had been charged with the murder of Pollie Johnson under Section 12.1-16-01, North Dakota Century Code, which said: "A person is guilty of murder, a class A felony, if he: 3. Acting either alone or with one or more other persons, commits or attempts to commit . . . burglary, . . . and, in the course of and in furtherance of such crime or of immediate flight therefrom, he, or another participant, if there be any, causes the death of any person."

218

The Olson team's contention was that there was no evidence introduced to prove beyond a reasonable doubt that the crime of burglary was involved because the evidence disclosed that nothing was missing from the house and that there were no signs of a forced entry having been made into the Johnson house. Olson did not "commit or attempt to commit" a burglary beyond a reasonable doubt according to any evidence introduced during the trial.

The court wrote that the statute did not require that something must actually have been taken in order for a burglary to have been committed. The court declared, "The statute does provide that a person is guilty of murder if he 'commits or attempts to commit . . . burglary . . . and, in the course of and in furtherance of such crime . . . causes the death of any person . . .' Forcible entry is not a necessary element of the crime of burglary as defined by North Dakota statutes, and in the Century Code it states, '1. A person is guilty of burglary if he willfully enters or surreptitiously remains in a building or occupied structure . . . when at the time the premises are not open to the public and the actor is not licensed, invited, or otherwise privileged to enter or remain as the case may be, with intent to commit a crime therein.'"

John Rowell also argued, however, that there were no signs of forced entry into the house and that neither of Pollie's parents had testified that Olson did not have their consent to enter the premises. There was nothing in the evidence that said Gary Olson was not invit- ed or otherwise privileged to enter. That was a case where one easy question asked by the prosecution of either of Pollie's parents during their testimony would have dismissed the likelihood Olson was "otherwise privileged." However, no such was asked. It hadn't seemed like a realistic consideration. But this really wasn't so minor a point, since the defense had a precedent to cite that supported reversing the conviction for this failure to have put the obvious in evidence. Following precedent was the guiding light in applying the law, so this could be it.

The Olson argument was that even if the court accepted the charge for Olson based on the incorrect stature, with no sign of forced entry there was insufficient evidence to prove the crime of burglary. Texas cases, *Williams v. State*, 429 S.W.2d 503 and *Wilson v. State*, 420, 328 S.W.2d 305 (1959) were cited as precedent. In the Williams case, the Texas Court of Criminal Appeals had reversed a conviction because of insufficient evidence and indicated that it was the responsibility of the state to prove the lack of the owner's consent to enter the property. It could not be proved by circumstantial evidence if the property owner was available to testify on the question. The Johnsons had been available but hadn't testified that Olson didn't have consent to enter their property. By the Williams rule, that should mean the outcome would be reversed. Precedent was fundamental to the legal system.

The court ruled, "We have found no cases in North Dakota which have adopted this rule for use in North Dakota, and we decline to do so now. Rather, we conclude that the element of entry for the purpose of committing a burglary may be proved by circumstantial evidence in the same manner as any other elements of the crime. The evidence introduced indicated that the Johnson family and Olson did not know one another. The jury could have found from the evidence introduced that Olson did not have the consent of any of the Johnson family to enter the house." So, the court's rejection of an out-of-state precedent and limiting of itself to whether the jury could have reasonably reached its conclusion meant Olson lost again.

The court found that the evidence wasn't overwhelming, but sufficient, so that a jury could have reasonably inferred that a burglary was in progress at the time Pollie was murdered and that the burglary was interrupted by Pollie being there, and the telephone calls from Kelly Rodgers and Pollie's mother.

Shakespeare's "Beware, the Ides of March" that was his soothsayer's prediction was again fulfilled in the Supreme Court's closing March 15 words:

"We find upon reviewing the evidence in the light most favorable to the verdict that the jury could have concluded that Olson was in the vicinity of the Johnson home on the day of the murder of Pollie

Johnson; that he observed the Johnson home for a period of time and determined that the family had left the premises, that he approached the home with the intent of burglarizing the home for the purpose of obtaining firearms or money; that he was surprised when entering the home to find Pollie there, and, after the telephone call from her mother, became frightened he would be discovered and killed Pollie Johnson. Although the circumstantial evidence of guilt is not overwhelming, the testimony that the spent cartridge by the body of Pollie Johnson had been fired from the same weapon which fired several of the cartridges found in two cars previously owned by Olson is substantial. Olson's admission that he killed Pollie Johnson was further evidence to be weighed and considered by the jury. We have examined the entire record and we conclude that the evidence supports the verdict, that there are no other grounds for reversal, and therefore the judgment of conviction must be affirmed."

It almost became a spring ritual, as Gary Dean apparently felt he knew his way around the courtroom. He missed the Ides by four days, but his next big court date came in 1981, when his case was submitted to the United States Court of Appeals, Eighth Circuit on March 5 and decided on March 11. Gary did *pro se*, and acted as his own legal representative in the case.

Olson claimed that a search of his cell had been done outside of his presence on March 22, 1979, that was an unconstitutional search under the Fourth Amendment and also alleged that during the cell search, personal legal materials were read by the person who had conducted it. The district court dismissed the case, and he appealed.

Olson's cell had been searched with the warden's approval by students in a jailer-training course conducted at the North Dakota State Penitentiary. Thomas Paulson, a student in the jailer-training program had conducted the actual search of Olson's cell. The search had been preceded by training, and the students had been given instruction on proper cell-search methods, which included not reading inmate's mail.

The Eighth Circuit Court reviewed the case and found little in Olson's complaint to be of merit, given his status as a penitentiary inmate. They wrote, "And even the most zealous advocate of prisoners' rights would not suggest that a warrant is required to conduct such a search." They said prisoners had minimal Fourth Amendment protection in cell-search situations, and prisoners' reduced measure of Fourth Amendment search and seizure protection stemmed from legitimate institutional needs as well as prisoners' diminished expectations of privacy. Permitting those incarcerated to observe the searches had only one conceivable beneficial effect, which would be to prevent theft or misuse by those conducting the search. The trainee who searched Olson's cell testified that he was the only person in Olson's cell during the search and that he did not knowingly disturb Olson's mail. He positively did not read any of Olson's mail. The district court's dismissal of Olson's complaint was affirmed.

So, Olson lost again, but that didn't mean he was resigned to his fate and wouldn't continue trying, once he had some fresh idea or something new came along.

15

WHAT ELSE IS GOING ON?

The state and the community had been undergoing changes as the 1970s progressed that were a challenge to the traditional economy and character. The early years had been prosperous for farmers and the industries they supported as massive sales of grain to the Soviet Union had driven prices up. By 1974 commodities were selling for record high prices. The prices of farm machinery and feed and other farming necessities followed suit, and when grain prices fell over the next two years, many farmers went bankrupt. Small farms, family farms, were being lost as big agriculture arrived, and small towns were becoming ghost towns. There was movement to the metropolitan areas where work was available, or out of the state, especially to "the Cities," of Minnesota, which meant Minneapolis-St. Paul.

Small towns and the small farmers that had supported them continued to diminish and the population that remained in state was congregating in fewer areas. Preeminent among them was Fargo-Moorhead. Young people who had been away at college were interested in the Saturday night life of bars and clubs rather than rodeos and wanted to be able to call out to order a pizza or live somewhere they could stop and pick up a video. The decimation of the country-side was self-fulfilling, as health care and social services also declined, leading to greater abandonment.

The Fargo-Moorhead metropolitan area had a population of 137,574 by 1980. The "twin town" area had grown most of all, with West Fargo on the fringe of that area and being absorbed more com-pletely. In the years after 1970, West Fargo grew and begun to devour the valuable farmland that had separated it from Fargo, and the sep-aration vanished that had once made Fargo-Moorhead urban and West Fargo more associated with its rural past.

Another change of the time was that the metropolitan area was reaching a size to attract a more diverse and current entertain-ment. Rock concerts arrived, and attending the ZZTop performance at the Fargo Civic Center was a first of a new type of experience for a number of West Fargo students. Alice Cooper, Blue Oyster Cult were other rockers who came along with James Taylor and John Denver for the adult set, as many entertainers made appearances in Fargo and concerts were common, as was live music at entertainment venues. The variety expanded from the county-western music of West Fargo and piano bars and easy-listening of Fargo, with rock bands increas-ingly popular at establishments for a younger crowd. In 1977 the hit movie with John Travolta, *Saturday Night Fever*, helped encourage the popularity of the disco fad in music that was crossing generations.

Left behind particularly by younger people, though his televi-sion show carried on, was Lawrence Welk, the most successful of all the state's musicians, the one who had come to represent North Dakota both admirably and in ridicule across the nation. The dichoto-my of North Dakotan culture was in many ways personified in this man a generation of residents had grown up watching regularly first on black and white then color television on Saturday nights. Many of that same generation had disassociated themselves from Lawrence

Welk or looked back on liking him as naïve nostalgia from their youth as they felt they had grown too sophisticated and joined in belittling him and his hick North Dakota ways. People from coast to coast mocked his "Wunnerful, wunnerful" after his Champaign Music-makers preformed and his "Tank you, tank you" to the audience following its ovation. Lawrence Welk had a national television show from1955 to 1982. He stated his show's goal as, "We try to bring it some joy, happiness, relaxation and always in good taste—the kind of entertainment that should come into the home." He launched the careers of area performers, including Lynn Anderson of Grand Forks, North Dakota, who won a Grammy for "I Never Promised You a Rose Garden."

Welk, who appeared to many as a caricature of "hick" was the real thing, a North Dakota pioneer, and his background explained his mannerisms and use of English. While he made North Dakota a joke or embarrassment in the minds of some, what he accomplished with what little he was given was the other side of his story, the struggle and trust in values. His parents were a German Catholic blacksmith and his wife who had come to America from the Ukraine to farm, and made a long trip by ox-drawn cart before settling on a land claim in North Dakota in 1893. They spent their first North Dakota winter underneath their overturned wagon, which they covered with sod. Welk was born in 1903, in the small town of Strasburg, North Dakota. The family's sod home remained on their farm, and Lawrence didn't learn to speak English until he was twenty-one.

TV Guide sent out Maurice Condon to capture Welk's early days for an April 1967 issue. Condon saw rural North Dakota. He called on the Reverend Father Mark Renner, who recalled, "Lawrence has had to combat all these years the enervating effects of a ruptured appendix in his youth. In that day—it was 1913, 1914—a ruptured appendix was usually fatal. In small Strasburg, then as now, there was no hospital. The nearest was in Bismarck, almost eighty miles away. And that's where he was taken, swathed in blankets, lying on the hard wooden floor of a horse-drawn wagon. It must have been a painful journey. But by the grace of God, he was alive when they reached Bismarck, and he survived, although for more than a year he was a bedridden boy."

The advice the *TV Guide's* reporter was soon given was, "If you want to know about Lawrence when he was growing up, we're too young for that. You see Uncle Pius. Everybody calls him that. He's everybody's uncle. Pius Kraft runs the store down the street, Kraft & Keller. He's been in business here since the Year One."

The scene Condon arrived on he described as, "Kraft & Keller, on Strasburg's main street, is a grocery supermarket, drugstore, clothing, soft goods, shoe, hardware, and confectionery store — in short, an establishment almost vanished from the rural American scene, best described as 'the general store.' Merchandise is displayed — 'spilled' would be the more exact word in profusion in the glass-fronted cases, on the floor, on shelves, appended to the walls, hanging from the ceiling in a splendid chaos. In spite of the seeming confusion, when you specify your need, it is met with speed and precision."

Pius was located and was incredulous at the question of whether he remembered Lawrence Welk as a boy. He responded, "I've been in business in Strasburg since nineteen-ought-six. Ask me about any baby born here, I can tell you.

> How did Lawrence get started on the accordion? Aha, you should have heard his father, Ludwig. Now he could play the accordion. When they came over here they had the clothes they wore, no more. Except for the accordion. It had been in the Welk family three, maybe four generations. Farming was hard then. Up with the sun, to bed with the sun. But when there was a wedding! In those days any respectable wedding took three days — they were real weddings! And there was Ludwig Welk with the family accordion, playing as long as there was anyone left to dance! Lawrence plays the accordion very good. But then, Ludwig taught him. You know how Lawrence got his own accordion? It cost fifteen dollars and he didn't have fifteen dollars. That was a lot of money then, he was just a boy. So he got the money by trapping. Muskrat, beaver, badger. He skinned them, sold the pelts, paid for the accordion.

226

I tell you, Lawrence has gone a long way, for a boy who had little education. He never finished fourth grade. Went to the boarding school over there; the Ursuline nuns used to teach there. Then he got sick, for a long time, never got back to school.

Lawrence Welk did go a long way for a boy who never finished fourth grade then trapped and skinned animals to buy his accordion and finally learned to speak English when he was twenty-one. His "Ah, one-uh an-uh two-uh" embarrassed some who didn't want to admit they were from the same state as the corny band director who did the polka with members of the audience. But to come from a sod hut on the prairie and reach a ranking of second to Bob Hope as America's wealthiest entertainer, have a star on the Hollywood Walk of Fame and a his photo with President Lyndon Johnson on his wall, plus having a marriage that lasted the sixty-one years until his death in 1992 was worth suffering a few chuckles. He was definitely a prominent figure in establishing a North Dakota image.

Welk's was an image of an old, fading North Dakota. Again, the warning Reverend Krangas had delivered at Pollie's funeral of the changing world, a more sophisticated and modern world where community members no longer knew or trusted each other was emerging. It came with more "evil in our time."

As DEMOGRAPHICS WERE CHANGING the Olson cases and their appeals had carried on, and the large investigation launched into solving the murder of Billy Wolf had been making little headway. Since the case against his father had been dropped, there had been no new suspect identified, and the number of agencies going off in different directions had increased. Overall control remained with Larry Costello, who ended many of his statements with, "you know what I mean?" He was a hardworking cop who doggedly followed the myriad possibilities, but they couldn't get a break. It just didn't make sense, but there had to be a solution.

Pete Graber, a Fargo officer assigned to narcotics described Billy as a "street urchin." He said he was just a guy without much money who hung around local bars and hoped someone would buy him a beer or possibly offer to share a joint. Not a tough or nasty kid. What could have made someone want to do what had been done to him? It wasn't a lover's quarrel, as one of his classmates observed.

In the winter of 1980 it looked like they might have caught a break. A twenty-four-year-old burglary suspect seemed to know something about Wolf, authorities believed. He had been questioned about Billy on January 11 and had refused to answer the questions. His refusing to say anything was only serving to convince people he had information to hide. Cass County authorities took him to court on February 2 to force him to respond to their questions about the Wolf murder. Assistant State's Attorney Robert Hoy told the court he hoped this man would provide the break that would lead authorities to the person responsible for the Wolf murder. The man's attorney, Bruce Johnson, advised his client not to answer anything, and Judge John Garass ruled that the man didn't have to answer anything incriminating. He said that a question that could go unanswered would be, "Did you see Billy Wolf being beaten before his murder?" However, Judge Garass said the burglary suspect would have to answer some questions, and the example he gave for that was, "Did you tell your aunt that you know who killed Billy Wolf?"

The day's hearing focused on whether the man would have to answer questions and a sideline case was being fought by local radio stations for a temporary restraining order to prevent the Cass County attorney from closing the inquest to newsmen and the public. The judge sided with the media and said if the county wanted such privacy when this suspect was questioned, it should call a grand jury.

Friday came and the questions about Wolf were asked. The news media was present, but the burglary suspect still refused to give any answers. Two weeks later he was found in contempt of court for his refusal to speak. The sentence was sixty days, and he was still in

228

custody awaiting trial on burglary charges. Garass said that setting the time when the sixty days were to be served would be determined after the outcome of the burglary case.

And just how much had the case missed out on by this man's defiance when the investigation was desperate for leads? Costello tried talking to him after considerable time and reported, "Years later we re-interviewed him, and he said the only reason he didn't talk to us, he had nonthin' to hide then, [was that] the public defender at that time told him not to say anything. But now of course, he's matured and moved on in life and thought, 'What a stupid thing this lawyer told me to do,' you know. He really didn't know anything."

They had run out of leads to follow, and the Billy Wolf case looked like a lost cause. It was time to put the resources of the departments back to work on other crimes.

One thing that had happened because of the tragedies that stuck West Fargo was that a great deal was learned about the changes that had taken place and the extent of criminal activity in the area that had existed under the surface. There was "evil in our time," and it was pervasive, and the world was changing beneath the feet of the children of all of those Schmidts and Kellers and those Johnsons and Olsons and Petersons and othersons, the mainly German and Norwegian descendants who populated the area. It was a transformed environment and not all change was for the better, even if it made the somewhat isolated and neglected North Dakotans' life-style more like the culture of the country that surrounded them, the TV and movie world they saw that was glamorous and sophisticated.

Earl Larson said, when he worked Pollie's case, "We were kind of turning over rocks. We put a lot of people in jail because of that investigation because we were leaning on everyone who might have been involved or might have been a logical suspect, so we arrested a lot of people. Which I guess, talking to people later on, if that happens on a tough case, it's because you're bothering so many people who come up with crimes to be solved."

One thing that was apparent was that drugs had made their way into common usage in West Fargo. Young people had generally reflected the community, smoking cigarettes and drinking beer as the favorites, while sloe gin and Strawberry Hill wine were also being consumed as cheap thrills for some. Things were changing from the protective small-town days of officers Smokey Stensrud and Lester Lindblad, who when they saw kids driving who had been drinking, would stop them and follow them or drive them home if they weren't driving well. Priority was getting the kids home safely.

But marijuana had come up in the investigation of Pollie Johnson's homicide. Kelly had been aware of local dealers and users as had another of Pollie's friends. During their first interview of Steve Skar, back in January of 1977, they had learned of "Dead man's speed," which was speed, or methamphetamine, being shipped in from Florida with dead bodies in caskets and sold in the area. Authorities learned of names of people using it and interviewed a girl who admitted to having tried it. Skar had later been counseled by the judge to observe his self-incriminating statements about drug sales and use. Users and dealers in West Fargo had been named in a number of interviews.

Some West Fargo youth were dealing in Fargo, investigators had been told, where the market was much larger. Even as they looked at West Fargo High School there were stories of students getting high during the day. The cliques in the school included some who were said to congregate on a drug-culture basis. There were the mysterious small bags being carried around that were the optimists' way out on getting pot cheap.

After the fall of the Philippines to the Japanese in 1942 the United States lost its main source of hemp, and the Agriculture Department encouraged diversification in North Dakota to replace it. Hemp was commonly used in rope and had since come to be used in a wide range of textile, body care, and paper and construction products. But the plant, a member of the same cannabis species as marijuana, later became an issue the government took seriously, at which time it was outlawed and an attempt was made to eradicate all existing hemp fields. Some wild hemp, known as "ditchweed," survived in patches and included some small amounts of wild marijuana. Hemp and marijuana have similar characteristics, but in hemp there is only a trace of delta-9 tetrahydrocannabinol, commonly known as THC, the psychoactive element in the plants. High school students would drive to nearby Richland County, hoping to find surviving plants, often returning to school with bags of wild leaves that they would sell, but it was considerable effort for what was likely to be only a low level sensation. Law enforcement took this seriously, but changes were taking place in the 1970s leading to more "evil in our time."

With a substantial population, the area had attracted more serious, large-scale drug operations. More than just the residents of the metropolitan area were being targeted. People came into Fargo for entertainment and shopping, and this created customers for enterprising dealers. The city developed into a location where drugs were being distributed over a larger area. Fargo Police Chief Keith Ternes was an undercover narcotics operative when he first started on the city's police force. As to how it became a distribution point for drug dealing, he said, "I think just the simple fact that Fargo is located at the intersection of two interstate highways [with] drugs coming and going from Fargo is something that has been going on for quite some time. The influence of drugs in our community comes from both near and far. There is certainly drug manufacturing, drug growing, that takes place within the immediate region and there's also an influence of drugs that come from as far away as both coasts and even internationally from Canada and as far away as Mexico."

Fargo sits on the intersection of east-west Interstate Highway 94 and north-south Interstate Highway 29. There was a great deal of open space surrounding both roads, and there were certainly homegrown operations in the area. That was noted by the Drug Enforcement

Agency, which began to look more closely at what was coming out.

Ternes said, "I don't recall there's ever been one particular set of individuals or one individual that has really controlled the drug trade here in Fargo." He went on to say that with drugs coming from so many different places and with different gangs around there had been no permanency to what he referred to as "the heap" of area dealers. He had started his undercover work dealing with downtown Fargo, where a large congregation of regional juveniles would gather to "cruise" or "drag Broadway" on weekend nights. He was doing street buys and not finding it extremely challenging. He explained, "It certainly wasn't the only part of the city where drug trafficking was taking place. But, you know, I think the fortunate part, at least for law enforcement, is that many, if not most of the people involved in the drug trade, especially on the lower ends of it, are just not that bright (Pete Graber, who had also been an undercover agent in Fargo enjoyed saying, 'There's a reason they call that stuff dope'). All they were interested in was making the sale and getting their money. And so, very seldom was I asked a question or was there any type of suspicion. Once the transaction was completed and they had my money, I moved on and processed the drugs I was able to purchase like any other piece of evidence."

There are several questions that come to mind that aren't commonly answered on television shows or in movies when it comes to undercover police and what becomes of their purchases after they end up in the police's hands. The police chief said, "Most of the time they're weighed, they're tested and if necessary they're sent out to the state lab for testing. And once the department or the prosecution no longer has any need, there's no evidentiary value, then they are taken out to an industrial incinerator here in the city and disposed of. There's a very strict process to make sure what needs to be destroyed is, in fact, destroyed." But buying drugs cost money, and who supplies that? "It comes from a wide variety of sources, but at the end of the line, it's obviously taxpayer dollars. The police department and all the agencies that are involved in those types of investigations allocate a certain amount of money as part of their budgets to investigate drug crimes. And, of course, in many drug investigations, quite often the cost of doing business is just incorporated in that money. In other words, if you come to me and are offering to sell drugs, I may have two, three, four different purchases into you where I've actually given you $100, $200 or whatever the case may be. So over the course of a year I've actually given you $500 or $600 that you've actually walked away from me with. But eventually it will culminate in your arrest. Quite often, I think law enforcement is able to recover their loss by maybe seizing property; your vehicle or anything else that you may have purchased with your drug proceeds, so to do it is a cyclical thing."

Entrapment was another concern of theirs as it was for all officers involved in drug investigations. Being careful that one only allowed the person he dealt with to break a law that the person had intended to break, and not convincing someone to break that law could be a fine line and could cost a conviction.

So that was in Fargo and the metropolitan area, but there was concern with a local operation that caught the attention of heavyweight drug enforcement. Included in "the heap" of people distributing drugs in the area during the time of Olson's appeal's and Billy's death was one local operation, the Samuelsons, two brothers, Jay and Robin, and a cousin, Jim, who were thought to be running a large methamphetamine operation, based on a farm outside of Moorhead, but distributing to a wide area. Their father had a manure business, and they were from the area and had some country background and knew the area's people and their tastes. Their specialty was minibennies, amphetamines sometimes called speed beans, which were being brought in from Mexico. The Drug Enforcement Agency, DEA, sent in Special Agent Charlie Lee, and the Samuelsons had met their match.

Charlie took his work seriously and those who worked with

him held him in high regard. A six-foot-one marathoner who had the stamina to follow a case as well, described by those who worked with him as a sincere man with true character, one who helped you no matter what was happening in his life, and a thrill seeker. Costello added, "His mind is just phenomenal." Charlie lived comfortably with danger. Being a federal agent, he did all his cases through the United States Attorney's office in Fargo.

Charlie worked undercover and was interested in being noticed so he could make his way to people who could testify in court about the actual operation. That required something different from the street purchases Curtis had described.

Charlie's initial buys were on a country road out past Fargo's Hector airfield on the way to West Fargo and started at $25,000. There was an informant who had helped set up his original contact, but after that, he operated mainly on his own, with some backup for surveillance on some of the sales and meetings and with analysis of the organization by Pete Graber and other local law enforcement personnel. He needed sufficient quantities before an adequate case could be made. He said the minibennies were good quality, which he knew because they smelled like urine. The important information he waited for soon came in, when he learned, "We got a bunch of ballistics on them and the punches were all the same. They were coming off the same rotary press. And we sent some samples, typically, to ballistics for testing, and sure enough, they were coming off the rotary press, it was more evidence, since this rotary press churned out more speed beans than any other press in the world, and they were down in Mexico."

By then he had worked his way into the organization until he was dealing with Tommy Hornbacher, who knew how it was set up. Then it was time to move. Charlie said, "I seized over a million minibennies from these guys, which was significant. It was the biggest seizure of minibennies in the country that year." And as far as recovering some of the money he spent, he said, "We got a bunch of

234

money. It was interesting, because . . . it was an old abandoned farm implement and there was a seed drill sittin' out there. There was a seed drill sitting out there and in the seed boxes was all this money. And then we seized that money. We had to get a warrant out there and then we seized that money. And then Hornbacher, he had a car parked at the airport. And we never got a warrant for that. It was an old Dodge, or a Plymouth. And in the trunk there was a bunch of money, and we missed it. We talked about that later. I never got a warrant for it. I missed a bunch of money, too.

"But eventually, Hornbacher turned the corner, and we got him to testify. And he did a bunch of grand jury work."

A story frequently told about Hornbacher's testimony was that he received a visit from an attorney for the Samuelsons to discuss what he would be saying. While Hornbacher was never threatened, the attorney had a pad of paper he kept in the interviewee's view and he slowly drew a stickman on it with a noose around its neck as they talked.

On November 12, 1979, charges were brought in the Southeastern Division, District Court of North Dakota that stated, "Jay Kenton Samuelson, Robin Jack Samuelson, James Samuelson and James Raymond Mimiaci knowingly and intentionally did unlawfully distribute approximately 750,000 tablets of dl amphetamine sulfate, a Schedule II controlled substance." The federal case was presented by the distinguished and authoritative Gary Aneaur, whose presence ruled the courtroom as he prosecuted.

Jay was tried and convicted by a jury on continuing criminal enterprise charges, or CCE, which required showing a series of violations of federal narcotics laws done together with five or more persons, by a person who occupied a management or organizing position in the group, and received a substantial income from his position. The Eighth Circuit Court of Appeals described Jay as "the central figure in the operation, which was based in Fargo, North Dakota."

Hornbacher was the key witness, and he had testified he had

"arranged to sell a large quantity of amphetamines to Dennis Siewert, who intended to sell them to Charles Lee, an undercover agent. The sale was not completed due to Samuelson's failure to supply the drugs to Hornbacher. In November Hornbacher again attempted to complete the deal with Siewert, and obtained the drugs pursuant to Samuelson's directions. Hornbacher and Siewert were subsequently arrested." Jay was sentenced fifteen years for engaging in a continuing criminal enterprise, a sentence not subject to suspension, probation, or parole. Some related charges, including six counts of unlawful possession of amphetamines with intent to distribute, one count of possession of cocaine with intent to distribute, to run consecutively, totaled twenty-four years, including a ten-year sentence for a conspiracy count. The twenty-four-year sentence was to run concurrently with the fifteen-year CCE sentence. The appellate court accepted his argument that the conspiracy conviction constituted double jeopardy, since it was a factor in the CCE conviction. That conviction was vacated.

Jay's brother Robin was indicted along with Jay as a co-conspirator on July 22, 1981, but Robin had escaped and was not caught until July 12, 1982. His trial began on September 15, 1982, in the United States District Court for the District of North Dakota, with the Honorable Paul Benson, chief judge, presiding, and he was charged with six counts of unlawful possession of amphetamines with intent to distribute, one count of possession of cocaine with intent to distribute, and one count of conspiracy.

After the jury was selected and the first day of trial ended, plea bargain discussions began. The next day the court approved a plea bargain in which Robin pled *nolo contendere*, or no contest, on three of the amphetamine charges, and the remaining four were dismissed. The court sentenced him to five years on each of the three counts, with sentences to run concurrently, except that two years on one count were to run consecutively to the five-year term, giving him a total seven years confinement. The court imposed a statutorily mandated two-year special parole term on each count, and he claimed he wouldn't appeal his conviction. He did, but to no avail.

Jim ended up in prison for conspiracy, which was a lesser charge than his cousins had faced, and his sentence wasn't as long as theirs. He was a little different from them, it seemed, more of what one officer described as a "happy-go-lucky, partier" type. Charlie noted, "Jim drove a drove a red Pontiac convertible. Jay and Robin, they were Cadillac guys, and they wore Rolex watches and, oh, they had the finest stuff." Robin and Jay added years to their sentences when they were individually called before grand juries several years later and refused to answer, claiming the right to plead the Fifth Amendment.

The size of the Samuelson operation made it clear how pervasive drugs were in the area, and they had specialized in one product. With all that was on the street and from what West Fargo law agents learned, there were many suppliers available, large and small, in that "heap" that operated in the area from where an enterprising dealer could get merchandise. It had been suggested because of the timing and the success of the DEA's operation that Billy had informed on the Samuelsons, but lead prosecutor, Ed Klinger said, "I don't know of any evidence tying them to the crime."

With drug availability and a drug culture in the area, several from West Fargo were trying to make some easy money by getting involved in the larger drug markets in nearby Fargo-Moorhead. Their world spilled over into the town that prided itself on its frontier association. It was a part of the changing world that was encroaching on the region, as one era and its necessities and beliefs began to fade while the world of more choices and temptations became standard.

16

WHAT DID HAPPEN TO BILLY?

The Billy Wolf Case had gone cold after his father had been dropped as a suspect. The other big investigation, the DEA's case, had been bought to a successful conclusion, and Gary Dean Olson still wasn't pleased with the outcome of his legal actions, but he seemed to have run out of steam, at least for the time being. Things were calm, at some new equilibrium, but Costello still hoped to see the Wolf case solved. His department was less enthusiastic, and he soldiered on, more and more with the cooperation of a group of other investigators from area agencies, including Pete Graber from Fargo narcotics and Budd Warren of West Fargo who were interested in getting to the answer. They thought perhaps it had slipped through their fingers earlier when they had twenty-seven investigators from nine different agencies on the case and the information was never put together fast enough. Billy had a record of possession of a small amount of marijuana that predated his murder but they knew he had moved on to a different level of drug involvement. They had learned that Billy was participating in the illegal trade and by 1987 a second

238

look at the case seemed to be in order from that perspective. The case was reopened, and since they were dealing with it from a drug angle, Charlie Lee was brought into the investigation.

An unexpected event really revived the flagging investigation. In San Jose, California, an arrest for car thefts led the individual taken in to make an offer, to play the card he had been holding for a desperate situation. He said that for the right treatment, he could provide some information about a North Dakota homicide that people would find very interesting. It sounded like it was going to involve drugs and that had been the recent direction the Wolf homicide investigation had turned.

Local narcotics agents like Graber had seen Billy around enough to know he was involved in the scene. What they had learned was that he was doing some dealing that wasn't quite as low level as they had previously thought. Budd Warren, who was a jailer at the Cass County Jail at the time, said Billy was bigger than people thought he was, but he was low level. He had to help keep himself financially afloat. He worked for his dad, did menial jobs, and sold drugs on the side and probably got in over his head with these guys.

The man arrested in California had made his knowledge sound promising enough to encourage Costello to think it was worth checking out, and he had seen nearly all but a small group generally decide to stand back and lose interest in the case by that time. Since it appeared there was a drug connection to it, he asked Charlie Lee of the DEA to come along.

Costello and Charlie flew out to California to interview the witness and the trip was worth it. They weren't sure they believed the story they were hearing, so they brought in a polygraph operator to determine whether it was the truth. The polygraph came out positive that the man was giving them details about the murder. Still cynical, they called in a second polygraphist to listen to the man's story and evaluate it. Again the answer was absolute; this was the true story. They knew what had happened.

The Billy Wolf investigation was again open, but their valuable information was not admissible in court. And that was only part of the problem, once things were really getting moving.

One thing they had learned was that the stories William Wolf, Sr., had told about Billy being abducted and driven off the road and other things they thought had been tales he had told to draw attention away from himself hadn't been imaginary. They had been true, and Billy's father may have only heard a part of them. Steve Gabrielson, a Cass County deputy sheriff who would become involved in investigating the events much later said, "When it comes to drugs, it's either you didn't pay for them or you took them."

Investigators from the time say Billy had gotten himself in debt, the sort of debt some people take seriously, over someone who claimed to have paid for six pounds of hashish that he hadn't received. Billy was frightened about what to do and how to take care of it. He had taken to carrying a knife, a fillet knife, in one of his boots, and he would take it out if he got into an argument. A classmate of his from West Fargo remembers seeing him not long before the murder and noted his curious behavior.

In Billy's West High School days, he had once played a small role in the school's production of *Harvey*. It was quite a different crowd for him, but Carin Noriega, who was one of the leads in the play said, "I liked him. I thought he was pleasant. We had a lot of fun putting on that play. We didn't socialize with them. The first talk was about drugs. He hung out with those people."

The star, who had played Vita Louise Simmons, the role Helen Hayes had performed opposite Jimmy Stewart, was Jan Maxwell. Jan pursued her acting and went on to Broadway where she twice achieved the stage's highest accolade as a Toni nominee. Looking back, Jan recalled seeing Billy shortly before he was murdered, and how strange he seemed. She had been with another member of their class at the time and said, "Dwight Grotte and I were in Ralph's Corner Bar (it was a Moorhead State University drama department hangout) where I had seen Bill just a few weeks prior to his death. Bill always seemed high whenever I'd see him there (and he was there a lot), but he was always very friendly to me, and that particular night that I saw him last, I mentioned something about going across the street to another bar and he said, 'No, I'm afraid to walk anywhere anymore.' I asked why and he said, 'I'm afraid someone is going to hit me with their car.'

"I thought he was just high and paranoid and I laughed. He said, 'No, I'm serious.' And it gets vague here, but there is a slight memory of him telling me that he had already had to dodge a car."

He was serious, and the investigators had heard of two bikers from New York in long coats with hand guns from both Billy's father and Billy that had him extremely frightened. They learned that Billy had been tied up and driven out in the country, and a bag put over his head. He was forced down between the headlights of the car and a gun held to his head as he was warned about coming up with what he owed. That was his final warning. The witness who passed the polygraph twice told what had happened and the condition of the body when it was discovered supported his story.

His next encounter was fatal. Billy had been taken to a farm in Cass County. A knife was held to his throat. It might have been the knife from his boot, though it was never found. He was poked in the throat repeatedly and seven times the knife entered the skin. Whether the intent of this was to scare him and a mistake was made, or the assailants had finished torturing him remains uncertain, but Billy's neck was sliced, which was the actual act of murder. Then he was then cut in half.

The stories of his being alive when he was cut in half that circulated the area were false. Also false was the story that the body had been frozen, then cut with an electric saw or power saw. Costello's statement that he had been cut by a band saw was equally incorrect. What happened was less sinister than that, in a perverted view of being practical. Billy had thrown the shot put and wrestled in high school and hadn't decreased from his 210-pound large frame. The killers made the mistake of leaving the large young man lying out, apparently extended. When it seemed like a good time to dispose of the body, they had a problem. Leaving the body meant that post-mortem processes had begun, and one is that the muscles and joints began to lock up. The process varies in how long it takes, but within several hours it is usually complete, and the body remains rigid for days. Rigor mortis had set in. Billy had become a large item to move, and one of them stumbled on him as they got him to the trunk of the vehicle they planned to use.

They found they couldn't get the stiffened body into the trunk because of its large rigid size. Determined to complete the job and find a way to dispose of the corpse, they took the stiff body back into a barn where they were and tied it up by the heels with a rope. They threw the rope up through the rafters and yanked on it as it raised the body to full extension, hanging in the air. Billy was then cut in half, and the marks on the vertebrae suggest they used the filet knife he carried to do the cutting.

With the mess made and the bloody corpse they needed to do something quickly. They had two body halves to dispose of from the fresh bisection, so they grabbed two garbage bags, not trash bin liners but the big green ones, and put a half in each. That would keep the blood stains out of the cars. Then they took the two bags to two different vehicles and didn't have problems getting them in the trunks.

From there the two cars were driven to the Sheyenne River, where the bags were dumped. The Sheyenne flows into the Red River. Not long after entering the Red River and being carried with the flow, the bags hit snags and eventually were discovered. They had separated and were caught in tangled roots of fallen trees on either side of the river, with one half caught first in a tree on the Minnesota side before the other half was wedged in tangled roots a mile north in North Dakota. Minnesota ended with jurisdiction. Federal prosecutor Gary Aneur had said that in Clay County they joked about how they should have pushed bag across to the North Dakota side, and West Fargoan Mike Lyman, who was involved in all three of the investigations as a Cass County agent looked at it from the North Dakota side and said, "Maybe we did."

Armed with this new knowledge, there seemed to be opportunities to move forward, but things weren't so simple. One problem was soon discovered when the investigators got excited about pursuing new possibilities. All of the information from the original investigation and evidence that had been located by the various agencies had vanished. This was no clever plot or inside operation. It was regular people doing their jobs and being overwhelmed while priorities had changed. Clay County Court House expanded, and in that expansion all the records had been transferred. During the remodeling many things were thrown out. Among those things had been not only the all the evidence gathered, but also the grand jury testimony from the first investigation of the homicide. Back to square one.

It had been Costello's investigation, and he said the boxes with the Wolf case information were probably just sitting there collecting dust over the years as new evidence from new cases kept coming in and needed a place to be stored, so "Somebody who probably didn't know anything about the Billy Wolf case probably saw a box with an old date, and tossed it out." The investigation would have been handled much differently today, all concerned agree, with DNA testing available. Finding the lost clothes and bags might not matter. Costello's view is, "I don't believe that any of the evidence that was lost in the Court House would have made a difference in this. Because we had nothing to match it to; we didn't have anything to match the rope to, the garbage bags or any of those things. I mean at that time, you know, let's face it, we didn't have the hot-shot pathologists that we have today, and we didn't have all the high-tech testing equipment that they have today, you know what I'm sayin'? Back in '78 it was a whole different era of crime scene and pathology than we have today. And finding it now, there is nothing. We have absolutely nothing to compare it to. If there was DNA on the garbage bag that may have been the suspect's, obviously it disappeared in the river."

Whether it would have been of any use, it was gone, and the grand jury testimony that vanished with the physical evidence might have provided some useful information. Without any physical evidence, investigators were looking at developing a case on circumstantial evidence, unless they could find others willing to step forward. Pete Graber said it was difficult to get anyone to step forward because the people involved were young and impressionable when Wolf was killed, and they believed that the judicial system couldn't protect them. "You could promise them the world, and they would know they're not safe." He mentioned one convicted man facing prison time. They told him they would get him out of his sentence if he testified. He told them, "I'll do my time."

This doesn't sound like something one was supposed to hear in North Dakota.

17

IT'S NOT OVER 'TIL IT'S OVER

W hen the 1990s arrived, Gary Dean Olson had recovered some of his eagerness to challenge the system. In 1991 he asked a federal magistrate in Fargo to overturn the North Dakota Supreme Court's decision that upheld his conviction for the murder of his wife. His attempt to bring the federal court system in to overturn the highest state court was based on his allegation that his civil rights had been violated, which afforded federal protection. Federal magistrate Karen Klein in Fargo ruled that the state court had not violated Olson's rights, specifically when affirming the decision that allowed his cellmates to testify against him at his trial. His attorney filed an appeal of Klein's ruling.

In 1992 his Bismarck attorney Gregory Runge told the panel of three judges on the Eighth Circuit Court of Appeals in St. Paul that the rights of his client had been, "trampled on by a district court's eagerness to convict him of murdering his wife." Olson's attorney had a litany of reasons why Olson's trial had been unfair, all familiar arguments wrapped up in another voice. Perhaps this new audience would finally understand. He didn't state his goals in modest terms, but said, "We're looking for total destruction of this case." A new trial was in order, Runge assured the judges.

Olson's trial held in Fargo hadn't been fair because the *Fargo Forum*'s stories included statements made by the informants, snitches who had been imprisoned with Olson, and the statements the paper reported about what they had said in the past could have created preconceptions or biases among the jurors. Considerable challenge was made to that testimony being admitted in court, with Neukom's testimony coming under attack for several reasons.

Olson's one-time cellmate Arnold Neukom had testified that Olson admitted murdering his wife to him, which had been corroborated by Lester Meddy, another of their cellmates. Neukom had read about the case in the newspaper, Runge argued, and the prosecution would never have known about him, but he came forward and used what he learned to get out of forgery charges outstanding against him. He had made a deal with law enforcement agents to supply them with information. When the officer accepted Neukom's offer to provide information, the state had created "agency status" for him, and he had the obligation to warn Olson of his right to counsel when they had discussions involving what had happened on the night of the murder of Gary's wife. Beyond that, Neukom had confessed to having committed perjury in a similar case in exchange for favorable treatment, and the evidence discovered for that showed him to be an untrustworthy witness whose testimony should not have been allowed. Meddy's corroborating testimony was argued as inadmissible, because he was added as a witness too late for the defense to prepare its cross-examination.

The appeal also challenged the influence of the ongoing coverage of the story in the *Fargo Forum* and statements included some that were later introduced as evidence in the trial. The dangerous offender statute, which extended Olson's sentences, was argued by Runge as being unconstitutional. After hearing the arguments decided several times in the past, the court took the case under advisement and said it would announce its decision within sixty days.

Near the end of December 1992, the circuit court announced its decision on Olson's appeal and the conviction stood. The panel of judges had not found the arguments any more convincing than had the many judges who had heard them before. Both cellmates had testified legitimately, and Neukom's conversations were not "interrogations by a government agent," so Olson had no Miranda rights. The judge had handled the issue of jurors reading the newspaper adequately, and Neukom's admission to perjuring himself in a different trial was not relevant, as "it has no direct bearing on truthfulness of his testimony in this proceeding." The court found no constitutional issue with the dangerous offender statute, so Gary's life term for his wife's murder remained intact.

Olson filed a writ of *habeas corpus* in *Gary Olson versus Thomas Powers, Warden, North Dakota State Penitentiary* on December 17, 1992, which the Eight Circuit Court rejected. It contained the same arguments as his appeal, and they found it no more convincing. *Habeas corpus*, Latin for "you have the body" is seen as one of the great writs that guarantees freedom from unlawful and arbitrary arrest, as it requires the party who has incarcerated another to prove that it was done with reason and with the rights of the victim observed. The issues had just been resolved in the appeal by this same court, so restating the arguments and rejecting them wasn't a time-consuming matter.

Gary could be labeled many things, but "quitter" probably wasn't one of them. A year after his failed appeal, he finally won a victory, though modest. This victory came not in court but from the pardon board, which consisted of the governor, the chief justice of the supreme court, the attorney general, and two citizens appointed by the governor. Like the federal government and many states, it often comes near the year's end when the pardon board announces decisions for all crimes except treason and impeachment. At the end of each legislative session, the governor announced the persons pardoned along with the crime committed and the reason for pardon. The process begins with a written statement requesting consideration, and selection was done though confidential means that could involve a review of the applicant's personal testimony along with his records.

On December 9, 1993, the pardon board announced that it had reduced the sentences of two convicted murderers. Both had been sentenced to serve two consecutive life terms in the penitentiary. One of them, Calvin Newman, had the substantial reduction of his two consecutive lives to one single fifty-year sentence. His situation had been a true "prisoner's dilemma," since he had ended up with the dire sentence because he refused to testify against Kevin Austin, who had been involved with him in a double murder. His greatly reduced sentence came at the price of his testimony against Austin, since the case against Austin had been dropped and until then he had gone free.

The other announcement of a sentence the pardon board made was also the reduction of the sentence of another double murderer serving consecutive life terms. Gary Dean Olson didn't have the prospect of perhaps breathing free air again in his later years, like Calvin Newman. Gary's victory had more of the look of a practical joke, as the pardon board reduced one of his two consecutive life sentences to ninety-nine years. It was life number one, Dixie's murder, so living to an old age could only get him to another life in prison. And it would have to be a very old age, since he received the first sentence, which was now reduced to ninety-nine years, when he was thirty-three. Even in the state with the most people over 100 there was little optimism in this and more salt in the wounds. Hardly the sort of victory he had been eager for since he was first incarcerated and hoping to overturn both trial results.

As this was going on and the second Wolf investigation fizzled, Charlie Lee had moved on to where the drug world was more active and dangerous. He headed to Pakistan to get closer to the production and distribution points and found the thrill-seeker life he enjoyed. At the time the Pakistan-Afghanistan border region was producing about a third of the heroin consumed in the United States and three-quarters of what Europeans used, putting it second to Southeast Asia's Golden Triangle. The opium from Afghanistan's and to a lesser degree Pakistan's poppy fields was being processed into heroin in more than 100 illegal laboratories in tribal areas of northwest Pakistan where the army wouldn't go at the time. Palaces existed that exhibited the wealth earned by tribal leaders, and Charlie was based in Lahore and Karachi.

Not deterred by the obvious dangers of dealing in remote areas, he did undercover work looking for poppies in Afghanistan and shopping for finished product in Pakistan. His time undercover in nearly inaccessible areas brought him into contact with other sorts of traders, and he did some dealing in things beyond heroin. He bought weapons-grade plutonium and stinger missiles that he found available from obscure mountain traders. He also discovered that some of the heroin trading was being carried on by government officials. Powerful people on both sides of the law were involved, and he was going after them. He recalled, "In Pakistan I got chased really hard. They tried to do a job on me."

They got on to him, and the NSA had a tape of plans to kidnap him, but a German was mistakenly taken. That didn't slow him down. The DEA took a few big operators and managed to get them out of the country by using an old extradition treaty from before the partition of India into India and Pakistan. He was also in on the arrest of two Pakistani air force officers who had come to the United States on official business but the DEA thought were headed to New York to sell heroin. There was a reprisal arrest in Pakistan of a DEA officer, Ayaz Baloch, and relations were a bit tense briefly. Charlie said Secretary of State Madeline Albright was unhappy with him, but he had lost his cover, and the government hid him out in Chicago for most of a year, since he had moved beyond the dangers of undercover with Fargo drug dealers, but had upset some people in powerful positions in the international trade. "'A curse be on your father' — they don't forget," he said, and to the present, "I don't prop up a shot gun by the door, but I keep alert."

Charlie's work in Pakistan had exposed the fine and murky line between law enforcement and crime, as drug agents often relied on informants. A 2004 United Press International story carried in several newspapers told the story of Charlie's working relationship with Mohammed Habib Rehman, whom he recruited as a DEA informant in the early 1990s in Lahore. Charlie said it proved to be a very successful relationship, and they paid him well for being fearless, while, "We had a pretty good run with him." When a suspected heroin smuggler discovered Rehman was working for the United States agents, someone was sent to kill him, and they had him and his family on their way to America within hours.

Charlie moved back to the United States in 1997, and Rehman came to see him, since things weren't going so well and Charlie tried to help out. He arranged a meeting between Rehman and FBI agents in the spring of 1999 and encouraged the agents to use Rehman in counter-terrorism investigations. Rehman's skills were found to be valuable. Rehman was the central figure in a very elaborate government operation, about which President Bush said to reporters, "The fact that we were able to sting this guy is a pretty good example of what we're doing in order to protect the American people." The United States government caught a British arms dealer Rehman had been working with, Hemant Lakhani, who was convicted of attempting to provide missiles to terrorists and related charges in 2005 and sentenced to forty-seven years in prison.

While Charlie had lived his Indiana Jones life of excitement, he hadn't forgotten about the case of Billy Wolf, and was one of a small group, some now retired, who no longer worked on the case, but maintained an interest in developments and hoped to see someone step forward or confess to involvement. Someone confessed to having shot Billy in an argument but since he wasn't shot, that wasn't taken seriously.

A story in the *Fargo Forum* in 1999 was surprisingly open about the Wolf case. After reviewing the grisly details briefly, it said that since the case was reopened in 1987, police believed it was drug related. That was followed with, "They think they know who killed him and possibly where, but don't have enough evidence to charge the suspects," and said to contact either the Clay County or Cass County sheriff if one had any information to add. There have been calls, but not from realistic sources.

Not everyone attributed the Wolf murder to drugs. The Internet made that apparent and gave access to claims being let loose into the ether, as Jim Stensland's recent posting, dated July 5, 2004, made clear. Stensland says he was the prophet Elijah, and heard directly from the Archangel Gabriel, and proclaimed William Wolf, Sr., was responsible for the murder. He went beyond that and claimed to have warned Billy of the very thing in advance. His website stated, "One night in May, 1978. I was shooting pool in the basement of the 410 bar. In Fargo, North Dakota. When I all of a sudden had a revelation about this guy who was shooting pool at another table next to me. And I told him about it. His name was Bill Wolfe. Although I don't remember exactly what I said I will say what I can remember. I told him that his father was going to kill him. Cut his body in half. Put the halves in two garbage bags and throw them into the Sheyenne River. And try to blame it all on the Mafia . . . I remember in August of 1973 that Gabriel told me that Bill Wolfe, Sr., was going to murder his son Bill Wolfe, Jr. . . . One thing I do remember from my visions back in 1978 is that Bill Wolfe, Sr., will be convicted of the murder of his son and sentenced to twenty years. In order to do this though you need an eye witness. And I will rise Bill Wolfe, Jr., from the dead so that he may testify as to who murdered him when and where . . . I am curious as to how old he will be when I raise him

PRAIRIE MURDERS

from the dead . . . I don't believe that I have the power to raise the dead as of yet. I think that God will give me this power at some future point in time."

The long discourse carries on to cover flying saucers, his previous lives, which included living on Atlantis, having been Abraham and Moses among others and an "immigrant who came to the United States during the potato phantom," which no doubt was some time near the potato famine. He stated that Chapter 11 of the *Book of Revelations*, "says that there will be an earthquake in Fargo, North Dakota," and he is, "Absolutely Certain That Jimmy Carter Is the Antichrist."

Those who read Stensland's site are told that he is the cousin of Jesus, and has the angel name Bo while the entity Peep is his angel wife. He plans "to write the true gospel. Which of course will make the Bible obsolete. And anything I say will supersede anything in the Bible that might disagree with me or what I say." Ultimately, this is a very serious matter, "Because when all is said and done, anyone and I mean anyone and everyone who doesn't listen to me is going to burn in hell."

So, whatever Jim Stensland sees and hears in his world, the Internet has given him a tool for spreading his ramblings and accusations to anyone worldwide who will read them, and while he suspects a Fargo police conspiracy against him, he has failed to revive the idea that William Wolf, Sr., was responsible for the death of his son.

18

HOW THINGS CARRY ON

T he local area had undergone considerable change from the time of the murders. The uncertainties of the weather and agricultural foundation that have characterized the state from its inception have remained, as this headline from the *Forum* of June 11, 2008 made vivid: "Severe Storm Headed for Fargo-Moorhead as Volatile Weather Nails Region; Flying Cows Reported Near Valley City."

West Fargo's population was over 21,000 by the most recent count, and the Fargo-Moorhead metropolitan area's population was 200,000. While nearly fifty percent still claim German ancestry and forty Norwegian, the numbers of ethnic minorities has grown and become more commonplace, and the universities have become large, and the variety of ethnic and cultural diversity has increased. An example of this was widely reported with the January 2009 arrest of journalist Roxana Saberi on charges of spying in Iran. Saberi was the daughter of a Japanese mother and Iranian father and grew up in Fargo, then attended college in Moorhead at Concordia. After being selected as Miss North Dakota, she continued her education with master's degrees in journalism from Northwestern University and international relations from Cambridge University. Working as a free lance journalist since 2003, Saberi was charged as being a U.S. spy and given an eight-year sentence. Following international pressure and active intervention by North Dakota's Senator Dorgan, Secretary of State Clinton, and President Obama, her sentence was overturned.

Urban life has arrived in several spots in the state, though within those metropolitan areas, pockets of rural life and rural communities continue to exist. North Dakota remains the least violent state in the United States. There had been seven murders in the most recent annual report which was up from the years of one, but the area hasn't changed dramatically. West Fargo has been completely absorbed into a metropolitan area and the urban benefits of greater exposure to a diversity of people and activities and wider range of ideas and attitudes has led to greater sophistication.

Reverend Kragnas alerting the trusting community to "evil in this world" could as well have been a statement that the area was moving from one era to another, and time was changing the isolation and adversity that had given the people their strength and values into a more aware and cosmopolitan people who were adopting the cultural norms mobility and technology allowed, which made their lives little different from those of people elsewhere. This was a refreshing change for the provincial prairie but there was a dark side. Rural North Dakota had at one time been closer to the Jeffersonian ideal of agrarian democracy, but the easy thrills and exploitation of a less challenging existence came with more cultural advantages accompanied by evil parasites.

Author-journalist Tom Wolfe labeled 1970s "the me decade" and the name had the most meaning where "me" was counter to the essence of successful living, being especially destructive when self-interest became the acceptable social norm in areas built on cooperation, as prairie life had been by necessity. Wolfe cited 1970s statistics, including that three in five marriages ended in divorce, a fifth of the child population lived in single-parent homes, declining SAT scores, the twenty-percent increase in sales of bran cereal that to him signified preoccupation with personal lifespan, while social concerns had lost favor, replaced by the quest for personal wealth. The "me" generation with its seeming sophistication included the prairie. This move away from rural values had come at a cost, and the 1970s witnessed the change with the growth of urban living and self-interest above community that characterized North Dakota and that was especially true in the Fargo-Moorhead area, where the grounding that many had in an earlier era became fashionably seen as simplistic and immature.

The darker side of urban life that included drugs and violent crime moved in, and neighbors weren't there to watch out for each other, but often to view with disinterest or suspicion. The criminal activity like that of the Samuelsons and the deaths of three people long before their times showed things had changed. Gary Olson may have been an aberration, but his behavior carried on too long for a close community not to have been aware of it and to have let it get to the point it did. And Billy suffered a fate unfit for any human, but while the answer sits silently known, his story remains untold. These aren't the qualities that "won the West," where danger in life hung by a thread, where a hailstorm could mean the loss of a summer's work, and suffering through the winter and flu could mean the risk of late planting or harvest. People bound together in times of hardship and the best and most selfless in them was brought out.

Some would say little had changed and the hard work that was born of facing challenging weather and uncertainty produced determined people who survived in any competition. The work ethic of the North Dakota culture remains as seen in its generally high academic achievement. It has the nation's highest high school graduation rate and sends a greater portion of high school students to college than any other state. *The New York Times* on November 14, 2007, reported, "On the most recent national assessment, the highest-performing state in math was Massachusetts, and in science, North Dakota." In his 2006 commencement address, the dean of Yale Law School, the nation's oldest and most selective law school, said, "And my favorite fact about the class of 2006: it includes not one, not two, not three, but four citizens of Fargo, North Dakota . . . Believe it or not, we have more students in this class from Fargo than we have from Chicago, LA, or San Francisco." Open spaces and open minds continue to produce many hard-working and achieving people. The North Dakota problem is that many of these achievers don't remain in the state.

In the murders, the Billy Wolf homicide remains an open case and has been taken on by both the North Dakota Attorney General's Cold Case Unit and the Cold Case Unit of Clay County, Minnesota. They work on homicides where no statute of limitations applies. The North Dakota unit was formed in 2005 and takes on two or three cases at a time, re-interviewing and applying technology to cases that didn't exist when the incidents occurred. There are currently fourteen cases, dated 1962 to 1996 on the North Dakota Cold Case list, and it has solved homicides from 1982 and 1987 and is working on Billy Wolf's 1978 case. They are tight-lipped about what they know regarding the case, and state, "Any chance of successful resolution of the matter is dependent, in part, upon keeping information concerning possible ongoing activities to a minimum."

The Cold Case Unit of Clay County continued its investigation of the Billy Wolf case under its Cold Case Unit, directed by Detective Bryan Green through 2007, but has left it to North Dakota since 2008. They still get occasional calls from "psychos" or people who have had "visions" but only follow up on anything they consider realistic possible leads. Green said Clay County was in a position where they could indict someone, but didn't have enough information or evidence to take the case to trial. Two witnesses had seen the body cut in half and put in the vehicles and the crime had been drug related. There were people who had information. Green believed the crime would be solved some day, because, "somebody will do the right thing." On the thirtieth anniversary of the homicide, Green was quoted in the newspaper as saying, "Somebody needs to clear their conscience before they die. They've had hard lives, and they'll have to face their maker," and also, "We're pretty certain we know who did it; ain't no doubt about that. We have to have enough to convince the jury, and we don't quite have that yet. It's still being worked at but you need that one solid bit of proof." He has visited Wolf's grave to keep the case personally real.

Detective Steve Gabrielson has 4,000 pages of investigation material on the Wolf homicide combined in four binders sitting on his desk at the Cass County Sheriff's Department and won't go quite as far as Green on saying he knows who committed the homicide. "I narrow it done to a few — I am not totally sure exactly who actually murdered Mr. Wolf," but "nothing that can tell us that here's the individual involved." Gabrielson said he hasn't spoken about the crime with any of the prosecutors from the past, though he traveled with Lyman to do an interrogation in 2007, "nor do I plan to at this time."

The *Fargo Forum*'s front page story on the thirtieth anniversary of the murder included the slightly ambiguous comments, "Several persons of interest have been in and out of prison over the years. Investigators remain watchful of at least two people in the Fargo area." This touches on Gabrielson's approach, perhaps, but earlier investigators directly involved have grown increasingly frustrated. Budd Warren had made a slightly less optimistic comment on a radio broadcast when he retired from law enforcement and entered business. He said, "We know who did it but are not able to prosecute."

Merv Nordeng, whose involvement in the Wolf case was limited, was most pessimistic, commenting, "I think it's solved but it will never get prosecuted." He didn't run for reelection as states attorney after prosecuting Olson for murdering Dixie. He explained, "I liked the prosecuting part, but not dealing with the press and the running of the office, the dealing with the county commissioners. I mean, the average I.Q. of the county commissioners back in those times must have been borderline mentally retarded."

As the years went by, he grew disenchanted with law, and late in his career he quit as a prosecutor to become a public defender. He said, "I enjoyed it. You deal with the dregs of society, but if I ever did anything that really saved someone's ass, and I guess a couple of times I did, it was worth it."

There have been several who were involved in the investigation of the Wolf case up to their retirement that have always held out hope a conviction would still result. Pete Graber went into security after retirement, but remained intensely interested in seeing this case closed, and Budd Warren, Mike Lyman, Larry Costello, and outsider Charlie Lee are among those who have known for years much of what the investigators of the cases now know. They can only sit back and leave it to the new team of investigators, but like them, hope that the positive inside one of the key participants, the Yin that had been suppressed for all these years by the Yang, will see that while they may have felt trapped by the changing world they were a part of thirty years ago, the only way to ever make amends is to step forward and say what they know.

The Wolf family's closure and grief has passed largely ignored, possibly because of the early events of the case when William Wolf, Sr., was considered a prime suspect. Little thought has been given to the Wolfs, and they have left West Fargo and generally avoid contact or the past. Perhaps some late measure of peace is still a possibility for the man in his mid-seventies and his wife if the perpetrator of the gruesome deed that was the end of their son could be exposed and brought to justice.

There has been some attempt to keep the memory of Pollie Johnson and her joyful existence alive at West Fargo High School with the awarding of an annual Spirit Award. Gary Clark, the school's principal who started there as a teacher in 1971, said he doesn't think students know why the Spirit Award is named for Pollie and perhaps should hear the explanation.

The investigators most involved in Pollie's Case, Earl Larson and Mike Lyman remain active. Larson is at the time of this book in his sixties, but continues his role as a West Fargo patrolman. Lyman left law enforcement to become a private investigator working for the Vogel Law Firm, the largest in the area. Others involved in area cases have moved on. Pete Graber retired from the Fargo Police and does work in security. Larry Costello and Charlie Lee have retired, and Budd Warren has entered the business world.

With the conviction of Gary Olson, the Johnsons may have found some closure, but they will always know that an irreplaceable joy in their lives was taken from them. They have their ghosts. Gene to the present has a special regret, as he noted, "I think of her every day, even after thirty years. She always wanted a trampoline, and I'd say, 'Pollie, we can't afford a trampoline,' and every time I see one I wish I would have got her one."

He retired from the Highway Patrol in the late 1989, two years before reaching the mandatory retirement age of sixty. He bought more pasture land for their horses and continued to maintain the yard at Maple-Sheyenne Lutheran, their local church. Recently they had Pollie moved to the cemetery there.

Norma found adjustment slow. It was ten years before she considered looking at slides of family that included Pollie, and she couldn't go to the cemetery to visit the burial site for an equally long time.

They live as they did before August 1976, with trust overcoming fear. They have not retreated behind locked, bolted doors, and often, when they look for their car keys, they often find them in the ignition. It is still JOHNSON'S HIDE-A-WAY nestled in its secluded peninsula along the Maple River.

Gary Dean Olson remains in the North Dakota State Penitentiary where he has spent nearly the last thirty years of his life. He is sixty-four and not in the best of health, working his way through his ninety-nine-year sentence so he can start his life sentence. Olson still hasn't given up on getting out, and 2007 was a banner year. There were challenges to both of his convictions.

In the summer there was a confession to the murders of both Pollie Johnson and Billy Wolf. Investigators from a variety of agencies gathered information from the time to interview the man who said he had kept it all a secret for all of those years. It didn't see plausible, but stories of false convictions being revealed years later and men being sentenced to death when DNA later proved the jury had been mistaken were common enough that this had to be taken seriously. The fact there had been mistakes made in trials didn't mean they were common, just newsworthy.

There was a major problem with this story, which was the math. Arden Archer, who confessed to killing both Pollie and Billy, had been twelve at the time of the Pollie's murder, which didn't make it impossible, but certainly unlikely. Mike Lyman and Steve Gabrialson from Cass County went to interview Archer at Stillwater Prison in Minnesota in late August. Before going, Lyman went over the layout of the Johnson home with Gene Johnson to be sure he had the details correct. They found the suspect only knew what he could have learned from law journals or publications, such as evidence about footprints. He didn't know enough about the physical layout of the house to have any credibility. Lyman didn't interview him about Billy Wolf. Billy would have been much bigger than Archer, who would have been fourteen. Bryan Green had been among those who had interviewed Archer in Nebraska about the Wolf homicide and Lyman learned that Archer said Wolf was shot with a 12-gauge shotgun.

So why was this man saying these things? Lyman believes, "He had a motivation or secondary game plan, I think. He wanted to get to North Dakota. My take on it was if Archer could somehow take a fall on it he'd end up in a North Dakota prison. The Stillwater Prison isn't a very comfortable nightclub atmosphere. It's a pretty cold, hard prison, and I'm pretty satisfied that that's what his motivation was."

Budd Warren's comment on the confessions and follow-up was, "Nothing happened except his wasting everyone's time. If you asked him he would tell you he was involved with putting Lee Harvey Oswald down after the Kennedy assassination. Those things come with the territory on the unsolved homicides. The freaks just seem to come out of the woodwork."

The year 2007 saw another of Olson's challenges to the conviction for the murder of his wife again reach the North Dakota Supreme Court. This was a new approach for challenging the conviction. It had begun late in 2006 when he decided to go the modern route and challenge the DNA of the evidence used against him during the trial. In his September, 2006 hearing, Olson was the only person to testify. He said that hair, fibers, fingerprints, and a blanket had been offered in evidence at the trial. A problem emerged when the December hearing was held and the Cass County clerk of court testified that while some of the physical evidence had been located, her office had not been able to locate the complete criminal file. Olson's own DNA expert had stated that DNA analysis of the found items "would not provide significant probative information and would not satisfy the criteria that additional testing would have the potential to produce new evidence relevant to the defendant's assertion of innocence."

North Dakota law on DNA required that the individual present a *prima facie* case showing that identity was an issue at trial and that "the evidence to be tested had been subject to a chain of custody sufficient to establish that it has not been substituted, tampered with, replaced, or altered in any material aspect." Olson had established that identity was an issue, but not chain of custody, since he asked that all possible evidence used in his trial, whether in existence or not, be found to have been sufficient as meeting the chain of custody requirement. The court added, "Without knowing whether evidence is still in existence, it would be impossible to make a determination on the chain of custody. Mr. Olson did not make a request to the district court that he be allowed to hire a private investigator to look into the whereabouts of any other physical evidence at the time of the district court proceedings. It appears that he is now trying to circumvent that oversight by requesting that this Court do it for him."

On June 5, 2008, Olson was back again, and the State Supreme Court was once more faced with a challenge to his conviction for the murder of Dixie from the importunate Gary on the basis of DNA testing. The same issues with the evidence were repeated, how the Cass County clerk of court had testified she discovered some hair but was unable to locate the entire contents of the criminal file. She had not found any bedding or clothing that had been introduced in evidence. She also testified that evidence was normally kept for approximately twenty-five years after sentencing.

Olson argued that evidence had been received at trial, so it should still be in the state's custody. The court was persuaded by the clerk's testimony that it was policy to keep evidence approximately twenty-five years following sentencing. They said they were not aware of any law requiring the state to keep evidence for a specific period of time. Their conclusion was that the existing hair would have met Olson's burden of establishing a chain of custody and DNA testing would not have potential to support an assertion of innocence. The Law Code required that the complaining party must present testimony or otherwise show that evidence exists.

Olson had opportunity to conduct discovery to locate such evidence under the Postconviction Procedure Act, and there was no evidence he had. The judgment confirming his conviction was affirmed. Once again his appeal failed, though what was at stake for him in rushing to a life sentence is unclear.

Looking back, regarding the choice to not include sexual charges against Olson in the case of Pollie Johnson, Judge Cynthia Rothe-Seeger, who had been a prosecuting attorney for the state at the time commented, "Awareness has changed, the public is much more familiar with these issues, probably because of television and movies, and science has given the prosecution new tools." To that she added one other comment about a long forgotten subject that has remained a well-kept secret for thirty years, "The issue of the reward money is confidential and will never be disclosed."

Jim Samuelson, cousin of Jay and Robin, and one of the Samuelsons that were prominently involved in the drug culture of past years, served his sentence and did an about face. He says, "Me going to jail saved my life." Speaking of his past, Samuelson reported that his drug use had begun when was on Ritalin in seventh grade, prescribed by a doctor who said he had Attention Deficit Disorder, or ADD, and in high school he smoked pot and used speed. He is open about being imprisoned for drug trafficking and says the turning point in his life came on December 2, 1981, when a Christmas choir came to the jail and sang. That started him and two other inmates reading the Bible. Following his release he became an evangelical minister and founded a church, "Springs of Living Water." They hold services that are televised and he does revival meetings that involve personal testimonials and healing. His church also does social service, including food distribution, for the needy in the community.

Kelly Rogers, who had been first to be concerned about Pollie and had gone to her house and found her dead, had been distinctly influenced by Pollie's father, Gene, who was a father figure to him. Kelly chose to go into law enforcement and became a Highway Patrolman, the same as Gene. In 2007 Kelly retired as a lieutenant, and Pollie's parents made the 200 mile trip to the capitol in Bismarck for his retirement ceremony. Kelly's message when he spoke to mark the end of his career was, "I just encouraged other people, younger ones that were there, that you know if they could mentor somebody to get into law enforcement, do the same thing Gene had done."

In the strange workings of the universe, who knows what Kelly would have become if it hadn't been for that tragic night, but Gene showing concern for him even at the most difficult time a father could experience and along with Norma, remaining his friend over all the years, brought things full circle in some small way when Kelly went out by recommending the example be a precedent.

While the area went through a change, its reputation didn't follow suit. An apparently random decision made by the Cohen brothers has outweighed news reports, FBI statistics, and Department of Education reports. The Cohens decided Brainerd wasn't a catchy title when they finished their screenplay fabricating a crime story that included some truth and was thought to be true. The setting for their story was Brainerd, Minnesota, which they made famous for Paul Bunyan, pancakes and prostitutes. Instead of using Brainerd as their title, they chose to call their script *Fargo*.

The area's reputation was twisted some and bloated by the highly successful and critically acclaimed Cohen Brother's movie, which imbedded the North Dakota "hick" image in a nationwide and eventually worldwide audience. With many "uff dahs" and "yas" and "you betchas," the speech, which has traces of accuracy local residents barely notice, was much exaggerated, while the bleakness of the prairie on winter days was precisely captured in a fanciful story that had only one scene at the beginning where the location was Fargo. The peaceful community image of the nation's safest state wasn't enhanced when one character put another's body through a woodchiper. The true nature of the community was more accurately revealed in its reaction to the movie.

North Dakotans inclination to mock themselves and play into others' stereotypes as they did with the Zip to Zap in 1969 hadn't changed, and the *Fargo* movie provided an ideal opportunity. Fargo's oldest movie theater continues to exist as a historic landmark and opened in 1926 with a custom-built Wurlitzer pipe organ and room for an orchestra to accompany silent films and Vaudeville Theater. Babe Ruth appeared that first November to hit baseballs hanging attached to a string and silent movie cowboy movie star, Tom Mix appearing on stage with his horse. When "talkies" were introduced in 1927 the Fargo Theater added sound equipment and films were shown in the theater with its arena of 1300 Spanish leather seats, large crystal chandelier, colored mirrors and panels of art. Seventy years later when the film *Fargo* appeared, there was a tradition at the theater that on Academy Awards night guests were invited to the theater in formal dress, evening gowns for women and tuxedos for men.

Margie Bailly, the theater's development director, came up with a different idea for the 1997 event, since *Fargo* had been nominated for seven awards. She got into the spirit and sent out invitations that read: "Join Ole and Lena and all their relatives around supper time (6:00 p.m. March 24) . . . It's Academy Awards night, don'tcha know. Dress warm (not fancy) and chow down on extra special lefse chips and lutefisk bits—all ya can eat! Arne Bjornson will o'course be playing his accordion in da lobby." Bailey encouraged people to dress "funky, flannel and furry," to overdo it and camp it up.

The national media got wind of Bailly's plans and converged on the city to cover the event, which the magazine *Entertainment Weekly* listed as one of the five hottest Oscar parties in the country in its March 21, 1997, issue. The idea captured the local population as well, as 870 free passes were reserved for members of the theater's society and media. The remaining 800 were given out on a first-come, first-served basis at the theater and were gone in ten minutes.

Julia Suits of Hawley, Minnesota, orchestrated what Bailly described as becoming "performance art" at the theater's entrance as national attention grew. When the big day arrived, the first event was *CBS This Morning* showing up at 6:40 a.m. to interview Bailey and actress Kristen Rudrud, who had lived in Fargo and played the part of a kidnap victim in the film. The theater had flown Rudrud back from Hollywood to be the celebrity attraction. A woodchipper was on display producing red snow and there were characters acting as misplaced ice fishermen, as well as a crowd acting like it didn't understand when the show started, which was 6:00 p.m. The exterior was decorated with "Ole," Fargo's version of the Oscar statues. Unlike the immodest Oscar, Ole was dressed with a coat and hat.

Bailly, who had to buy overalls for the event, added that Julie Lee and the White Rose Band would play polkas on the theater stage and there would be a short concert featuring the theater's Wurlitzer pipe organ. True Midwest comfort food would be available at the "Fargo Theatre Church Basement Café," where the hungry patrons could stop by for pickled herring, lime Jell-O, lefse, and *rommegrot*.

When evening arrived and the real event approached, representatives from *People Magazine* and television crews from *Entertainment Tonight, Inside Edition, Access Hollywood* and "E!" cable networks along with local and regional media were there to cover it live. Rather than limousines, the crowd arrived in wagons pulled by John Deere tractors. At 6:00 p.m. Kristin Rudrud pulled up in a blue pickup truck. Since along with the other media exposure, the event had a live feed to KABC in Los Angeles to be used as a cut-in during the live Oscar coverage, Bailly had said, "The crowd has to be prepared to be seen by two billion people," and reminded everyone attending to wear "your most elegant snow shoveling outfit—flannel, jeans, fur hats. Try to be a little understated."

The live television broadcast patched in the Fargo activities twice during the Oscar presentations, but continuing wins for the *English Patient* put a damper on the local crowd's festivities. They received satisfaction when the Cohens won for best screenplay and when Frances McDormand took the award as best actress. The name "Fargo" is likely more associated in the broad public conscious with that movie than with anything else, and by extension, the image of North Dakota. A simple decision, said to have been made because the Cohens thought "Fargo" sounded more interesting than "Brainerd," has been a forceful factor in the psyches of a generation in forming attitudes about an area.

What hasn't changed in the area is that the values of community and cooperation, neighborliness, and friendliness remain common to many and give them security and comfort with each other unlike what is seen in many urban areas. That cooperation was evident in Fargo in March 2010, when thousands of volunteers joined to fill and transport millions of sandbags that could defend the city from being flooded, as the Red River rose to its highest level in 112 years. People don't look at each other with suspicion, though it is no longer the pre-1970 world where depending on others was assumed. It is still a prairie area isolated in some ways, and the stories of what happened to Pollie, Dixie, and Billy have tarnished it and lessened the trust and innocence.

But the people of the cold empty state and West Fargo are maintaining something now three generations old, but still in their blood. They still have values from their past that were earned through challenging lives and not being indulged. Their survival required cooperation and hard work, and they were sustained by faith. They have accommodated to the present era while retaining cohesion that makes the events like those of the 1970s stand out as shocks in a contemporary world that has become anesthetized to mistrust and to the "evil in our times."